FURTHER ADVANCE PRAISE FOR *CREATING DEMAND*

"How much is a good idea worth to you? Take whatever dollar figure you came up with, subtract $19, and you now have your net profit from reading Tabío and Beamer's new book. And that's a conservative estimate, because *Creating Demand* will probably help you generate dozens of good ideas. I can't imagine a better or more timely investment."

Andy Goodman
Director, the Goodman Center

"It's worth the money when a business book gives me one idea I can use. Tabío and Beamer not only gave me pages of them—they showed me how to make more!"

Steve Stockman
President, Custom Productions, Inc.,
and director, writer, and producer

"Finally—a book that makes the connection between concepts with behaviors and in doing so outlines for us a step-by-step road map to creating effective marketing ideas that actually work."

John I. Coulter
Managing Partner, the Content Factory

D1569825

Creating
DEMAND

GERARDO V. TABÍO & SALLY BEAMER

Creating
DEMAND

Generate
Cool, Custom
Marketing
Ideas

Prometheus Books

59 John Glenn Drive
Amherst, New York 14228-2119

Published 2009 by Prometheus Books

Inquiries should be addressed to
Prometheus Books
59 John Glenn Drive
Amherst, New York 14228–2119
VOICE: 716–691–0133, ext. 210
FAX: 716–691–0137
WWW.PROMETHEUSBOOKS.COM

13 12 11 10 09   5 4 3 2 1

Library of Congress Cataloging-in-Publication Data

Tabío, Gerardo V., 1954–
  Creating demand : generate cool custom marketing ideas / by Gerardo V. Tabío and Sally
Beamer.
        p. cm.
  Includes bibliographical references and index.
  ISBN 978–1–59102–755–3 (pbk. : alk. paper)
  1. Marketing. 2. Marketing—Psychological aspects. I. Beamer, Sally, 1958– II. Title.

HF5415.T23 2009
658.8—dc22

                                                        2009021872

Printed in the United States

To Sandy and Mel

CONTENTS

5. THE MARKETING ANALYSIS   75

13. PREPARATION　277

ACKNOWLEDGMENTS

Not one word of this book could have been written were it not for the opportunity our clients have given us over the years to contribute to their success. Everything we teach we have learned from the thousands of students who have attended our workshops and who have—some more patiently than others—helped us see the difference between the elements that really create results and the ones that should be discarded.

Kandice Herndon, Lori Sheridan, and Crystal Hardy make up the rest of this small band of zealots we call the Creative Resources Group. We love their devotion to our clients and their passion for our process. Crystal gets a special thank-you for making herself available at all hours to help us complete this project. Kandice is our company's director of facilitator development. She lived up to her title by painstakingly reviewing every chapter and insisting that the book be a practical tool for present and future facilitators.

We could not do what we do without the unconditional love and support of our families. Thank you to Sally's husband, Mel; and to Gerry's wife, Sandy, and children Charlie, Crystal, and Victoria. Thank you to Sally's parents, Dick and Libba Beamer, and to Gerry's parents, Gerardo L. Tabío and Nilda Rodriguez.

Sandy Tabío was a very important part of the writing effort. She typed every word of the book, often improving on Gerry's chicken scratchings. Her love and her belief in the project fueled the process and moved it forward, especially when the going got tough.

It is a rare individual who can generously offer guidance and support, expecting little or no credit in return. Richard A. Reis is such a person. Rich was in the room when our company was born. For more than two decades he has known exactly when to offer praise and when the best prescription is a firm kick in the butt. We love him madly.

We thank Claudia Gere, our book coach, agent, and friend, who is guaranteed a place in heaven for her patience and persistence in keeping us focused on finishing the book. Claudia believed in the book sometimes more than we did. Without her help we may never have finished the project.

We have been very fortunate to work with two gifted editors who really made this book much better than we ever imagined. First, we want to thank Linda Regan for seeing the potential in our book. More than a great editor, Linda is a smart marketer, whose point of view was invaluable in fine-tuning the book. Then we want to send a big bear hug to Meghann French, who took the book apart sentence by sentence and made sure we said what we really wanted to say.

One final thank you from Gerry to George Sard for withholding my paycheck until I finished writing those exasperating Allen Fund reports. You taught me so much more about writing than I appreciated at the time.

PREFACE

IDEAS ARE THE
NEW CURRENCY

In the business of marketing communications, ideas are the only currency.

The job of creating demand for a given product or service comes down to this: coming up with an idea that will get a target consumer to believe something about a product or service or do something with that product or service.

One of the challenges facing the typical marketer is that today's target consumer is not necessarily sitting still, waiting to be persuaded. Rather, target consumers are playing a game of "catch me if you can." As a matter of fact, the entire field of integrated marketing communications (IMC) is based on the simple premise that technology has given target consumers of all ages complete control over when and how they receive the information they need in order to make a purchase.

The answer, according to IMC, is integration. Surround the target consumer with an integrated campaign that coordinates all your communication tools and engage the target consumer in a conversation that will lead him or her to choose your products over those of your competitors.

As if the target consumer's new sovereignty were not enough of a challenge, there is the sometimes overwhelming explosion in the number of

23

communication tools available to the average marketer. It wasn't too long ago that all the major media industries were neatly categorized into discreet silos. If you wanted to send your customers and prospects a video message, you advertised on television. If instead you wanted to talk to your customers and prospects on audio while they drove to work in the morning, you advertised on the radio. Looking to hire new employees or maybe sell an old motorcycle? Just place a small classified ad in your local newspaper.

Today you can run that thirty-second video message on Web sites owned by newspapers or radio stations. Magazines offer radio-type programs called podcasts. You can auction your motorcycle on eBay, and those pizza coupons you were going to send via the US Postal Service can be delivered more quickly—and probably more narrowly targeted—directly to your customers' cell phones.

Marketers looking to create demand for their products and services have an unlimited number of communication tools from which to choose. Even at the local level, the dramatic increase in new kinds of media has created seemingly infinite ad space inventory on the market.

In all the excitement over the new communication options available and the uncertainty about how to purchase and use the tools most effectively, it is no wonder some marketers have lost their way. We have seen their marketing programs fail for a variety of reasons. Some marketers, seduced by a new communication tool, forget the original marketing objective. In our experience, most marketing programs that fail are missing the one most important ingredient: an idea.

Creating demand for your product or service is based on these three premises:

1. Ideas are at the core of all successful marketing programs.
2. Ideas are the outcome of a creative process.
3. The creative process will be most productive when managed by a facilitator.

We believe that at the core of all successful integrated marketing campaigns there is a cool, custom, and effective idea. It is this belief that has driven us to write this book.

WHAT IS A MARKETING IDEA?

A marketing idea is the communication a target consumer experiences that causes him or her to do something or believe something about a product or a service. Marketing ideas have to meet three specific standards. They have to be cool, custom, and effective.

Cool

Marketing ideas have to be cool to the target consumer. "Cool" implies relevance. Ideas, and most especially marketing ideas, have to be relevant to the target consumer. But relevance doesn't totally capture the essence of cool. "Cool" also means that the idea has immediate, novel, and cutting-edge appeal. A cool idea has the best chance of breaking through the cacophony of messages in our culture and capturing the attention of a consumer. Only a cool idea has the power to cause that consumer to want to engage with any given brand.

Custom

Marketing ideas have to be customized to the marketer's brand. Custom ideas let the target consumer know which of the millions of brands out there is responsible for this cool idea. Only a custom idea can illustrate— even prove—to the target consumer that this particular product is different from all its competitors in a way that is valuable to a target consumer.

Effective

Marketing ideas have to be effective. Only an effective idea has a chance to cause a target consumer to do or believe something about any given product. An effective idea lays out the path for the target consumer to follow as he engages with a brand. Effective ideas give that target consumer reasons to stay engaged with the program and reasons to believe in the benefits offered by a specific product or service.

The winning formula for a successful marketing program is a cool, custom, and effective idea executed with the right communication tools.

IDEAS COME FROM A PROCESS

There is no question that there are people who are more creative than the rest of us. People like Pablo Picasso, James Joyce, and Wolfgang Amadeus Mozart generated ideas that are more brilliant, more beautiful, and more innovative than the ideas most of us will ever conceive. In every company there are people who are more creative than everybody else, and there is a natural temptation to defer all idea generation to the handful of people to whom ideas come naturally.

You, however, are trying to run a business, and a business needs to take control of its own idea-generation process. When you need a solution to a problem, you should be able to pull your team together and generate a lot of ideas. But all too often we forget that most of us are as creative as anyone else. Look around your company. Every one of the people you work with—the receptionist, the delivery driver, the accountant—are all valuable creative resources. Yet they rarely get drafted into the cause of generating ideas for your business. So they take their creativity home and they invest it in the way they help their kids with their homework, the way they decorate for holidays, or the way they plan a romantic evening with their spouse.

We believe that when you keep the creativity solely in the hands of those people labeled as "the creatives," you make your organization smaller. So, although we make no claim that we can make you more creative, we know that if you and your team follow the process described in this book, you will generate cool, custom, and effective ideas when you need them, and not only when it is convenient for the creatives in the organization.

David Packard, the co-founder of Hewlett-Packard, once said that marketing was too important to be left to the marketing department.[1] We feel the same way about idea generation. The generation of ideas is too important to be left only to those deemed creative.

Back in the 1940s, Alex Osborn, of the advertising agency Batten, Barton, Durstine, and Osborn (BBDO), coined the term *brainstorming*. What began as a simple yet revolutionary idea-generation technique was developed by Osborn and Dr. Sidney J. Parnes into a full-fledged creative problem-solving process.

We first encountered the Osborn-Parnes method of creative problem-solving about twenty-five years ago. We found the process to be tremendously powerful, yet somewhat academic in its approach. Over the last twenty-five years we have adapted it—maybe rescued it back—to the world of marketing. The result is what we refer to as the Creative Resources Process. It is sequential and repeatable and has a proven track record of helping marketers generate ideas that create demand for products and services of all kinds.

THE CREATIVE PROCESS NEEDS TO BE FACILITATED

Just as it is true that every company has some people who are good at coming up with their own creative ideas, it is also true that every company has people with the leadership skills to incite others to be creative.

The Creative Resources Process requires a leader. The leader of a creative process is called a facilitator. This is the person who manages the process that makes it easy for a team of people to work together to create marketing ideas.

It requires leadership to get a client, your colleagues, or even your own boss to focus on a narrow marketing objective. It requires leadership to convince a team of people—often from different departments—to temporarily abandon their own agendas and work together to come up with a variety of marketing ideas. It is leadership that gives those team members the confidence to express their ideas—even ideas that might be perceived as stupid or inappropriate at first—in a public forum. And it is leadership that gets a decision maker to select the idea with the most potential for success, then commit to a timeline with actions and deadlines.

Over the years, we have trained thousands of facilitators who currently hold a wide variety of positions with companies all over the world.

Once they are trained, they become the go-to people within their companies whenever anyone—a supervisor, a colleague, or a customer—needs help coming up with marketing ideas.

In this book, we will share with you the Creative Resources Process as we have taught it to them—and as they have taught it back to us—over the last twenty-five years.

THE VOICES YOU'LL HEAR

Two authors, Sally Beamer and Gerardo V. Tabío, who developed the Creative Resources Process, have collaborated to write this book.

The primary voice you hear in this book is mine. "I" am Gerardo V. Tabío (my friends call me Gerry), president of Creative Resources.

From time to time Sally Beamer, my business partner and coauthor, will illustrate an important point, and then I'll let you know it's Sally's story.

"You" are the person reading this book: the business owner who hopes, even during difficult times, to find a way to create demand for your products or services; the manager who wishes you could get your people to work together as a team; the general manager who doesn't have the budget to hire a big-time marketing consultant; or the team member who wants to make an even bigger contribution to your company. All of you are potential facilitators of the creative process.

THIS BOOK IS ABOUT BEHAVIOR

A few years ago, we met a man who told us this story.

The senior managers of his company gave him and one of his colleagues this assignment: read all the current, popular books on creativity and idea generation and distill them down into a training program that will teach our people how to come up with better ideas.

So this man, whose name was Bob, and his colleague went out and bought two copies of every popular book on creativity, innovation, and creative thinking that they could find. Each of them read the books independently. They scheduled a series of meetings to review their findings and to figure out how to organize what they were learning into a series of training experiences for the management and the staff of their company.

After a couple of very frustrating meetings, Bob and his colleague had to regretfully report to the senior managers of the company that they could not move forward. The project was abandoned. Why? Because Bob and his colleague discovered that all the books they purchased, although popular, were full of concepts and abstractions and devoid of concrete behaviors.

It is concrete behaviors—not abstract concepts—that help us to learn. Imagine that you are at a party having a conversation with another adult who brought his two kids to the gathering. If, in the middle of your conversation, one of his kids were to walk between you, interrupting the conversation, odds are that the parent would say to the child, "Say, 'Excuse me'!"

That parent will probably have to repeat that lesson a handful of times before the child begins to excuse himself every time he walks between two people. But can you imagine how long it would take the child to learn to say excuse me if, every time the child interrupted a conversation, the parent said, "Remember to be polite"? For it to stick, the lesson needs to be articulated as a behavior as well as a concept.

We are obsessed with behavior. We have written this book from the same point of view that we have used in all the training we have delivered over the last twenty-five years: *People act their way into a new way of thinking.* As we were writing this book, we kept coming back to one phrase over and over again: "Make that behavioral!"

Our mission is to deliver to you first the concepts and then the behaviors that will help your company create demand by generating cool, custom, and effective marketing ideas.

CASE STUDY: WOODLAND NURSERIES

Throughout this book we will refer to the case study of Woodland Nurseries, a high-end gardening supply store based in Atlanta, to illustrate the Creative Resources Process.

Although we have endeavored to make Woodland Nurseries as real as possible to enhance the learning experience, we are required to let you know any similarity to any gardening stores, named Woodland Nurseries or not, is purely coincidental.

We will introduce you to a talented facilitator named Alesia, and we will follow her every step of the way as she helps Woodland Nurseries accomplish its marketing objective with a cool, custom, and effective idea.

MAKING LISTS AND MAKING CHOICES

"Good morning everybody." The man speaking is standing at the head of the table. To his left is an easel with lots of flip chart paper. He has a blue Crayola® marker in his hand. His official title is regional sales manager for his company. But not right now. Right now, he is playing the role of facilitator. And he's on a mission.

"Good morning!" the group responds with anticipation.

"Before we begin our session today, I would like to ask you guys to help me make a list of all the different names you might give a dog."

The group is silent for a few seconds, as if waiting for the first participant to break the ice.

"Lady."

The facilitator writes the word *Lady* on the flip chart.

He has barely had a moment to turn around when he hears a burst of names.

"Trixie."

"Spot."

"Buddy."

"Honey."

The facilitator is writing so fast it is becoming difficult to read his handwriting.

"Snoopy."

"Ziggy."

The torrent of names begins to slow down until there is silence in the room again. As the facilitator writes down the last name on the list, he turns around and says, "Let's pretend it's a really big dog. What are we going to call it?"

A new flood of ideas begins as the participants call out names for really big dogs.

"Cujo."

"Beethoven."

"Marmaduke."

The facilitator begins a second column on the page and feverishly writes down all the names as quickly as the participants call them out. With his back turned toward them, he repeats, "Big dog!" and it seems to spur the group to give even more names.

"King."

"King Kong."

"Goliath."

And just as it happened with the first list, the calling out of names slows down, then stops. The facilitator captures the last item and turns to face the group again.

"Okay, I want you to forget that it is a big dog. Let's imagine that we are going to name one of those yappy little lap dogs. What are we going to call it?"

Once again, the participants become rejuvenated by the question and new names begin to pour out. The facilitator turns his back to the group once again, attempting to write the names down as the participants call them out.

"Cuddles."

"Fifi."

"Jenny."

The group bursts out laughing when they hear this name. A smallish woman in the room, whose name is Jenny, says, "Thanks a lot!"

Five or six names later the facilitator has filled the second column of names and begins a third column on the same sheet of paper. Predictably, the flow of ideas again begins to slow down. And again the facilitator turns around, this time saying, "Okay, one last question; let's forget about the small dog. Let's pretend now it is the typical family dog. Imagine the kids named it. What names would they choose?"

Just as if he had flipped a switch, the names pour out quickly.

"Benji."

"Pepper."

"Luke."

"Puff."

"Barney."

"Missy."

The facilitator writes the last name at the bottom of the third column of the flip chart page and takes a deep breath. "Look at what a great job you've done! In just under five minutes you filled this sheet of paper with names we might give a dog.

"Our next job is to make choices from this list. I need you to pretend you are getting a new dog. Of course, when you get a new dog you have to give it a name. In a moment, we are going to go around the table. I am going to ask each of you to give me three pieces of information: I want you to tell us your first name, what kind of dog you are getting, and then what you are going to name your dog. The only requirement is that the name of your dog has to come from this list. I'll give you a moment to review the list and then we'll begin."

The facilitator pauses for a few seconds, giving the participants a short time to look over the list and then says, "I'll start. My name is Richard. I am going to get a Labrador and name her Honey."

As he mentions the name he's chosen for his dog, Richard picks up a red marker and puts a red check mark in front of the name Honey, which appears around the middle of the first column.

One by one, the participants introduce themselves, saying their name and the kind of dog they are getting, and choosing one of the names from the list. And, as he did at the beginning, Richard puts a red check mark in front of each name as it is chosen by a member of the group.

Once he has heard from everyone, he puts down the marker and stands aside to let the participants look at their choices. The flip chart looks like figure 1.

Lady	Cujo	Benji
Trixie	Beethoven	Pepper
Spot	Marmaduke	✓Luke
Buddy	King	Puff
✓Honey	King Kong	✓Barney
Snoopy	Goliath	Dino
Ziggy	Cuddles	Missy
Bubba	Fifi	Elmo
Diego	✓Jenny	Bert
Rocky	✓Duke	✓Ernie
Fido	Duchess	Daisy
Badger	Penny	Tinkerbell
BD	Sonny	Blackie
✓Simon	✓Cher	Rudy

Figure 1. Long List of Dog Names with Choices

FIRST MAKE A LIST. THEN MAKE CHOICES.

Whenever a facilitator conducts an idea-generation session, he begins the session with a simple exercise like the one just described. Whether the task is to name a dog or to come up with places to go on vacation, he first asks the group to make a long list of different ideas. Then he asks each member of the group to read the entire list and choose one option. The results are always the same: three columns of ideas and check marks all over the page.

The results are so predictable, in fact, that we use a similar exercise to teach the group the fundamentals of idea generation. And the fundamentals are disarmingly simple: The most effective way to come up with a new idea is to first make a list of ideas and then make choices from that list.

WHY WE MAKE A LIST

We make a list of ideas for at least three reasons:

1. When you get in the shower you turn the hot water on first, right? You do that because it takes a few minutes for the water to get really hot. Once the water is nice and hot, you turn on the cold water and adjust the temperature to what feels best to you.

    Idea-generation sessions need to warm up as well. At first, most of the ideas generated are conventional and familiar. This is especially true if the marketing objective has been addressed before. It takes a while for the participants to get conventional ideas out of their system and begin to explore possibilities they had not considered previously.
2. A good list of ideas contains variety. One of the tasks of an effective facilitator is to make sure the client has a variety of ideas to consider. By definition, variety can come only from quantity, which gets us back to the need for a long list.
3. Making a list works. Put a list of options in front of someone and watch her make choices from all over the list instead of limiting herself to the first few choices. The list of names for a dog shown in figure 1 is a very accurate representation of what most idea-generation sessions really look like. You can see how the choices were made from all over the list.

HOW TO MAKE A LIST

Alex Osborn first proposed the notion that idea generation is the result of two separate actions (first making a list, then making choices) in his book *Your Creative Power*,[1] which was published in 1948. Osborn described his new technique as the act of first generating ideas without evaluation or judgment, then choosing the ideas that were best suited to accomplish the objective at hand.

Knowing that it is difficult to create an environment free from judgment or evaluation, Osborn proposed four rules that should be followed by any team of people engaged in brainstorming. We have borrowed those four original rules and taken the liberty of adding three more that, in our experience, complete the job of setting the right expectations for a productive list-making or idea-generation session. And although we refer to them as the "Seven Rules of Brainstorming," we see their usefulness as far beyond idea generation.

Seven Rules of Brainstorming

As you will see when you follow the Creative Resources Process, the Seven Rules of Brainstorming should be followed whenever any individual or group wants to make a long list, regardless of the contents of the list.

Rule #1

During the list-making or idea-generation session, there will be no judgment of ideas, no evaluation, and no criticism. By writing the ideas down and not judging them—positively or negatively—we encourage more ideas to be generated. When people don't feel judged and when they recognize that anything they say will be written down, they generate more ideas, resulting in a longer list.

Rule #2

Freewheeling is allowed and encouraged. Wild and outrageous ideas are welcome. People often don't believe us when we say this. They think to themselves, "I bet they won't write down this idea." Then they say something that's distasteful, illegal, or unaffordable, or something that's been done before. Our response is always to celebrate the idea, whatever it is, by writing it down with confidence. What we are communicating is, "We want anything and everything you can think of, because when we write it down it is going to make a connection for someone else; it's going to lead to all sorts of possibilities and ultimately make our list longer."

Rule #3

We are going to make a long list. Remember that we're striving for quantity rather than quality, because when making lists, quantity leads to quality. Your job as a facilitator is to get quantity, because if you have quantity, you can offer your client options. It is your mission to get a long list. And this can be difficult. When you're learning to be a facilitator, there's a tendency to think that all the ideas on the list have to be good or you're not doing a good job. This isn't the case. When you go for quantity, you're assured of having cool ideas on the list from which the client can make choices.

Rule #4

We are going to take detours and make connections that create quantity, novelty, and relevance. We have added this rule because we want to set the expectation with the group that from time to time the facilitator will change directions and he will want the group to follow along and explore any opportunity to search for additional ideas to place on the list.

Rule #5

We need ideas to be specific and clear so that all participants can understand them. Specific ideas have a higher likelihood of becoming reality. As facilitators, when we are given an incomplete idea, it's our job to help the group fill it in with enough specificity that everybody in the room—especially the client—can visualize the idea in action.

Rule #6

All ideas must be written down. Choosing not to write an idea down would be a violation of rule #1. We recommend that facilitators set the expectation with the group that everything they say in an idea-generation session deserves to be captured on the list, even if it has been said before. Sometimes a participant comes up with an idea that is almost identical to one that has already been captured on the list. It is much better to write it down again than to waste time looking for the earlier version to compare the two.

Rule #7

Everybody participating in the list-making or idea-generation session is equal in rank. There are no bosses. There is no hierarchy. Idea-generation sessions need to be devoid of rank because rank suggests that the ideas offered by the boss are better than those of others. Groups appreciate when the facilitator reads this rule in the presence of the boss. It reminds everyone that all ideas will be considered equally, which elicits a longer list of ideas.

INTRODUCING DETOURS

As you read rule #4, you likely noticed the word *detour* and wondered what we meant by it. Detours are a very important tool for generating ideas. The best way to introduce detours is to show you how they work.

Let's say we ask you to make a list of things you can do with a chair. Your list will likely look like this:

- Sit in it
- Lean back in it
- Stand on it

We have a few responses but we need more. So we take a detour. We ask, "Please imagine you were five years old. What might you do with a chair?"

Suddenly the direction of the idea-generation session changes:

- Stand on it to reach a cookie jar
- Build a fort with it
- Color it with marker
- Hide under it

A detour is a technique the facilitator uses to help a resource group generate more quantity, novelty, and relevance in a list. As the term implies, it causes a person's mind to go in a different direction and search for new ideas in new and often unexpected places.

In its simplest form, a detour is a question, suggestion, or piece of information that serves as a spark to inspire the generation of ideas.

As you saw when Richard helped his resource group make a list of names for a dog, detours are generally used by facilitators when the number of ideas being generated slows down or when the facilitator would like to explore a different way of looking at the problem being solved.

Later in this book, we will discuss how detours can be complex, full-fledged techniques that completely distract the resource group by engaging them in a separate endeavor with the intention of bringing them back to the original objective with entirely new insights.

Whether they are simple or complex, detours help a resource group make fresh new connections they may never have considered otherwise.

MAKING CHOICES

We have found that making choices is one part heart and one part brain.

Most clients have enough experience in their own business that a choice based on their gut should not really be considered a reckless shot in the dark. And this is fine when we are asking the client to make the first cut from the list. However, we know that not everything that feels right is going to work. Once the client has selected the ideas that feel good, the Creative Resources Process calls for the use of criteria to more thoroughly vet the ideas before selecting the one that will ultimately be executed. Criteria will be discussed more thoroughly in chapter 9.

Now that you understand the basic premises of the Creative Resources Process, let us introduce you to the cast of characters that you encounter in the typical idea-generation session.

THE CAST OF CHARACTERS

Our session began at eight-thirty in the morning. By the ten o'clock break we were well into our idea-generation session. Paige, the woman I thought was my client, gestured for me to join her in the back of the room where she was speaking with the man who'd snuck in the back door just as we were getting ready to take a break.

"Gerry, I want you to meet Bill. He's our new executive vice president. Bill is going to be responsible for all the offices in our region."

And that's how I met Bill, my *real* client.

Sometimes figuring out the dynamics of a facilitation session is a lot like watching people play a sport with which you are not familiar. You can guess that every player is probably playing a different role; you just don't know what the roles are. This is true even when you are facilitating a project within your own company. One of the most common mistakes is assuming that the person with the biggest title is the client. You may think you are familiar with all the players and how they fit into an organizational chart, but your success as a facilitator may very well depend on your ability to clearly identify who is playing which role for any given project.

The facilitator manages the people through the process

The client, the ultimate decision maker, wants to accomplish an objective

The agent wants to help the client accomplish his objective

Objective

The resource group makes the lists from which the client or the agent makes choices

Figure 2. The Cast of Characters

In every marketing project there are all sorts of people involved to different degrees, with different levels of interest in the outcome and different power or influence over the methods used to accomplish that outcome. When it comes to the generation of ideas, all these people are generally playing one of four roles in a consistent cast of characters. We want to teach you how to recognize them quickly to save you a lot of time and heartache.

There are four primary roles being played in an idea-generation session: the client, the facilitator, the agent, and the resource group. We begin by describing the roles of client and facilitator because the overwhelming majority of idea-generation sessions require those two roles as a minimum. Take a look at figure 2 as we review all four roles.

THE CLIENT

Every project has a client. The client is the person who is looking to make something happen. We describe the client as the "engine" of the process because it is his need to accomplish a marketing objective that drives the process forward. One would think that identifying the client should be simple enough—you just talk to the person in charge. But the truth is that there are a variety of reasons why identifying the client can become quite tricky. We'll expand on this in a moment.

It is unfortunate that the word *client* often has connotations of an outside customer. The overwhelming majority of the facilitators we train facilitate projects for clients within their own companies. The client can be an executive of your company, a supervisor, a colleague from another department, or a customer of the company. In our context, facilitators need to focus their attention on clients who need help creating marketing plans, so the client is simply the person who is looking for new ideas to create demand for a product or a service and not necessarily the person with the highest rank. Think of him as the client of the facilitator rather than the client of the company.

The client is the person who:

- Needs to accomplish a marketing objective.
- Gets to make choices off the list.
- Is the only one who can say yes to a specific idea.
- May or may not be in the room for all steps of the process.
- May or may not ever meet the facilitator.

The best clients are forthcoming with information about their situation. Imagine that you come across a client who wants to introduce a new product, but doesn't want to tell you what it is; or a client who wants to sell more cars, but doesn't want to tell you how many cars he is currently selling. There is nothing more frustrating than the client who tells you he needs help and then makes you drag every piece of information out of him.

A helpful client suspends judgment. As difficult as it might be to hear outlandish suggestions, a good client will not reveal acceptance or rejection, either verbally or through body language, but will instead encourage free thinking. A client who is too attached to the problem can be difficult to manage. He needs to be willing to allow the facilitator and the resource group to remove himself from the problem, to help him consider other possibilities, and to be open to looking at the situation in different ways. Some clients have very clear objectives and can state them quite clearly. Others are stuck and need help to identify and clarify the problem. The process gives the client other perspectives about what the objective might be, how that objective might be solved, or what idea might be best. That is why the best client is one who can suspend judgment and allow a facilitator to help him explore a variety of marketing objectives and possible solutions.

THE FACILITATOR

The facilitator is the person who manages people through the process that will get the client the desired outcomes. Everything that is connected with the facilitation project—whether it happens before, during, or after the session—is the responsibility of the facilitator. This does not mean the facilitator has to do it all. But it does mean that the facilitator needs to know that everything is being done.

The facilitator is the person who:

- Manages the process.
- Generally does not stay involved in the project beyond the job of facilitator.
- May or may not ever meet the client.
- May or may not be part of the client's company.

The facilitator has to have enough familiarity with the fundamentals of marketing that even when she may not be completely familiar with the specifics of the client's business, she at least knows the questions that need to be asked. (We will get very specific about the marketing questions we recommend when we review the marketing analysis in chapter 5.)

The most effective facilitators have a strong enough ego that they can command the attention and respect of a group, but know when to stay out of the spotlight during a session.

One of the central responsibilities of a facilitator is to organize the project in such a way that when the time comes to generate ideas, the resource group is ready to make a long list of options that contains a wide variety of ideas to accomplish the client's marketing objective.

An effective facilitator is always putting herself in the shoes of the other members of the cast of characters. When it comes to the client, she is always asking herself, "If I were the client, would I have a wide enough variety of ideas on this list from which to choose?"

When it comes to the resource group, the facilitator is always asking herself, "If I were a member of the resource group, would I have enough information to help me come up with ideas in this situation?"

When it comes to the agent, the facilitator is asking herself, "If I were the agent, would I have a clear path to follow after this session so I can continue working with this client without the help of this facilitator?"

The facilitator needs to behave as if she is getting paid for the job whether or not any money is exchanging hands. Often the facilitator is engaged in a project for which she is not compensated. The most common illustration of this is the facilitator who works in the same company— even in the same department—as the client. It is important to remember in this situation that the client may be a CEO or a higher-up with great authority. But regardless of her usual relationship with the client, the facilitator should take care to always do as good a job as she would if she were being paid for it.

THE AGENT

If you're a facilitator, there is a good chance you have been recruited by an agent to help him solve his client's problem. Agents play a specific role, but we have found they come from many different situations.

The head of sales for a bicycle tire company is responsible for two separate and parallel sales divisions. One of the divisions is very successful; the other is having trouble this year. So the head of sales calls his director of marketing and requests that one of the people in the marketing department facilitate an idea-generation session to help the struggling sales division. The head of sales is the agent because he arranged for the session and recruited the facilitator. The client is the person in charge of the struggling division. The facilitator is the person recruited from marketing.

In another example, a good friend, who happens to be on the board of directors of a civic group, asked me to facilitate a session for her organization. It seems her group had evolved over the years and needed to change its name, and she wanted a facilitator to run the session. She played the role of agent, and the executive director of her civic organization was the client; I was the facilitator.

In a third situation, a salesperson for a television station is in danger of losing an important advertising account. She needs some cool ideas for this particular account. One of the production directors at the station is a trained facilitator. He is called in to run an idea-generation session for the client. The salesperson is the agent who needs ideas for her advertising client. The facilitator is the production director who was recruited by the salesperson. The client, who was never in the room, was the advertiser.

These three real-world scenarios help to illustrate the role of the agent. The agent is a person, inside or outside the client's or the facilitator's organization, who has a vested interest in helping the client accomplish his objective. The agent:

- Is engaged with the client before and after the facilitator's involvement in the project.
- Often recruits or hires the facilitator for the project.
- Represents the interests of the client when the client is not in the room.
- Can recommend to the client that an idea be implemented.
- Takes responsibility for moving the project forward on behalf of the client.

THE RESOURCE GROUP

Either the agent or the facilitator assembles the resource group for any given project. The resource group makes the lists from which the client or the agent will make choices. The most important job of the resource group is to follow the directions given by the facilitator. Precisely what those directions are will depend on the project and also on the step of the process for which the resource group has been assembled.

In general, the resource group:

- Follows the directions given by the facilitator.
- Asks questions as needed of the client or agent.
- Generates a long, deep list of ideas.
- Prepares before all sessions.

Matching the Resource Group to Target Consumers

Sally was once hired to facilitate an idea-generation session for a major beverage company. The marketing objective was to get seventeen- and eighteen-year-olds to sample the company's new product.

The agent had casually chosen the resource group from among the people in her company. As Sally was about to start the session, she looked around the room and discovered that the entire group consisted of middle-aged men and women—not the seventeen- and eighteen-year-olds the beverage company was targeting to drink a specific new product. Sally proceeded with the session but later talked to the agent about scheduling a second session in which the resource group was made up of individuals in the client's target age group.

Not surprisingly, the ideas generated in the second session were much more relevant, more fun, and better connected to the seventeen- and eighteen-year-old lifestyle. The members of the resource group were using words the target audience uses, not words that middle-aged people use.

This example points to the importance of making sure the resource group is familiar with the topic of the project. Whether they know the subject matter because it is part of their job or because the facilitator and the agent gave them the information, the members of the resource group need to come to all sessions with enough domain knowledge to make a significant contribution.

Now that you've met the different players and the roles they can play in the cast of characters, let's take a look at the four situations where you can see them in action.

3

FOUR APPLICATIONS OF THE CREATIVE RESOURCES PROCESS

The Creative Resources Process can happen in four different situations: an event, a round robin, one-on-one, and in a solo session. We refer to them as applications because they represent four different contexts where the Creative Resources Process can be applied to help a client accomplish an objective.

Think of these four applications as tools the facilitator can choose depending on the circumstances. For instance, an all-day strategy session for a client calls for a different kind of meeting than a client who wants a facilitator to help her work through a problem she is having within her department. The facilitator may decide to use more than one of these applications during her work on any given project.

THE EVENT

If I say, "I'm on my way to a brainstorming session," most people will visualize a meeting in a conference room with a dozen people in attendance and flip chart paper all over the walls. That's why we call it an event. In an event, we get together in a conference room with a client who needs help, a facilitator who helps the client make a list and make choices, a resource group who generates the ideas, and an agent who helps the client make his idea a reality. The event calls on the facilitator to orchestrate the entire process; she needs to manage a resource group, have a relationship with the agent, and interact effectively with the client.

Meetings in the event context are both larger and longer than the other applications. On the one hand, the event can be a great tool for impressing a client or for giving everyone in the department a chance to contribute to the solution of a problem. On the other hand, it can be like driving a ten-team stagecoach in that it requires a tighter rein than the other applications.

THE ROUND ROBIN

The round robin is another application that uses the basic steps of the Creative Resources Process. The difference is that everybody at the table takes turns being client and resource group member. A good example is when a company's facilitator leads a meeting of department heads. Once the group is assembled, one of the participants assumes the role of client. In this case, the person in charge of sales talks about the challenges she's facing getting salespeople to create interest for a specific new product her department has just introduced. The facilitator now leads the other department heads in generating a long list of ideas from which the sales director can make choices. Once the sales director has enough ideas, she thanks the resource group and the focus of the session rotates to a different person. Next it's the human resources director's turn. As he assumes the role of client, he gives the resource group an overview of his particular situation and then states the objective with which he wants help. Just as he did with the sales director, the facilitator leads the resource group in an idea-generation session for the human resources director. Once the human resources director is happy with the ideas he has received from the team, he rejoins the resource group and the next department head assumes the role of client.

Round robin is an effective format for meetings that happen on a regular basis. Compared to the event—where the facilitator, the client, and the resource group could all come from different disciplines and therefore could be relatively unfamiliar with each other—the round robin is a much more intimate meeting. This makes it an ideal setting when there are several colleagues who all need help at the same time. The round robin is usually appropriate when everybody knows each other and all participants are familiar with the issues at hand. This means the facilitator doesn't have to spend a lot of time educating the resource group. Round robin is also used when the issues are low-risk, because the group typically spends only about fifteen to twenty minutes generating ideas for each person.

ONE-ON-ONE

The third type of meeting is the one-on-one. As the name implies, a one-on-one session involves only two players, a client (or an agent representing a client) in search of a solution and a facilitator whose job it is to help the client get through the process successfully. When the time comes to make a list, both people become the resource group. When the time comes to make a choice, the facilitator is there to help the client, just as she would in any other situation.

A facilitator may choose the one-on-one situation when the nature of the client's problem is sensitive, emotional, or confidential.

Sally recently led a one-on-one session with a long-time client. The client walked in asking for help with a work-related problem. She was part of an organization that had gone through an ownership change, resulting in a lot of stress and tension. There had been a partial turnover of the company's managers, and in the turmoil Sally's client had lost the support of her team—and had lost confidence in her own ability to be effective.

The client started out wanting Sally's help in organizing a marketing meeting with her staff, but Sally noticed right away that this was not the real issue her client needed to solve. Sally said, "You did not come over here at six o'clock for me to help you invent a marketing team meeting. There's got to be more to it than that. What else do you want to make happen here?"

Finally, the client stated her true objective: "How do I get my team to believe that I can help them bring the two corporate brands together? I need tools that I can use to get my staff out of their separate corners and working together."

The ideas Sally and her client generated were geared toward winning back the confidence of her staff. The client had walked into the room thinking, "I'm scared I'm going to have to find another job," and walked out of the room relieved, knowing she had options on how to deal with her team.

Over the years, we have heard many stories vouching for the power of one-on-one facilitation in solving personal problems. One mom told us, "I facilitated an idea-generation session for my teenager last night. She hadn't opened up to me like that in years!" Going through the process one-on-one can be a powerful tool for anyone who needs help.

SOLO SESSION

The process of self-facilitation is referred to as a solo session. Once you learn the fundamentals of each step of the Creative Resources Process, you can sit down and say, "Okay, what do I need help with? Let me figure out what my objective is, and then I'll make a long list of ideas and make choices from that list." This is a powerful way to work through a problem by yourself and generate a good solution.

Once you know how to make a list and make choices, you don't need to wait for a facilitator and a resource group in order to solve your problems. You can apply this process whenever you need to generate an idea for yourself. That is the true power of working solo.

CHOOSING THE APPROPRIATE APPLICATION

The choice of which application of the process to use can be made by the facilitator, the client, or the agent, either individually or after consulting with each other.

The choice will be to decide whether the inclusiveness of the event, the egalitarianism of the round robin, the intimacy of the one-on-one, or the privacy of a solo session is most appropriate for the situation at hand. Here are other considerations to explore when choosing the most appropriate application.

- The facilitator can arrange an event when she wants the help of a big resource group, for instance, when there are many stakeholders involved, all of whom want their ideas considered.
- The round robin is a great application when there are a handful of people who need ideas for their own projects, but don't want to invest the time or the expense of scheduling an event.
- If the meeting needs to be more intimate, or if there is some confidential information the client needs to express, then it is appropriate to use the one-on-one application.
- If the client doesn't have access to a facilitator, or if there is a part of the process that he can take on himself, then it may be enough to do a solo session.

You will notice that most of the illustrations in this book happen in the context of the event. We have deliberately chosen the event as the context of our illustrations because events contain the entire cast of characters (facilitator, client, agent, and resource group) so you can see how they interact with each other in real-world situations.

Now that you know the four applications of the process you are about to learn, we might as well get right into it. The Creative Resources Process begins when a client makes a wish.

4

WHY YOU CAN'T GET
WHAT YOU WISH FOR

Y ou and I sit down over a cup of coffee and you notice that I am a
little nervous, perhaps distracted. "What's up?" you ask.

I say, "Man, I have a lot going on!"

"Like what?"

So I say, "Well, let's see, I have job stress and personal stress. So take
your pick."

"Which would *you* pick?"

Of course, I don't want to pick, so I say, "I want both of them to go
away!"

You don't let me get away with that. "We can definitely work on both
of them. We just need to resolve them one at a time."

Finally I say, "Okay. In that case I want to reduce my personal stress."

A CURE FOR STRESS

Without a moment's hesitation, you—like the overwhelming majority of
the people to whom we have described that identical situation—immediately start throwing out suggestions to relieve stress: "Take a vacation . . .
drink a glass of wine . . . get a massage . . . do yoga . . . have sex . . . take

a sedative." The list of ideas can become quite silly—and, even more important, predictable.

After a couple of minutes of casually offering me suggestions, you can see in my face that I'm not particularly excited about any of your ideas. So you decide to change your approach.

"Okay, why don't you tell me all the factors that are causing you stress?"

I ask, "Do you mean at work or at home?"

"You said you wanted to resolve your personal stress. Let's start there."

I begin by explaining that I just moved from Seattle to Providence to take a new job, and that I had to move before selling my house in Seattle. The mortgage on my old house is costing me $2,500 each month, which puts a real strain on my bank account. It also means that the house my family is renting in Providence isn't as nice as the house we left in Seattle.

My wife is unhappy about moving all the way across the country. Providence is a very nice city, but it's far away from her relatives in Seattle. Not only that, but my children—who used to be A and B students—are doing poorly in their new school.

When I drove my car from Seattle to Providence, it broke down several times along the way. Every time I tried to fix it something else went wrong. I took it to a mechanic who told me it's a real lemon and that I need to get a new car.

"Wow!" you say. "I don't know where to start!" So you grab a piece of paper and begin to make a list. Except this list is different from the list of suggestions you were firing at me a minute ago. This list includes all the different facts I have given you about my situation. I blurted them out at you so quickly that you ask me to go back and review them, as there are a couple you missed. Here is the list of facts you captured:

1. Moved from Seattle to Providence.
2. Paying a $2,500 mortgage in Seattle.
3. Wife is unhappy.
4. Kids doing poorly in school.
5. Car is a clunker.

"What do you think?" I ask.

Without answering me, you begin to write again.

"What are you writing now?"

"Objectives."

"My objective is to reduce my personal stress."

"No, that is your wish."

"What is the difference?"

"Let me explain. First, you told me that you had job stress and personal stress."

"Don't remind me!"

You continue, "Then you chose personal stress to work on first."

"Right."

"The wish is vague. We need something much more specific to work on. That's why I asked you to give me some facts. So you told me about the house in Seattle, your wife being unhappy, the kids, the car, and so on. But those are just facts. We don't have anything we can work on yet. What we need to do is to turn the facts into objectives so we can work on them one at a time. Let me show you what I mean."

With that you begin to read the list of objectives back to me. Here are the objectives on the list:

1. How do we sell the house in Seattle?
2. How do we get your wife excited about living in Providence?
3. How do we help the kids do better in school?
4. How do we get a new car?

At first glance it looks to me as if you are just writing the same things over again, but then I catch on to what you are doing. You are using each of the facts—such as "Wife is unhappy"—and converting them into objectives: "How do we get your wife excited about living in Providence?"

You turn to me and say, "I know we can figure out how to solve each one of these. But we should probably take them one at a time."

I protest, "Again with the 'one at a time' thing!"

You explain, "I promise we can go back and work on the other objectives if you want. But right now, I just need you to tell me which you want to work on first."

I think about it for a brief moment and respond, "I think the key here is to sell the house in Seattle."

"Why that one?" you ask.

"First of all, I won't have to pay a $2,500 monthly mortgage anymore. Next, by selling the house, I communicate to my family, 'We're burning the bridge. We are not going back to Seattle. I want everyone to realize that we're making a go of it here in Providence. We're going to be happy. I know that we're going through a difficult time right now, but we're going to be okay.' Then, once I've sold the house, I can take the $2,500 and send my wife to Seattle to see her family two or three times each year so she continues to be in contact with them. So I want to sell that house in Seattle and I want you to help me come up with ideas on how to sell the house. Will you help me?"

"Absolutely!" you say. "I can give you some ideas."

Let's stop here and take a look at what has happened in this conversation. When you and I sat down, you asked me what was going on, I gave you two vague statements like "job stress" and "personal stress." Then you made me pick one. As soon as I picked one, you began to give me a bunch of ideas to help me resolve this vague situation I called "personal stress."

If we were to map the conversation up to that point, it would look like figure 3.

First of all, notice that the first column contains two statements: "Reduce Job Stress" and "Reduce Personal Stress." We call them wishes because they are vague statements of desire. Also notice that there is a check mark next to "Reduce Personal Stress" because that is the wish I chose to work on first.

Now take a look at the fourth column, which is labeled "Ideas." That's where we listed all the ideas you gave me before you asked me any questions about my personal stress. When you noticed that I wasn't reacting well to the ideas you were giving me, you decided to ask me some questions. That's when you discovered that this vague situation I called "personal stress" contains a lot of other issues that need to be addressed. As the conversation progresses and I begin to tell you all the things that are causing stress in my personal life, suddenly we see that we need to change the map of the conversation to look more like the illustration in figure 4.

Wish			Ideas
1. Reduce Job Stress. ✓2. Reduce Personal Stress.			1. Take a vacation. 2. Drink a glass of wine. 3. Get a massage. 4. Do Yoga. 5. Have sex. 6. Take a sedative.

Figure 3. Ideas to Reduce Personal Stress

The second column in figure 4 shows the list of facts that was, in essence, hidden inside the wish "reduce personal stress."

The third column contains all the objectives suggested by the facts of the situation. Finally, you will notice that we have placed a check mark next to the first item on the list—"How do we sell the house in Seattle?"—because that is the objective I chose to work on first.

Now take a look at the fourth column, which contains all the ideas you gave me before you did any fact-finding about my situation. You can see very clearly that the ideas you gave me to solve my wish ended up being completely irrelevant to my objective, which is to sell the house in Seattle.

In a moment, we are going to replay this conversation in a business context. But before we do that, let's take stock of what we learned from the first conversation about the process of getting a client from a vague wish to a specific objective.

Wish	Facts	Objectives	Ideas
1. Reduce Job Stress. ✓2. Reduce Personal Stress.	1. Moved from Seattle to Providence. 2. Paying a $2,500 mortgage in Seattle. 3. Wife is unhappy. 4. Kids doing poorly in school. 5. Car is a clunker.	How do we... ✓1. Sell the house in Seattle? 2. Get your wife excited about living in Providence? 3. Help the kids do better in school? 4. Get a new car?	1. Take a Vacation. 2. Drink a glass of wine. 3. Get a massage. 4. Do Yoga. 5. Have sex. 6. Take a sedative.

Figure 4. Facts Lead to Objectives

The first lesson is perhaps the most painfully obvious one. When you generate ideas to solve a wish, the ideas end up being completely irrelevant to the client's objective. The obvious question is: *What is the likelihood that if I asked you to come up with ideas to sell my house in Seattle, you would tell me to get a massage?* The flip side of that is: *What is the likelihood that if I asked you for ideas to relieve my personal stress, you would come up with an idea that would help me sell my house in Seattle?*

Here are other lessons that we have learned so far:

- Most people—and clients are no exception—state their needs in the form of vague statements of desire, like "reduce personal stress" and "reduce job stress." We call those vague statements wishes.
- It is very common for clients to have several different wishes they want help with. A good facilitator needs to help the client make a list of wishes and then choose the one he wants to work on first.

- Once a client has chosen a wish, the facilitator needs to do some fact-finding to discover all the factors that contribute to the wish the client has chosen.
- Even though the client had more than one wish on the list, the facilitator needs to focus her fact-finding only on the wish chosen by the client.
- The facts of any situation suggest objectives the client may want to focus on.
- The facilitator will help the client make a list of objectives and, just like she did when she helped him choose a wish, she will ask the client to choose the objective he wants to focus on first.

GROWING MY BUSINESS

We are about to listen in on a conversation similar to the one above, except it will be in the context of marketing a business. Because the conversation is happening in a marketing context, you will notice that although the steps of the process remain the same, the facilitator needs to be more thorough in a couple of spots to help the client move from a wish to a marketing objective.

Let's say I own a small restaurant called Louie's. You and I sit down over a cup of coffee and you notice that I am a little nervous, perhaps distracted. "What's up?" you ask.

I say, "Man, I have a lot going on!"

"Like what?"

I say, "My business is growing in several directions at once. Sometimes it's hard to figure out where I should be spending my time."

You say, "I might be able to help you."

To which I say, "Great! What do we need to do?"

"Well, do you think you can state all your different priorities in the form of wishes?"

"You want me to make a wish?"

"Yes," you say, "make a wish."

"Well, okay. Let's see . . . I wish I had more time."

"Good. What about a year from now. What do you wish you have accomplished in a year?"

"In a year, I wish my new function room were booked all the time."

"Great. What about sooner, say in ninety days. What do you wish?"

"In ninety days, my restaurant better get more traffic or I'm in trouble!"

"Okay. Now let's think about the different parts of the business. Are there any other wishes there?"

"I'm glad you reminded me. We have a catering business that we are trying to grow."

"Great. Is there a wish there?"

"Yes," I say, "I wish we had a really successful catering business."

Now you look at the list of wishes and say, "I can help you with these."

"Great!"

"But we need to do them one at a time."

I protest, "But I need help with all of them!"

"Yes, I know. Still, we need to work on them one at a time."

"I don't know where to start!"

"I can help you make a choice. I am going to ask you to think about three questions before you choose one of your wishes to work on. Okay?"

"Okay."

"First, I want you to think about importance. Which of the wishes on the list are more important to you at this time than the others? Let's work on the more important ones first.

"Second, do you need an idea? What I mean is, don't choose a wish if you already know what you are going to do about it. Pick something where you really need a new idea.

"And third, is it under your influence? Whatever wish you choose needs to be in an area that is under your responsibility so you can take action on the ideas we come up with."

That last question catches my attention because not all of the wishes on the list are my responsibility. So I say, "Well, I'm in charge of the restaurant and the function room, but the catering business is my brother Charlie's problem."

You push ahead, "Okay, so you have four wishes. You wish you had more time, and you want to grow the catering business, get people to the new function room, and increase traffic to Louie's. Which do you want to work on first?"

"Since the catering business is not my problem and the function room hasn't opened yet, I say let's get more traffic into Louie's. Now, I should warn you that the other day I had a little meeting with the staff and they started spitballing some ideas . . ."

"Really? Like what?"

"Well, stuff like drop the price of the burgers . . . hand out flyers . . . get a mascot . . . sponsor the little-league team . . . get somebody famous to endorse the restaurant. You know, the same old stuff."

"You don't sound excited."

"No. It was the same stuff I've heard before."

"Okay. Why don't you tell me all the factors we need to consider if we are going to get more traffic to your store."

I explain that I have noticed that I have three different types of customers. "There is the guy who likes to come in for lunch. He's a blue-collar guy who probably works in construction and he wants a hearty hamburger.

"Then I have the mom with a couple of kids. She likes to come in because her kids can have small burgers while she has a Caesar salad. Louie's is a good compromise between the fast food moms consider unhealthy and the salad place the kids consider boring. She ends up spending more money than the blue-collar guy because she buys for more people.

"Then I have the teenagers who come in the evenings and especially over the weekend. My place becomes sort of a kids' hangout, not only in the restaurant but in the parking lot as well. Most merchants would mind that, but I don't. The truth is that they don't bother my other customers and it makes my place look hip—although it would be great if I could get them to spend a little more money. Sometimes they come in and just buy a pop or a milkshake and it would be great if they would also buy food.

"Oh, and I forgot to tell you that we are going to start serving frozen custard in the summers."

"Wow!" you say. "You really *do* have a lot going on!" So you grab a piece of paper and begin to make another list.

1. Blue-collar guy comes in for lunch.
2. Mom uses us as compromise, spends more money.
3. Teenagers on weekends.
4. Serving frozen custard this summer.

"Well, let me ask you. Are there some facts that matter more to you than others? Any key facts that we should keep in mind?"

"Yes. I think the blue-collar guy and the mom are critical. They both make me money. Then the frozen custard is a new thing, so I want to keep that in mind as well."

"What do you think?" I ask.

Without answering me, you begin to write again.

"What are you writing now?"

"Objectives."

"My objective is to increase traffic."

"No, that is your wish."

"What is the difference?"

"The wish is vague. We need something much more specific to work on. That's why I asked you to give me some facts. You told me about the blue-collar guy who comes in for lunch, the mom who uses your restaurant as the compromise place, the teenagers who make your place feel hip, and the frozen custard you are going to serve this summer. Now there are three key facts here you said are critical. But they are still just facts. We don't have anything we can work on yet. What we need to do is to turn them into objectives so we can work on them one at a time. Let me show you what I mean."

With that, you begin to read the list of objectives back to me. Here are the objectives on the list:

1. How do we get more blue-collar guys to come in for lunch?
2. How do we get more moms to bring their kids for dinner?

3. How do we get moms and dads to bring their kids for frozen cus-
    tard this summer?

At first glance, it looks to me as if you just wrote the same things over
again, but then I catch on to what you've done. You used each of the key
facts, like "Blue-collar guy comes in for lunch" and converted them into
objectives, like "How do we get more blue-collar guys to come in for
lunch?"

Now you turn to me and say, "I know we can figure out how to
accomplish each one of these objectives. But we need to take them one at
a time."

"Again with the 'one at a time' thing!"

"Yes, you need to choose one. Do you remember the questions I asked
you earlier when you were choosing the wish?"

"What were they again?"

"Is this objective important? Is this an objective for which you need
an idea? And is this objective under your influence, so that you can take
action on any ideas we generate? So which do you think makes the most
sense to work on first?"

I think about it for a moment and respond, "I think the big opportunity for me is to focus on the frozen custard. Here's my thinking. First of
all, summer is almost here and this is a new product that most people
don't know I serve. Now, if I can get families to come out in the evenings
and weekends for custard, I'll bet you we can come up with ways to get
them to try the rest of the items on the menu. That ought to create traffic
throughout the rest of the week." And then I ask you, "Do you think you
could help me come up with some ideas to get moms and dads to bring
their kids to my burger joint in the evenings for frozen custard?"

"Absolutely!" you say. "I can give you some ideas."

Let's stop here and take a look at what has happened in this conversation. When you and I sat down and you asked me what was going on,
I had all sorts of things swirling around in my head.

Then, you asked me to make a wish and I gave you some vague statement of desire ("I wish I had more time").

Then you started asking me questions to help me generate more wishes. You asked me questions that were time-based—"What would you like to accomplish in a year?"—and you also asked me questions about my different areas of responsibility, like, "Think about the different parts of the business. Are there any wishes there?" These questions helped make a list of four different wishes.

Then you asked me to choose one of the wishes from the list. But instead of just asking me to pick, you asked me three questions you wanted me to keep in mind:

- Is it important?
- Do you need an idea?
- Is it under your influence?

After I thought about those questions, I chose one wish: "Increase traffic for Louie's."

As soon as I chose that wish, I mentioned that I had had a meeting with the staff at the restaurant and they had come up with a bunch of ideas that were, quite frankly, kind of boring.

If we were to map the conversation we just had, it might look like figure 5.

First of all, let's notice that the first column contains four different wishes and that we have put a check mark next to "Increase Traffic for Louie's," which is the wish I selected.

Then, let's notice that the fourth column contains all those ideas my staff generated, which I was not very excited about.

As the conversation progressed, you asked me for facts that have an impact on the creation of traffic for my restaurant. You even asked me to focus in on the key facts on the list.

Finally, you turned all the key facts into objectives and ended up with the different ones. Now we need to change the map of the conversation again to look like the illustration in figure 6.

The wishes—"Have More Time," "Get People to Use the Function Room," "Increase Traffic," "Grow Catering Business,"—are on the left-

Wish			Ideas
1. Had more time. 2. Get people to the new function room. ✓3. Increase traffic to Louie's. 4. Grow the catering business.			1. Drop the price of the burgers. 2. Hand out flyers. 3. Get a mascot. 4. Sponsor the little-league team. 5. Get somebody famous to endorse the restaurant.

Figure 5. Ideas to Increase Traffic to Louie's

Wish	Facts	Objectives	Ideas
1. Had more time. 2. Get people to the new function room. ✓3. Increase traffic to Louie's. 4. Grow the catering business.	✓1. Blue-collar guy comes in for lunch. ✓2. Mom uses us as compromise, spends more money. 3. Teenagers on weekends. ✓4. Serving frozen custard this summer.	How do we... 1. Get more blue-collar guys to come in for lunch? 2. Get more moms to bring their kids for dinner? ✓3. Get moms and dads to bring their kids for frozen custard this summer?	1. Drop the price of the burgers. 2. Hand out flyers. 3. Get a mascot. 4. Sponsor the little-league team. 5. Get somebody famous to endorse the restaurant.

Figure 6. Facts Lead to Objectives.

hand side because they were the first things I said—the things that started the conversation to begin with. The next column contains the list of facts that were, in essence, hidden inside the word *traffic*. Notice that three of them have check marks because I chose them as key facts.

The third column contains all the different objectives that were suggested by the key facts of the situation. Finally, you will notice that we have placed a check mark next to the third item on the list of objectives— "How do we get moms and dads to bring their families out to Louie's for frozen custard?" because that is the objective I chose to work on first.

Let's stop again and take stock of the lessons learned in the Louie's conversation.

Here again, we see very clearly that when you generate ideas to solve a wish, the ideas will end up being completely irrelevant to what the client's real objective is. Look at the ideas in the fourth column in figure 6. These are the ideas generated by the staff of Louie's to "increase traffic." The obvious question is: *What is the likelihood that if I asked you to come up with ideas to get moms and dads to bring their families out to Louie's for frozen custard, you would tell me to drop the price of the burgers?* The flip side of that is: *What is the likelihood that if I asked you for ideas to increase traffic, you would come up with an idea that would help me get moms and dads to bring their families out to Louie's for frozen custard?* The Louie's conversation reveals a structure that you—as the facilitator in the conversation—used to help me get from a vague wish to a specific marketing objective. We are going to review that structure next.

TURNING WISHES INTO MARKETING OBJECTIVES

The world would probably be a better place if all clients were in the habit of developing clear and concise marketing objectives on their own. But the reality is that most clients—regardless of their perceived level of marketing sophistication—come to a facilitator with a suitcase full of goals, desires, facts, fiction, issues, concerns, opinions—and, somewhere in there, the makings of a marketing strategy.

It is often the job of the facilitator to sort through all the things that are keeping the client up at night and figure out how to help him arrive at a well-crafted, focused marketing objective.

What follows is the sequence of three steps that a facilitator can use to help a client get from a vague wish to a specific marketing objective.

Finally, we will finish the chapter showing you how a facilitator might apply that sequence in the context of a business called Woodland Nurseries.

Step 1: The Client Makes a Wish

The process begins with the facilitator helping the client make a list of wishes. As you saw in the Louie's conversation, the person playing the role of facilitator asked time-based questions ("What do you want to accomplish in a year?") and areas of responsibility questions ("Are there other parts of the business that might need help?") to make the list of wishes longer.

Here are other questions the facilitator might ask the client at this point in the process:

Time-Based Questions

- Pretend we are sitting here one year from today. What do you wish you had accomplished?
- Let's change the time frame a little. In the next six months or so, what wishes do you have for your company or your department?
- Are there challenges you face for the next ninety days or so, and could you state them in the form of a wish?
- Let's think more urgently. Are there immediate or "hot" issues that you want to add to our wish list?

Questions Based on Areas of Responsibility

- Think of the different products, services, or departments you are responsible for. Are there any wishes there?

- Do you have any wishes motivated by any new markets or target consumers you are thinking of pursuing?
- Are there any specific areas of your business that have not yet reached their potential?

Then the facilitator asks the client to select one wish to work on first. To help the client choose a wish, the facilitator asks three questions.

1. Is the wish important? Every wish list contains some wishes that are more important than others. With this wish, the facilitator wants to help the client select from among the more important wishes.
2. Is it a wish for which you need an idea? The facilitator uses this question to avoid working on wishes for which the client already has an answer but is procrastinating on taking action. After all, this process is designed to generate ideas. Let's use it for that purpose.
3. Is the wish in your sphere of influence so you can take action on the ideas we generate? You saw in the Louie's example how this question saved us from working on the catering business, which is under someone else's sphere of influence.

Step 2: Fact-Finding

Now the facilitator embarks on a fact-finding mission on the wish the client has chosen. As you saw in the Louie's illustration, the client listed several facts about his customers, his products, and so on. Sometimes there is a resource group involved in the session. In most cases, the facilitator will invite the resource group to take part in the fact-finding and ask all the questions to which they need answers.

Then the facilitator asks the client to select the key facts. Again, the facilitator wants to bring to the surface the facts the client considers to be the most critical.

This is a good place to point out that in marketing, the fact-finding mission on which the facilitator embarks is called the marketing analysis.

We will cover the marketing analysis quite thoroughly in the next chapter.

Step 3: Creating the Marketing Objective

Having heard all the information generated during fact-finding and especially paying attention to the client's key facts, the facilitator's next task is to make a list of marketing objectives. Here again, in cases where there is a resource group present, the facilitator will invite the resource group to add to the list of marketing objectives. Then, the facilitator asks the client to select the marketing objective he wants to work on first.

Just as you saw in the Louie's example, the client will usually resist making a choice because he wants help with all of them. So the facilitator will again use these three questions to help the client make a choice: *Is this objective important? Is this an objective for which you need an idea? Is this objective under your sphere of influence?*

When the client selects a marketing objective, the facilitator will have completed the first step toward coming up with a marketing program.

We are going to conclude this chapter with the beginning of the Woodland Nurseries case study. You are about to see how Alesia, the facilitator for this project, helps her client make a list of wishes and select the first wish he wants to work on. The Woodland Nurseries case study will continue to appear throughout the book as an ongoing illustration of how a facilitator leads a client through the Creative Resources Process.

WOODLAND NURSERIES MAKES A WISH

Alesia is the manager of the Landscape Services Department at Woodland Nurseries, a nursery and landscape company with three locations in the suburbs of Atlanta. She has been asked to facilitate an idea-generation session for Sam, her boss and the owner of the nursery.

The person who asked Alesia to facilitate the session is Eric, the sales and marketing manager for the entire company and Sam's right-hand man. When Eric recruited Alesia to facilitate the session, he confirmed what she had already heard in a recent meeting of department heads: Woodland Nurseries is a very successful business, but Sam is looking to grow it to the next level. Alesia remembered thinking at the time, "I wonder what *that* means?" Little did she know that she was about to get the chance to help Sam and Eric figure it out!

Being a smart marketer—after all, she actually runs a small business within a business herself—Alesia knows that Sam is ultimately going to grow his business by getting a large enough group of target consumers to do or believe particular things about his products or services. But since she doesn't know which consumers he wants to target or what he wants them to do or believe, she is going to follow the Creative Resources Process all the way from the beginning. The first step is to help Sam make a wish.

Before her first meeting with Sam and Eric, Alesia spends a great deal of time preparing so that she is ready to help Eric and Sam. As the facilitator of the process, Alesia's first mission is to get Sam to make a list of wishes and then select the one wish he wants to work on first.

The Client Makes a Wish

Alesia and Sam are sitting in Sam's office having their first cup of coffee of the day.

Alesia says, "Sam, Eric has asked me to facilitate an idea-generation session for you."

"Yes. We really appreciate you taking the time. He and I are looking for some new ideas and we get kind of stuck."

"Okay. Well, maybe I could get you to start with some of the issues that have brought us to this conversation. What is it that you need help with?"

Sam has played this game before, so he is ready with a couple of answers, "Well, my wish is to grow my business. So that is number one. But of course, a huge part of that growth is going to come from the spring, so my second wish is to have a successful spring season."

Alesia asks, "Let's think a little more long-term. What about any wishes you have by the end of the year?"

"Well," says Sam, "we always hope to have a strong fall season."

"So what's the wish?"

"Well, maybe the wish is to increase sales in the fall."

"Good." Alesia has been capturing Sam's wishes on a legal pad. She has three so far. She knows she is nowhere near done, so she asks, "Let's think about all the different products and departments around here."

Sam immediately remembers a new product he is introducing. "Well, we need help selling the new rose we are introducing this spring."

"Okay."

"And let's not forget that we need more people to know about our award-winning landscape design services."

Alesia smiles, as she is in charge of landscape services. She wants to say, "Great wish!" but bites her tongue.

"What about any other challenges or opportunities that you have already?"

Sam says, "Those apartment complexes." They can see them from this office, so he points at them. "I wish we could take advantage of the fact that all those new potential customers have moved in a few miles down the street."

"We have six different wishes."

"Good list!"

"Good list," Alesia repeats, then reads the list of wishes back to Sam.

1. I need to grow my business.
2. I want to have a successful spring season.
3. I need to increase my sales in the fall.
4. We have this new rose we are introducing and we need help selling it.
5. I need people to know about our landscape services.
6. Take advantage of the new apartment complexes that have opened up a few miles down the street.

Alesia said, "Sam, I want you to imagine that we are going to work on all these wishes that you have listed here. But we need to take care of them one at a time, so I am going to ask you to consider three important questions that will help us decide which one you want us to address first. Think about all three questions before you make a choice.

- First, please choose a wish that is *important* to you. We want to be sure we are working on the more important wish first.
- Second, pick a wish that requires an *idea*. This process is designed to help you come up with cool and effective ideas, so choose a wish for which you need some ideas.
- Finally, please make sure to pick a wish over which you have *influence*. We don't want to solve someone else's problem today. We are interested in working on a challenge that is within your sphere of influence so we can take action on the ideas we generate.

Sam said, "There are a lot of promising goals on that list, but my bread and butter is the spring. So if I have to choose one place to start, I would say, let's work on item number 2."

Beautiful! Sam has a wish: "I want to have a successful spring season."

Now that she has helped Sam choose the wish he wants to work on first, Alesia is ready to move forward with a marketing analysis of Sam's wish. First, she is going to go spend some time with Eric, who is playing the role of agent. We will see them again in the next chapter.

We have seen the steps that a facilitator can follow to help a client get from a vague wish to a focused marketing objective. Once the client has chosen a wish to work on, the next step is to do some fact-finding, which in marketing is called the marketing analysis. That's where we are going next.

5

THE MARKETING ANALYSIS

In chapter 4, you saw how a facilitator helped a client make a list of wishes and then helped him select the wish he wanted to work on first. You also saw how a wish contains facts that, when explored individually, can lead to a list of objectives from which the client can select the one objective he wants to work on first. At the end of chapter 4 you saw how a facilitator, Alesia, succeeded in helping her client and boss, Sam, generate a list of wishes for Woodland Nurseries. Alesia then helped Sam select the first wish on which he wanted to focus: *I want to have a successful spring season.*

Alesia's next assignment—and the focus of this chapter—will be to go on a fact-finding mission into the wish Sam selected. Knowing the discussion would probably take a couple of hours, Eric arranged for a working lunch with Sam and Alesia. The meeting was held in the nursery's conference room, where Alesia could have access to a flip chart.

We are now going to introduce you to an organized and sequential method of exploring the facts of a marketing situation. We call it the marketing analysis.

The marketing analysis is a series of ten questions that are designed to expose the most critical elements of any marketing situation and make it easier for all the players in the cast of characters to begin to create a list of marketing objectives.

The marketing analysis prevents the facilitator from making assumptions about what the client wants to focus on. After all, we are at the very beginning of the process. All we know is that the client wants to have a successful spring season. But we know that vague wishes lead to vague ideas that have nothing to do with the client's real objective. This is why our next step is to embark on is this fact-finding mission we call the marketing analysis.

Another important benefit of the marketing analysis is that clients know some—but often not all—of the information they need to make marketing decisions. Your client will benefit from a simple, linear approach to arriving at a marketing strategy.

Let's first take a look at the ten questions of the marketing analysis; we will explore each one in depth later in this chapter:

1. What is the product?
2. Who is the target consumer?
3. What is the trigger that puts the target consumer in the market for this product?
4. What is the purchasing process?
5. What are the benefits sought by the target consumer?
6. How does the product compare to its competition?
7. How is the product positioned?
8. How is the product distributed?
9. What is the price of the product?
10. What are the product's seasons?

It is important to highlight the fact that the marketing analysis is a series of questions that need to be asked and answered in sequence, because the answers build on each other. For instance, the first question, "What is the product?" identifies the product as the client wants to define it for the project at hand. The second question, "Who is the target?" seeks to identify the target consumer for the product as it was defined in response to the first question. Once the product and its target consumer have been identified, question #3, "What is the trigger?" seeks to identify what specific event in the life of the target consumer puts him or her in the market for purchasing the product we have identified, and so on.

When you look at the marketing analysis questions in sequence, it becomes obvious that asking the marketing analysis questions out of sequence would be a complete waste of time. A powerful question like "What is the trigger?" makes sense only once we have identified a product and a target.

You can also see that if at any time during the project the client decides to change the definition of the product, all the other questions need to be asked again, as they are dependent on the answer to the first question.

To help you see how the questions work in sequence, we will follow the Woodland Nurseries example throughout the chapter. Even in cases where we use examples from other businesses to illustrate a point, we will always come back to the Woodland Nurseries illustration so that you can see how the process moves, from start to finish, in the context of the same example.

FACILITATING THE ANSWERS TO MARKETING ANALYSIS QUESTIONS

In the real world you will find that clients have clear, concise, well thought-out answers to some of the marketing analysis questions and no answer at all for others. For instance, let's take question 2: "Who is the target?" You might come across a client who can easily tell you, "We know his name, his age, where he works and we have reams of research containing everything you need to know about him." Great. You have your answer. More often than not, however, clients give vague answers, like, "My customers are generally adults, twenty-five to fifty-four"—or a client like the grocery store owner who told us with a straight face that his target consumer was "everybody who eats." In those cases, the facilitator needs to be prepared to lead the client through the process of selecting the most appropriate answer to the question.

MAKING LISTS AND MAKING CHOICES

The behaviors of making a list and then asking a client to make choices from that list is the most fundamental and powerful decision-making tool at the facilitator's disposal.

Now, as we embark on the marketing analysis, you will see the behavior of making lists and making choices employed as a fact-finding tool. Whenever a client needs help answering one of the questions in the marketing analysis, the facilitator will help him by having the client first make a list of possible answers and then choose the one answer he wants to use for his project.

As in all cases where a list needs to be made, the facilitator will be expected to take detours in order to help the client make the list longer. As we saw in chapter 1 when the facilitator helped the team make a list of dog names by suggesting the team members think about big dogs or little dogs, the facilitator will introduce detours into her interaction with the client to make the list longer.

The detours will come in the form of questions and prompts. A question might be: "What are all the things we know about the woman who buys flowers?" while a prompt might be: "Think of the physical layout of your store and help me make a list of things your target consumer could purchase." As we will cover in much greater detail in chapter 8, both questions and prompts are considered detours because they help the facilitator encourage the creation of a list from which the client can make a choice.

Whenever it is appropriate, we will give you some suggested detours you can use to make a list. Please note that you do not have to use all the detours we suggest. You will want to choose the detours from the list that are most appropriate for your situation.

LET'S TALK ABOUT RESEARCH

The process of fact-finding using the marketing analysis can become iterative; that is to say, it could happen that the facilitator begins the marketing analysis and discovers fairly quickly that some of the crucial information needed to complete the project is not available. In those cases, it would probably make sense for the facilitator to suggest that the client, and possibly the agent, do some research to secure the information before the process continues. It is conceivable, for instance, that the client truly does not know anything, insightful or otherwise, about his target consumer. The facilitator knows that such information is always available when looking in the right places and has the prerogative to suggest a recess in the process that will give the client and the agent time to gather more information before proceeding.

When it comes to research, there are two generally accepted types of research and several methods of gathering the information. The two types of research are primary and secondary research.

Primary research consists of research studies that are specifically commissioned, designed, and paid for by the client's company to find new information that is not currently available. Because the client has complete control over the questions asked, this kind of study commonly reveals most, if not all, the answers to the questions in the marketing analysis.

Primary research can be conducted using a variety of methods. Perhaps the most reliable method is to administer a telephone or online survey to a representative sample of the target consumer population. This sort of strategic study can be purchased from any one of a long list of research companies. It is common for trade associations and trade magazines to publish resource directories with the names of the most prominent research companies that specialize in that particular industry. A less expensive option might be to contact the marketing department at a local university. There, you might find a professor who would be willing to conduct a study for your company as a class project.

Of course, these days pretty much any company can conduct its own customer surveys very inexpensively using online research tools such as SurveyMonkey.com.

Another common method for investigating the preferences and values of target consumers is to meet with them in groups and engage them in discussions about issues that matter to the business and to them as customers. Formal group discussions are called focus groups, while informal groups take the form of advisory groups. The difference generally is that focus groups are "masked," which means they happen in a neutral facility and the identity of the company sponsoring them is not revealed. Advisory group meetings are "unmasked" and everyone knows what company is asking the questions; in fact, the meetings are usually held in the company's facility.

Secondary research consists of information that is generally available to everyone. The same trade associations and trade magazines that can lead you to a primary research vendor also customarily publish secondary research. Secondary research takes many forms. It can come in the form of white papers published by trade associations, trade magazines, and industry experts. Sometimes colleges with a specialization in a particular industry publish articles that offer insights into the decision-making process of a particular group of target consumers.

Perhaps the most important difference between primary and secondary research is in the specificity of the information it reveals.

For instance, where a primary research study commissioned by Woodland Nurseries to study women who love to garden will reveal how those women feel about Woodland Nurseries specifically, a secondary research study commissioned by the trade association for the nursery industry will reveal how all women who garden regularly feel about nurseries in general.

Another difference between primary and secondary research is the ease with which the information can be found. A primary research study contains all the answers in one document. In the absence of a primary study, one might have to search through several different sources to answer all the questions posed by the marketing analysis. Marketers who have the patience for thorough online searches will be rewarded with a surprising amount of information in almost every business category.

Our experience—and we have seen this in many different businesses—is that trade associations usually produce very valuable information that their members do not always know how to use.

One final note before we get into the marketing analysis. While a thorough marketing analysis is valuable for determining a good marketing objective, it also nets the facilitator at least two important assets to use when generating marketing ideas:

1. *Facts* are pieces of information that the facilitator and the resource group can use to create a list of marketing objectives.
2. *Detours* are pieces of information that the facilitator introduces into the list-making effort to add quantity, novelty, and relevance to the list.

Taking the time to do research, whether primary or secondary, is worth the effort—and it is essential for a more accurate marketing analysis.

MARKETING ANALYSIS QUESTIONS

The textbook way to begin a marketing analysis is by identifying a target consumer. However, in the real world, the analysis of any marketing situation can begin in one of two places: Either the client already has a product or service that needs to be marketed to a target consumer or the client has a target consumer who needs to be served by a product or service.

Products and Targets—Targets and Products

When the first question is "Who is the target?" the second question is always "What is the product?" Conversely, when the first question is "What is the product?" the second question is always "Who is the target?"

In the overwhelming majority of cases, clients have existing products and services that need to be marketed to target consumers. For that reason, we will begin our marketing analysis with the question "What is the product?"

1. WHAT IS THE PRODUCT?

Many businesspeople are under the erroneous impression that they have only one product. For instance, a convenience store owner might think his product is his convenience store. However, if you take a walk through a convenience store you see that even the smallest ones have a variety of products targeted to different consumers. And while the entire store is certainly one way to define the product, it is only one of several products that could become the focus of a marketing project. In the marketing analysis, the word *product* can be defined in a variety of ways:

- A brand (De Beers diamonds®, Scotts® gardening products). The scope of any given project could be to build brand equity for a specific brand. One way to think of this product definition is simply as the name of your business. The scope of a marketing project could be to give meaning to your company's name so that when your customers and potential customers hear it, they associate it with a benefit that matters to them, like when Verizon buys advertising to get all of us to believe they have the most reliable network.

- A store (Sterling Jewelers, Woodland Nurseries' southside location). A project could focus on one specific store. In a company that owns several locations, a grand opening of a new store is an illustration of how a project could focus on one store.

- A product category or department (all engagement rings, all lawn mowers). A large store like Wal-Mart which has a wide variety of departments, could conceivably need help with different departments at different times. You can see how the things that could be done to promote the automotive department would be different from the things that could be done to promote the toy department.

- A specific item that already exists (a tennis bracelet, Scotts® Turf Builder®). A project could focus on the sale of a specific item. A car dealership might have ten Mustangs® it needs to get rid of before the new models arrive; a real estate company might need to rent one particular building.

- A specific product or service that the client is about to introduce (a new anniversary ring, a new zero-radius CubCadet® lawn mower). A project could focus on a brand-new product that the client is introducing. Please notice that this definition of a product is the same as the last definition (a specific item), except in this case we are speaking about a specific item the client is about to introduce that is currently not available. We have given new items their own product definition because we want the facilitator to remember to inquire about any new products the client might be getting ready to introduce.

We have been involved in projects where we discover late in the process that the client is considering introducing a new product or service that was never mentioned because the question had not been asked. We also created different product definitions for existing items and new items because the new item might require a more thorough explanation, given the fact that it is new.

- An ingredient (cotton, honey). Pretty much every raw material used in the manufacture of products has a trade association interested in increasing the consumption of that product. It is common, for instance, for Cotton Incorporated—the trade association for the cotton industry—to fund marketing programs in collaboration with retailers. A project could consist of convincing a customer to visit a store such as J. Jill or Brooks Brothers to purchase garments made of cotton.
- A local group or association (Hoboken Merchants Association, Antique Dealers Group). This definition of the product is very common among retailers who band together for a common cause.

As mentioned earlier, it is possible—even likely—that the product question has already been answered even before the marketing analysis is begun. For instance, the client may have chosen a wish such as "I need help selling the ten Mustangs I have on the lot." Or, in the case of the Woodland Nurseries, the client could have chosen the wish "We have this new rose we are introducing and we need help selling it." In either one of these examples, a reasonable facilitator might say, "Great, we have our product; let's go to the next question."

Making a List of Products

Earlier in this chapter we mentioned that facilitators need to be ready to help a client make a list of options and then make choices to answer any of the questions of the marketing analysis. We also said that whenever a facilitator needs to make a list, she needs to take detours to make the list longer.

Below is a list of detours in the form of prompts and questions. The facilitator can use these to help a client make a list of products to consider for a given project.

- Could you help me list the different brands you sell that might become the focus of this project?
- Could you please list any other brands that have not yet lived up to their potential?
- Do you have any particular stores or locations that need help or attention?
- What about the different departments over which you have responsibility? Are there specific departments with which you need help at this time?
- What about a specific item or service? Are there specific items or services with which you want help?
- Are there any new products or services that you are about to introduce for the first time?
- Let's look further out: What new offerings or product introductions might be in the wings?

The questions above will likely generate a nice long list of all the products a client might want to focus on to grow his business. Now the facilitator can help him make choices.

Choosing the Product

A facilitator can help a client select the product definition by suggesting criteria the client might use to make the choice. Those criteria might include:

- Profitability: Which product is likely to make you the most money?
- Timeliness: Which product needs help first?
- Personal interest: Which product are you most excited about?
- Leverage: Is there one product that if we market it effectively will have a positive impact on the sale of other products on the list?

We have just seen how a facilitator can help a client make a list of products and then help him select the product he wants to work on first. Once the product has been identified, the next assignment is to explore its characteristics.

Create a Profile of the Product

The product needs to be looked at in detail because every piece of information about the product or service can be used later as a detour to generate ideas. From the colors of the logo to the street address of the building to the way the product feels when you hold it in your hand, every piece of information can inspire new ideas to achieve a marketing objective.

Making a List of Product Features

To make a list of product characteristics, the facilitator might use detours like these:

- Help me make a complete physical description of the product, including sizes, colors, and all other distinguishing characteristics.
- Help me make a list of elements that make your product or service different from its competitors. This needs to be a thorough list. The key question is "What is different about this product?" The questions below will help you make this list longer:
   ○ What do your current customers mention consistently about your product?

° What do you find yourself having to demonstrate or point out to a new customer about your product? (Anything you need to make a special effort to demonstrate probably means customers are not used to seeing it in a competing product or service.)

° What element of the product or service do you feel protective about so that you don't want your competitors to imitate it?

° What would your sales staff say are the most common questions your customers ask about your product? (Customers' questions give you insights into what the target consumer might be noticing about the product.)

WOODLAND NURSERIES CHOOSES A PRODUCT

Alesia followed the process we suggest in this chapter and helped Sam make a list of products. Here is what the list looked like:

1. Woodland Nurseries as a brand name
2. Extensive collection of roses
3. Perennials
4. Container plants
5. Landscape design
6. Landscape installation
7. Garden design classes
8. Annuals
9. Trees and shrubs

When asked to select the product on which to focus this project, Sam chose his extensive inventory of outdoor plants, with his main focus being perennials. Now that we have a product, let's create a product profile.

Woodland Nurseries, as its name would suggest, is laid out over several wooded acres in such a way that you would not think you are in a store but rather in a beautiful garden.

To the left as you walk into the perennial section, you see a series of hothouses organized by plant type. The plants that prefer shade, like azaleas and hydrangeas, are clustered together under huge shade trees. To the right are the perennials that prefer sun, like the butterfly bushes.

Woodland Nurseries plants are clearly larger and happier looking than the plants you might find elsewhere. Everything is fastidiously labeled with the correct name of the plant, along with the scientific name and the sun and water requirements of the plants.

There is no escaping the impression that whoever runs the place is a neatnik. All the walkways are swept and the edges are neatly trimmed. Everywhere you look there are green signs indicating the different types of plants in the specific areas of the nursery.

Now that a product has been chosen and profiled for Woodland Nurseries, the next step is to identify a target consumer.

2. WHO IS THE TARGET CONSUMER?

Remember when we said the marketing analysis questions have to be asked in sequence? Here you can see why. Now that we have a product, when we ask, "Who is the target?" we mean "Who is the target *for this product?*"

The target consumer is a type of person, not a demographic segment or an age range. As noted earlier, the client might have the answer to this question on the tip of his tongue, but some clients need a bit more help to figure this out.

The target consumer we are looking for is the person most likely to make a purchase in this product category, whether or not she is purchasing the client's product. So rather than focusing on the client's current customers only, we want to identify all the customers who would be inclined to purchase products like the client's, regardless of where they are purchasing them.

To make it more concrete, let's use Woodland Nurseries as our example. Given that the product has been defined as outdoor plants, specifically perennials, the target consumers we are looking for are the people most likely to be in the market for perennials, regardless of where they are currently purchasing them. Of course, the client will be very curious about the opinions of his current customers, but those will be considered a subset of the total universe of target consumers for this product.

The universe of all the target consumers who might be in the market for a specific product or service is rarely homogenous. In fact, there are usually distinct subgroups or segments into which the total group can be divided. The target segments can be separated by demographic characteristics (gender, age group) and also by the way they might interact with the product (women who intend to dedicate a lot of time to their garden, women who want the garden to take care of itself).

This is why the facilitator begins by identifying all the different target segments that might have an interest in the product.

Making a List of Target Consumer Segments

If the client has conducted a primary research study, it is very likely the market segments have been identified. If, however, such a study does not exist, the facilitator will need to help the client create a list of market segments. Here are detours the facilitator can use to make a list.

- Imagine that all the people who would be likely to purchase this product are in a room. As you walk around the room, you notice they have naturally gathered in groups made up of people who have similar characteristics. Help me make a list of the different target groups and tell me what they have in common.
- Define the different segments by their gender and age as well as how they use the product.
- Help me get a sense of the relative size of each market segment.

Once the facilitator has helped the client consider all the different target consumer segments, a choice needs to be made.

Choosing a Target Consumer Segment

Let's imagine that, as a response to the detours above, the facilitator helped the client see a number of different groups of target consumers. The facilitator's next job is to help the client zero in on the target consumer for this project. Below is a list of selection criteria the facilitator will want the client to consider before he makes a choice.

- *The Heavy User.* In some product categories, consumers can make a lot of repeat purchases over a year. For these categories, it makes sense to select the heavy user of the category: those who purchase and consume the products in this category frequently or in large quantities. Examples include the woman who buys a lot of chicken, the man who plays a lot of golf, the professional who eats a lot of business lunches, and so on.
- *Ideal Customer.* There are companies that have established a profile of the ideal customer with whom they prefer to do business. This profile is usually arrived at by analyzing the company's best customer; the profile is then used to zero in on their best prospects. Examples include a financial adviser whose ideal customer has a minimum number of dollars to invest and an insurance company that wants to focus on married couples with young children. In the case of the Woodland Nurseries, the definition of the ideal customer is a forty-five-year-old woman who owns her own home and loves to garden. The ideal customer profile might also include a minimum number of dollars that she spends on plants every year.
- *Lifetime Value.* In some product categories, such as cars or home stereo equipment, the average purchase is large and the amount of time between purchases is long. In these cases, the client may be looking for the customer who is likely to spend more per purchase, or who is likely to make more purchases over her lifetime.
- *New Opportunity.* A facilitator might come across a client who is looking to pursue a new market segment, even if it is not the largest or the most profitable at the time. Examples include the car

dealer who has never focused on his female customers or the clothing store that has a new line of clothing for a more affluent man. In the case of Woodland Nurseries, it could be those young professionals who just moved into the apartment complex a few miles from Woodland Nurseries' main location.

Establishing the Profile of the Target Consumer

Once the target consumer is chosen, the next step is to create a profile of the target consumer so that you can know him or her as a person. All too often, the information gathered about the target consumer is so generic that it borders on the boilerplate (they are men, they love sports, they drink beer, etc.). When we ask for a profile of the target consumer, we are proposing that you get enough customer insights to develop a persona of this consumer. We will discuss customer insights and personas next.

Customer Insights

Customer insights are especially important in the world of new product development. The concept is fairly straightforward: If you know that the passengers who sit in the backseats of cars wish they could control the air-conditioning or that they had their own cup holders, then you design a way for those customers to get those things, and you sell more cars.

In marketing communications, customer insights are useful because they help a marketer establish a common ground and open up a dialogue with the target consumer.

Here is an illustration. Imagine a television spot that opens with a woman who appears to be wearing workout clothes. She looks at the camera and says, "I don't want to have to put on makeup when I go to a gym to work out." Other target consumers like her—those who are sick of going to the type of health club that seems more like a pickup joint than a gym—say to themselves, sometimes out loud, "Hey, that's me!" This relevant message allows the marketer an opening to transmit the full message, almost as if to say, "Now that we have established that we know what is important to you when choosing a gym, let us tell you how ours is different from all the others."

Customer insights come from conversations with target consumers. In addition to using formal research techniques like surveys and focus groups, a company can harvest customer insights by interviewing its own employees. The inspiration for the television commercial we mentioned above came from comments made by target consumers who look a lot like that woman. The comments were probably gathered in a formal focus group environment, but they could also have been picked up by astute employees of the gym and fed back to the marketing person in charge of television advertising. If you think about it, customers come in contact with a variety of the employees of the companies with which they do business: from the salesperson who sold them the product, to the person who helped them carry it to the car or delivered it to their home, to the customer service and technical support personnel with whom they inter-acted after the product was installed. All those staff members have a wealth of information about the target consumer. We are big believers in interviewing those employees in search of information about the cus-tomer as a person.

Other methods are primary research—always the preferred source of information—as well as focus groups and advisory boards to which target consumers can be invited from time to time, and reading secondary research articles and surveys conducted by third parties.

Personas

We can take the concept of customer insights even further by creating personas to represent target consumers. A persona is the compilation of the traits most often found in a target consumer group, represented as if they were all observable in one person. Using the customer insights gath-ered over time, a composite is created of the typical target consumer. He is given a real name, a family, a career, habits, beliefs, and so on. The objective is to create a persona that is real enough that one can imagine him or her interacting with the product in question. Because, in our view, personas are used most effectively as idea-generation tools, we will revisit them specifically during idea generation and development.

WOODLAND NURSERIES SELECTS A TARGET CONSUMER

Because of its considerable product offerings, Woodland Nurseries serves a variety of target consumers. From the older couples who hire Alesia in her regular role as head of the Landscape Services Department, to the young women who come in to buy container plants for their apartments, Sam and his staff see all sorts of people walking in their door every day.

That said, there is no question that when it comes to Sam's collection of perennial plants, the bread-and-butter target consumer is the forty-five-year-old woman who owns her own home and who loves to garden. For the purpose of beginning to create a persona of this target consumer, they agree to call her Sandy. When Alesia asks for more of a profile than just her name, Sam has a wealth of information.

"We know a part of her enjoys the whole process of digging, planting, mulching, feeding, and all that. She gets great satisfaction when she stands back, fairly exhausted, and beholds the fruit of her labor. Then there is the decorator in her. It is the decorator who lays out the garden and selects all the colors and textures. Finally, we know that she likes to see her garden evolve. That is why she loves perennials. She wants to see the plants grow and the garden take shape. And she is not afraid to move established plants around because she is always looking for ways to improve her garden."

3. WHAT TRIGGERS THE TARGET CONSUMER TO ENTER THE MARKET?

Triggers are the events, large or small, that thrust a target consumer into the market to shop for products or services she may not have considered the day before being triggered.

There are broad recurring triggers, such as New Year's for starting diets and joining health clubs and the Super Bowl for purchasing wide-screen televisions and pizzas, and then there are triggers that happen at different times and are determined by each individual's situation. For example, the day a woman decides to have a baby, she suddenly finds herself in the market for a whole slew of products she would never have considered the day before. And on the day the baby is born, a whole new trigger occurs for a new line of products and services.

It is amazing that the street vendors in New York City understand this concept while much more sophisticated organizations continue to fight against that brick wall that is the natural order of things. If you are ever in New York City when it begins to rain, you will be struck by the incredibly efficient retail operation that gets set up on practically every street corner and in front of every hotel. It is unclear where they come from or what they were doing up until the moment it began to rain, but all of a sudden there are what seem like hundreds of street vendors selling practically disposable umbrellas for three times their value. And we pay it! I can't remember how many such umbrellas I bought before I figured out that a person who travels as much as I do should probably have an umbrella permanently packed in his suitcase. We can all learn a lesson from the New York City street vendors. People want to buy umbrellas when it rains.

Identify Triggers from Different Life Stages

The life stage event theory[1] helps marketers anticipate when the conditions are opportune for a specific triggering event. According to this theory, life is a series of lessons and challenges that motivate us and help us grow. Let's suppose a young man entering college falls within a life stage in which most people find themselves in the market for, say, a new computer. However, that is not really the trigger. The actual triggering event might be that his old computer chokes when attempting to play a new video game. Now we can come up with a communication idea that depicts a young man starting college that will be relevant to young men starting college—but it might be more powerful and more direct to depict a young man whose computer has choked on a new video game trying to decide whether to add a new video card to his current computer or to simply purchase a new computer.

Sometimes when there is not a natural trigger to put a target consumer in the market for a product, marketers have to manufacture one. For instance, the lack of a natural trigger was the inspiration for oil change stickers—how else would you get drivers to remember to change their oil on a regular basis?

Making a List of Triggers

Here are a couple of questions a facilitator might use to identify the trigger in any given business:

- Do you have any research or have you heard any anecdotes that would tell you what happens in the life of the target consumer that puts him in the market for this product?
- Could the triggering event be tied in to the purchase of a different product, like when people get in the market for chips when they buy a sandwich?

WOODLAND NURSERIES IDENTIFIES A TRIGGER

Years ago, when Sandy was just beginning to get into gardening, she made the mistake of buying a bunch of plants too early in the spring, just because the weather looked like it was getting nicer. But she learned her lesson, and even though it might look safe, she no longer plants in March.

Sam has been in this business long enough to know that his target consumers, especially the ones who are going to spend a lot of money on perennials, are keeping an eye on the date of the last frost. They will not be in the market for Woodland Nurseries' products until the danger of frost is over. While there are occasional anomalies, everyone in her area of Atlanta and the surrounding suburbs begin serious planting during the second week in April, specifically after April 10.

4. WHAT IS THE PURCHASING PROCESS?

The last question helped us to identify the trigger that puts the target consumer in the market for this product category. Now we want to know, in detail, all the other steps the consumer takes in the process of making a purchase in this category.

We have seen this step referred to in books and articles as either the sales funnel or the touch points of a sale. The term *sales funnel* is not satisfying to us because it is typically used to describe the activities of a sales organization as it puts "prospects" into the top of the funnel and moves them along until they come out at the bottom of the funnel as first-time customers and eventually repeat customers. It is true that sales activities are important, but they are not what we are attempting to describe here.

With this question, we are attempting to create a story—a storyboard, if you will—of the natural steps a consumer takes as she makes a purchase. Once the target consumer has been triggered, what does she do next? And then what? What we generally find is that in every industry or product category there is a different sequence of steps a customer follows as she makes a purchase.

Every product category has its own acquisition process. With cars, for example, it might be that consumers spend time on the Internet before visiting a dealership. In home remodeling, a consumer having her bathroom redone might get design ideas by looking at dozens of magazines full of pictures of bathrooms before beginning the process of identifying potential contractors and getting bids from each of them. On the other hand, if the product is a pair of tickets to the Super Bowl, the acquisition process probably does not include getting bids from different vendors.

The Purchasing Process Map

Every step that is taken in the acquisition of a product or service gives marketers an opportunity to present a relevant idea to a target consumer and possibly to exert some influence over the direction of the rest of the sequence. We are looking for steps and influencers that create a complete map of the process of making a purchase.

Let's imagine for a moment that a typical mom takes the following steps before she goes grocery shopping:

- *Trigger*. She looks in the cupboard or the fridge for one specific item and when she notices it is missing, she realizes it is time to go shopping.
- *Step 1*. She looks at the current state of the staples that are not meal specific: "Do we have enough cereal? How are we doing on milk . . . coffee . . . and so on?"
- *Step 2*. She looks at her calendar and makes a rough estimate of how many meals she will need to buy for, as well as the kind of meals. For example, her daughter has dance on Wednesday nights after school, so this is a quick meal: "Maybe we'll pick something up on the way. Thursday night, on the other hand, everybody's home, so we can sit at the table."
- *Step 3*. Now she decides which specific products to purchase. This is a spot where her children's taste in cereal, for instance, becomes a huge influence.
- *Step 4*. If she has a coupon box or a habit of checking for coupons on the Internet, she does so at this point. Moms who don't have a coupon habit skip this step.
- *Step 5*. Trips to the supermarket are part of a cluster of other errands. For instance, she checks for any dry cleaning that needs to be dropped off.
- *Step 6*. Armed with her list, coupons, and the dry-cleaning, she gets in her car and goes to the grocery store.

If we assume the above sequence is accurate, you can see how grocery stores and food manufacturers could benefit from every single item on the list. What you have created is the purchasing process map for how the target consumer prepares to purchase a product.

First of all, a skilled facilitator can use all the information in the purchasing process map to encourage a resource group to generate a list of marketing objectives. For example, Step 1 of the purchasing process map indicates that this mom looks through her kitchen to check for staples before she creates a shopping list. That particular fact might inspire a marketing objective like "How do we get moms to check for Pop-Tarts™ every time they are preparing a grocery list?"

Later in the purchasing process map we see that some moms check for coupons in Step 4 of the purchasing process. That fact might inspire a marketing objective like "How do we get a mom to register for an All-K Pass™ from Kellogg's?" (The All-K Pass gives members access to special features, contests, and coupons from all the Kellogg's Web sites.)

Facilitators could also use the information in the purchasing process map as detours when the time comes to generate ideas. For example, in Step 3 of the purchasing process we learned that once the mom has created the list of staples, she begins to think about what specific products to purchase. One can see how this piece of information could inspire an idea for a television commercial where a little boy has made a colorful shopping list for his mom, highlighting his favorite cereal.

Facilitating a Purchasing Process Map

If the client doesn't already know the complete purchasing process map for the purchase of a particular product, there are questions the facilitator can ask in order to develop one. We are looking for two things in this investigation: steps and influencers. So there are a lot of "What happens next?" questions, immediately followed by questions like "Is there another person involved who has an influence over the direction the target consumer takes in this step?" Here are questions the facilitator may ask.

- What are the steps that your customers typically take when they are making a purchase in this product category?
- Are you aware of the natural influencers that might have an impact on the way the target consumer makes a decision in this category?
- Which are the spots in the process sequence where the target consumer is swayed by natural influencers?
- Are there predictable questions that your salespeople get from

target consumers that might give us insight into the steps they are following to make a decision in this category?

Choosing the Steps of the Purchasing Process

Now the facilitator uses the questions below to help the client narrow down to the most essential steps in the purchasing process map. The final map will include the most important steps and influencers that lead the target consumer to make a purchase in that product category. By "most important steps" we mean any steps that increase the likelihood of a purchase. For instance, if it is true that when a person test-drives a Jeep® Wrangler® the likelihood of a sale increases dramatically, we need to know that. If it is true that when customers ask for a free sample of ice cream, they are likely going to buy a larger cone, we need to know that.

By "most important influencers" we mean people whose involvement increases the likelihood of a purchase or of a larger purchase in this product category. For instance, if it is true that when a man walks into a men's clothing store accompanied by a woman the average sale goes up, we need to know that.

- Are there specific steps that matter more than others?
- Are there specific influencers that matter more than others?

It is important to consider two final notes on this particular question before we move on.

We have arbitrarily decided to stop mapping the process of the mom with her arrival at the store. However, in the real world, we could map the process all the way through her supermarket experience—and even further. In a wonderful article in the *Harvard Business Review* called "Discovering New Points of Differentiation," Ian MacMillan and Rita Gunther McGrath describe what they call the *consumption chain*.[2] MacMillan and Gunther McGrath suggest that you can map the entire relationship a consumer has with any given product or service from the moment the consumer becomes aware of his need for the product (what we are calling the trigger), all the way to the time he discards it after it has been used.

The authors suggest—and we strongly agree—that every business should involve all its employees in answering this type of marketing question. As we suggested when we discussed customer insights, the staff who interact with customers should be taught to observe customer patterns. Regular staff meetings could generate a great deal of valuable information about the way customers behave, what they ask for, and how they make decisions.

WOODLAND NURSERIES MAPS THE PURCHASING PROCESS

During their marketing analysis meeting, Alesia asks Sam and Eric, the marketing director, to help her map the process Sandy might follow as she makes her purchases in the spring. Eric says, "That's a question I can answer. Here is how Sandy would describe the steps she takes:

- *Step 1.* 'Well, I go outside with my little notebook and I survey my garden. I see what made it through the winter and I also note the plants that need to be replaced.'
- *Step 2.* 'Next, I decide what colors I want to see in my yard and where.' This, by the way, is consistent with the secondary research we have read from trade associations. These women are not farmers; they are decorators.
- *Step 3.* 'I usually make a little rough drawing of each section of the garden and I show what plants I want to plant and more or less where I want them. The little rough drawing helps me figure out how many plants I'm going to need to buy.'
- *Step 4.* 'Now I can create a shopping list of the plants I need to purchase. I make two lists. There are annuals that I can get pretty much anywhere. And then there are perennials that I am willing to pay a lot more for that I need to purchase at a quality nursery staffed with people who know what they are doing.'
- *Step 5.* 'I will probably visit three or four places during the first week or so. When I am buying flats of annuals, I am checking out everyone's prices. When I am buying perennials and nice plants, I am not as worried about price.'

- *Step* 6. 'I don't ask for help when I'm buying annuals. If I ask for help, it is usually when I am looking at a perennial, especially something new or interesting. I usually ask the staff about a particular plant's need for sunlight and water. My yard is a little tricky because I have a lot of shady spots and I always want to make sure I'm not going to put a plant in the wrong place, so I like to get advice on that from the staff.'
- *Step* 7. 'When I get to the nurseries and I am ready to shop, I look for one of those four-wheel wagons on which I can load all my plants. If there are no wagons outside, then I know the place is too crowded and I come back later or another day.'
- *Step* 8. 'When I am in the store, part of me is all business. I have my list of plants and I am on a mission. I find the plants, check for the happiest-looking ones, put them in my wagon, and check them off my list. Then there is another part of me that likes to browse. A good nursery always has surprises and I don't want to miss them.'
- *Step* 9. 'When I am done picking out the plants I want I head to the cash register. I always pay with a credit card.'"

We have seen Woodland Nurseries identify its ideal customer. We know what puts her in the market and what process she follows when she purchases her perennials. Next, we will find out what goes through her mind when she is deciding where to go to make her purchases.

5. WHAT ARE THE BENEFITS SOUGHT BY THE TARGET CONSUMER?

Consider this image: A target consumer is driving down the road, having decided that he is going to purchase a product. He sees two different stores across the street from each other, both of which are likely to sell the item he seeks. How does this target consumer decide whether to go to the store on the right or the store on the left?

Target consumers choose one product over another in the same category because they believe the product they have chosen is superior to other comparable products in delivering the benefits they seek. We have heard benefits sought referred to as "buying considerations." We like "benefits sought" better because the target consumer is actually seeking a benefit by purchasing a product. Also, when the time comes to establish a position for the product (coming up in question 7), we will see that a position needs to be based on a key benefit and that is what we are about to define here.

Benefits can be tangible:

- I choose it because it has a handle that makes it easy to carry.
- I choose it because it has leather upholstery.
- I choose them because they always finish the job quickly.

Benefits can also be intangible:

- I choose it because it makes me look cool.
- I choose it because it makes me look young.
- I choose it because it is healthier.

In the traditional literature, you will see that this phase of the buying process is generally referred to as the "information-gathering phase." However, that may be a misnomer. If we look at the real behavior of a customer, it is probably more accurate to describe it as a "benefits-checking phase." Unless the field is completely unfamiliar to the target consumer, she approaches this phase of the acquisition process with a set of questions in mind: *What sort of warranty do they offer? How far will I have to drive? How much is it going to cost?* and so on.

The questions consumers ask are important because they reveal the benefits these consumers are really seeking when they purchase a product or service in any given category. Of course, in every product category, there is a list of benefits that people seek and, as with all sets of criteria, they may work against each other. That's why you hear customers say things like, "It's more expensive, but it's a lot faster." In that statement you just heard a customer say that both price and speed are on the list of desired benefits, but speed is higher on the list than cost.

So what we are attempting to discover with this question is: (1) What are the benefits that customers seek to get from products or services in this category? and (2) Among those benefits, which are the most important ones (the key benefits) that need to be present in order for a product to be chosen consistently over its competitors?

Making a List of Benefits

A facilitator attempting to make a list of benefits only has to get one question answered here, and that is, "When the target consumer is in the market for this particular product or service, what are all the benefits they are thinking about that help them choose between two comparable vendors?"

At this point the facilitator is simply looking to make a list, so the answers to the question do not need to be ranked in any order. And because the facilitator is not looking for the benefits to be in rank order yet, the question can be asked in a variety of contexts. One simple way to get an answer to the question is to have the company's staff interview the next few dozen customers they interact with and then combine all the answers into one master list. A more formal way to get a list is to do it in a focus group or advisory board environment where the company invites ten or twelve people who customarily purchase the product to a meeting. During the meeting, the facilitator could ask the participants to make a list of benefits they seek when purchasing the product in question.

Whether the questions are asked individually or in a group, the result will be a list that includes items like, *I don't want to drive too far*, *I need a place where the staff knows what they are talking about*, *I don't want to pay too much*, and so on. The list might include ten or twelve items. While it is okay for the list of benefits to come from a variety of sources and from informal conversations, the choice of the key benefits needs to be made more formally.

Choosing the Key Benefits

As we get ready to choose the key benefits sought by the target consumer, let us go back to the image we used to introduce this question. A target consumer is driving down the street on his way to purchase a product. Ahead he sees two comparable stores where he could make the purchase. He decides which store to visit based on his perception of which store is superior at delivering the key benefits he seeks. It is because the key benefits play such an important role in the purchasing decision that we need to make sure we pick the right ones.

Perhaps the best way to characterize how we would like to see the choice of key benefits sought is: The more people involved, the better. By that we mean that if the client has the money to field a survey to a representative sample of all the forty-five-year-old women in Atlanta who love to garden, that would be best. If we can find the results of a national study in which women thirty-five to fifty-four who love to garden were asked to identify their key benefits sought, that is actually not bad at all. If we can send an e-mail questionnaire to people in the Woodland Nurseries database and a couple of hundred recipients answer the question, that is pretty good. If we can get four groups of a dozen forty-five-year-old women who love to garden to take part in a series of focus groups where we ask them to choose the key benefits they seek, that's okay. If all we have is the opinion of one person who owns the business, we'll take it—but we will work hard to convince him to pay for the biggest survey he can afford.

Keep in mind that the key benefits sought are the target consumer's "musts." They are important enough to cause the target consumer to choose one vendor over another. They are, therefore, important enough to cause a vendor to steer his entire business in one direction or another. It makes sense to take the time to get it right.

Woodland Nurseries Identifies the Benefits Sought by the Target Consumer

Alesia gets right to the point, "If we ask ten women shopping for plants to decide on the top three things that are most important when purchasing products at any nursery of the quality of Woodland Nurseries, what would they say?"

"Well," says Sam, "I think they like that the place is clean. My store is well organized, and they really like that everything is color coded." As Sam continues, Alesia begins to realize that Sam is making a list of things *he* likes about his nursery. So she has to bring him back to what his target consumer, Sandy, might be looking for. In this case, Eric can help.

Eric says, "Alesia, a couple of years ago we read a research paper that was published by one of the trade associations to which we belong. The study was conducted because there had been some concern among the nurseries and garden centers that the big box discounters and building supply centers were beginning to take business away from companies like ours, whose sole focus has been the plant business.

"In any event, the trade association conducted a study that showed that nationally, this particular female target consumer wants three things when she goes out shopping for plants."

Alesia inquires, "And those are?"

Eric continues, "And those are, first, a wide variety of plants from which to choose; second, a staff that has a lot of gardening expertise; and third, plants that are happy and healthy."

Sam reiterates, "No question. If you are talking about the big things they care about, the answer is: variety, knowledgeable staff, and healthy plants."

We are five questions into the marketing analysis and Alesia, our facilitator, has learned a lot—even some new information—about her company's target consumer.

TAKING STOCK OF WHERE WE ARE

Let's stop here for a moment and take stock of how far we have come in the marketing analysis.

We know the product the client wants to promote.

We know the target consumer who is most likely to purchase that product.

We know about triggers that cause target consumers to decide to make a purchase in this product category, and we also know the steps she takes when she is in the process of making that purchase.

Finally, we know the benefits she is seeking when she wants to make a purchase in this product category.

Notice that up to now the questions we have asked have helped us learn about this target consumer and about how she goes about making a purchase in this product category. So far, the focus of the investigation has not been Woodland Nurseries or any of its competitors. As a matter of fact, if instead of working for Woodland Nurseries we were working for any one of its competitors, as long as the product chosen was perennials, the information we would have gathered in this marketing analysis up to this point would be identical.

The next two questions are going to shift the focus of the fact-finding mission. Alesia and her client, Sam, are now going to establish how Woodland Nurseries is fundamentally different from all its competitors in a way that matters to their target consumer.

Perhaps the best way to approach the next two questions of the marketing analysis is to visualize Sandy, the forty-five-year-old homeowner who loves to garden, getting ready to purchase perennials for her garden. As we said a moment ago, her deliberations have been entirely about herself and her garden. She has not had a need to consider any vendors. However, as the time approaches for her to get in her car to go plant shopping, she is faced with the simple decision of where to go first.

Two things are going to happen in Sandy's head at lightning speed. First, she is going to think about all the stores where she would consider purchasing perennials for her garden. Second, she is going to choose the first place to visit based on how well she believes the store delivers the key benefits she is seeking.

As we are about to discuss, every one of us takes those same two mental actions that Sandy took to select the first place to go in search of perennials. We just don't make all decisions at the same speed.

6. HOW DOES THE PRODUCT COMPARE TO ITS COMPETITION?

The question of how the product compares to its competitors is really two questions in one. First, we need to get a handle on which other businesses might provide the same products or services that the target consumer might seek from our client. And second, we need to figure out how those products compare to our client's product when it comes to delivering the key benefits sought by the target consumer.

Establishing the Competitive Arena

The question of which companies might provide the same product as the product being offered by our client has been referred to in marketing literature as "frame of reference" and also as "consideration set." Actually, both phrases are useful as explanations of the same phenomenon. Frame of reference is useful in context of the question "Who would the target consumer consider to be in the same category, so that if she were to compare the client's product with someone else's product, the two could serve as frames of reference for each other?" The concept of consideration set is also handy because it communicates that the target consumer will really only consider a limited set of vendors—usually three to five—who have similar credibility as providers of a given product or service.

For instance, in Sandy's case there is only one other vendor that, in her opinion, carries the quality perennials that she demands for her garden. This other vendor, which we will call Whisper Hill, is another full-service nursery that has only one location and is about seven miles farther south from Sandy's house than Woodland Nurseries. If we were to ask Sandy, "Imagine you were on your way to Woodland Nurseries and discovered that for some reason they were closed, where else might you go in search of the same things you would expect from Woodland?" The answer would not likely be any of the big box discount or building supply stores, even though technically they do sell perennial plants and are closer to her house. The answer would be Whisper Hill.

The question, in the case of Woodland Nurseries, is how do we know that? And that is exactly what Alesia asked Sam. Sam's answer was fast and confident. For years Woodland Nurseries has conducted brief customer surveys at its store. One of the questions asked many times is, "What other nurseries do you visit when you are searching for quality plants for your garden?" The most frequent answer has always been "Whisper Hill." Yes, there is a growing percentage of people who mention the big box discount and building supply centers, but nowhere near as often as Whisper Hill.

Facilitating the Definition of the Competitive Arena

If a facilitator needs to help a client identify the competitors who fit the same frame of reference, she might ask questions like these:

- Imagine you are closed or your product is temporarily not available. What other options does the target consumer have?
- In your (or your salespeople's) experience, what alternative products does the target consumer consider before buying from you?
- In your (or your salespeople's) experience, in cases when the target consumer does not buy from you, from which competitors is she likely to buy?

COMPARING WOODLAND NURSERIES TO ITS COMPETITORS

So it has already been established that, at least when it comes to perennials, there are really two credible players for our target consumer: Woodland Nurseries and Whisper Hill. Next, we need to determine how our client's offering compares with the other companies in the same frame of reference when it comes to delivering on the key benefits sought by the target consumer.

When Alesia asks Eric about how Woodland Nurseries compares to Whisper Hill, it becomes clear that he has very strong feelings about his competitor. "This is an area where we have paid a lot of attention over the years. I spend a lot of time in the stores talking to customers, and they consistently tell me two things about Whisper Hill: The place is a complete mess, and I can never get anyone to answer any of my questions."

Alesia needs to know more. "What does 'a complete mess' mean?"

Eric elaborates, "If you want to know how we compare, I can tell you that there is no question that Whisper Hill is recognized for having a wide variety of plants. The site is much larger than ours, and everyone knows that. Now, I will tell you that this particular target consumer has to rummage through a lot of damaged plants to find one that makes the trip worthwhile. That's the first weakness. The second weakness, according to the customer comments we have gathered, is that Whisper Hill hires kids who are paid minimum wage and don't really know anything about the plants. So, while Whisper Hill has us beat on variety because of the size of their location, we have always received higher scores for our knowledgeable staff and also for the health of our plants."

Eric is being so specific with his answers that Alesia feels compelled to ask where he got his information. It seems that a couple of years ago Eric, in his capacity as marketing director, hired a marketing professor from one of the local universities in Atlanta to do some consulting work for Woodland Nurseries. This marketing professor was very helpful in refocusing the Woodland Nurseries marketing effort.

The first project he suggested was a customer survey to identify how Woodland Nurseries was perceived by its forty-five-year-old target consumer. First, a letter signed by Eric was sent to the entire database asking the customers if they would be willing to take part in an e-mail survey in exchange for a hanging plant worth a little under $15. A huge number of e-mails were returned as undeliverable. However, about 250 existing customers agreed to take part in the survey. Eric and his marketing consultant designed a simple questionnaire consisting of about twelve questions, which could be completed by the target consumer very quickly. In the survey, respondents had to identify their gender and age, along with a few of their gardening habits, like how many hours per week they dedicated to gardening projects.

There were three central questions in the survey designed to discover what perceptions the target consumer held about Woodland Nurseries. The questions were phrased like this:

- What store comes to mind when I say the phrase "the store with the best variety of perennials"?
- What store comes to mind when I say the phrase "the store with the staff that has the most knowledge about plants and gardening"?
- What store comes to mind when I say the phrase "the store that sells the healthiest plants"?

Two hundred different women fitting the description of Woodland Nurseries' forty-five-year-old target consumer (the survey asked about age in ten-year increments, so the age range became forty to forty-nine) answered the survey. Their responses were tabulated and displayed in what we will call a Key Benefits Report Card like the one shown in figure 7.

Creating the Key Benefits Report Card

If you take a look at figure 7 you can see it displays three columns, one for each of the three key benefits sought by the target consumer. You also see it displays two rows, one for Woodland Nurseries and one for Whisper Hill.

	Wide Variety	Knowledgeable Staff	Healthy Plants
Woodland	35%	✓62%	✓55%
Whisper Hill	57%	20%	40%

Figure 7. The Key Benefits Report Card

You can see that Whisper Hill was mentioned by the overwhelming majority of the survey respondents as the place with the biggest variety of plants. Whisper Hill's command in that particular category was significant enough that it could be said it "owned" that perception in the mind of the target consumer. For its part, Woodland Nurseries received more mentions than Whisper Hill as the store with the most knowledgeable staff as well as the store with the healthiest plants.

In the end, the survey ended up costing Woodland Nurseries about $2,000. A number of women never redeemed their certificates for the hanging plant. Sam and Eric consider it the best investment they ever made.

Alesia is thrilled to have such concrete information at her disposal. Now that she knows how the target consumer perceives Woodland Nurseries as well as its competitor, Whisper Hill, she is ready to ask about the nursery's positioning statement.

7. HOW IS THE PRODUCT POSITIONED?

We have arrived at a pivotal point in the marketing analysis. So far, we have been told by the client—or we have helped the client figure out—how to define the product, how to define the target consumer, what triggers the target consumer to become a potential customer, what process the target consumer follows to make a purchase in this category, the criteria the target consumer uses to choose one product over another, and the competitive environment for this product. The next logical question in the sequence is: "How is this product positioned in the mind of the target consumer?"

A position is a piece of real estate a product earns in the mind of the target consumer. Positions are intrinsically neither good nor bad; they are simply composite images target consumers create in their minds. They are made up of the consumers' own experiences with the product and its competitors, the product advertising they have seen, and the stories they have heard about the product from friends, family members, and even total strangers.

In our view, a strong positioning statement creates a clear, vivid image of how a product is different from all other products in the marketplace in a way that is valuable and credible to the target consumer, expressed in a compelling way. Let us first define each element of a positioning statement. Then we will illustrate them using the Woodland Nurseries example.

Different

Being different—how do so many companies miss this? It is astounding how many advertised products claim they can do pretty much the same thing their competitors can. It is worth repeating: A product that is not different from its competitors in a valuable way has no logical reason to exist and probably won't for very long. After all, how many auto insurance companies does the market need whose central claim is that they can save you a pile of money on insurance? The challenge here is to find different territory on which to stake a claim. For instance, recently we saw a commercial by an insurance company that claims it will keep its customers legal by selling them the absolute minimum insurance they need. The "We keep you legal" claim is fundamentally different from the "We save you money" claim. These two companies are staking out different territories.

Valuable

It is not enough to simply be different. The product needs to be different in a way that matters to the target consumer. In question 5 we identified the key benefits sought by the target consumer when purchasing a product in a given category. For instance, for our forty-five-year-old female gardener, these are the top three key benefits in order of importance: variety of plants, expert advice from the staff, and healthy plants. A strong positioning statement for Woodland Nurseries needs to be based on one of those key benefits or it will not be perceived as valuable to the target consumer.

Credible

Strong positioning statements satisfy two different credibility requirements:

1. The claim needs to be something that is contained in the product or that the product obviously does. For instance, you should not claim something is "indestructible" if it can break.

2. The claim has to be believable, or plausible. It is not believable that both Chevrolet® and Ford® trucks are "the best-selling trucks in America." It is not believable that a cell phone company *never* drops calls. On the other hand, "Fewer dropped calls than all other companies" is a claim we can believe, whether or not it is true.

Compelling

A compelling position is communicated in a way that makes it easy for the target consumer to remember and maybe even repeat to peers and family members. "When it absolutely, positively has to be there overnight" is much more compelling than "We guarantee overnight delivery."

It could be argued that requiring the positioning statement to be stated in a compelling fashion really gets into the medium that will be used in communicating it to the target consumer. After all, FedEx has not used the slogan "When it absolutely, positively has to be there overnight" in a long time (the current slogan is "The World On Time") but its core positioning statement has not changed. We include the requirement that the positioning statement be compelling here because we want to make the point that the way the statement is communicated both inside and outside the client company is as important as having one. Positioning statements cannot be boring. They have to be communicated so clearly and succinctly that the power of the message does not get lost. Look, for example, at Wal-Mart's slogan: "Save Money. Live Better."

When designing a positioning statement, make sure it communicates how your company is different from its competitors in a way that delivers a key benefit to the target consumer, make sure it is credible to the target consumer, and make sure it is communicated to all your stakeholders in a compelling way.

Identifying a Strategic Opportunity

In question 5 the top three key benefits sought by the target consumer were illuminated. In question 6 we learned how the target consumer perceives our client and his competitor. Now we need to figure out where there is a strategic opportunity for the client in the form of a key benefit that the target consumers do not currently attribute to the client's competitors. To be clear, what we are looking for is a hole—we are seeking to find a key benefit the client can own that is not currently claimed by any other competitor.

Let's return to the Woodland Nurseries example to illustrate what the facilitator needs to do next.

REVIEWING THE WOODLAND NURSERIES POSITIONING STATEMENT

For years, the Woodland Nurseries positioning statement was "Where Beautiful Gardens Begin." Although the phrase seems nice, it is not a positioning statement, as it does not meet the requirements we outlined earlier. The phrase really was a blank canvas that could be interpreted in a number of ways.

Improving the company's positioning statement was the second suggestion made by the marketing consultant Eric hired. He got Sam and Eric in a room and, armed with the results of the customer survey they had just fielded, engaged them in a conversation about their strategic opportunity.

Alesia asks Eric for some background on the choice of a positioning statement and Eric responds, "We were looking for a key benefit that was not already owned by Whisper Hill and that Woodland Nurseries could deliver differently and better than Whisper Hill." The first thing they did was look at the information we have now organized in the Key Benefits Report Card in figure 7. There they confirmed what we learned in question 6, which is that Whisper Hill has already laid claim to the "wide variety of plants" perception in the minds of the target consumer. Then they looked at the other two key benefits and discovered that those held more promise. Woodland Nurseries has a commanding lead over Whisper Hill in the perception of having a knowledgeable staff. Of course, Woodland Nurseries has a lot of credibility in this area, with ten people on their staff with degrees in horticulture and seven with master's degrees in the subject. Woodland Nurseries also has a commanding lead in the perception of having healthy plants. This happens to be a perception that Sam, specifically, has nurtured. A number of things at Woodland Nurseries have been done to support that perception, like replanting plants in larger containers, spraying them with water several times a day so they look fresh, and keeping the plants clean of dead leaves. It's very common to see the staff at Woodland Nurseries picking dead leaves off of plants as they walk by them, something that would never happen at Whisper Hill.

Having reviewed the information contained in the Key Benefits Report Card, the three men engaged in a very spirited conversation about which of the two positioning opportunities to pursue (the store with the most knowledgeable staff or the store with the healthiest plants). They finally decided that the position that made the most sense for Woodland Nurseries was to become the store with the most knowledgeable staff. It seemed to all three men that the expertise of the Woodland Nurseries staff would always be a decisive strategic advantage over any competitor. In retelling the story to Alesia, Eric remembers commenting that even if one day the big box discounters and building supply centers were to improve the quality of the plants, they would never be able to match Woodland Nurseries' command as employing people who can answer your questions and help you grow your garden as beautiful as it can be.

On that day, they decided that they would begin using a new positioning statement, which they have been using for the last couple of years: "Deep Rooted Wisdom to Help You Grow Your Garden."

8. HOW IS THE PRODUCT DISTRIBUTED?

Products go to market through distribution channels, which is a fancy way of describing all the different ways in which a company can make its products available for its customers to purchase.

Think of the different channels of distribution as pipelines through which a product can get to a customer. One company will only sell its products directly to the consumer—Woodland Nurseries is a good example of this—while other companies sell exclusively on the Internet.

Still others, like life insurance companies, sell their products through a network of agents.

Of course, there are companies that have evolved over time, adding new channels of distribution to stay current with their customers and prospects. Dell® Computers is a good example. For years, Dell sold its computers exclusively over the telephone. Then it expanded into the Internet, and then to direct mail catalogs. In July 2002 Dell began opening kiosks in malls and airports where consumers could see, touch, and feel the computers before ordering them. Later, Dell began selling its products on the QVC shopping channel, and more recently the company announced that two different computer models would be available for purchase at Wal-Mart, which is Dell's first foray into the retail channel of distribution.

Choosing a distribution channel is an important strategic decision. Not only are there costs involved in adding channels of distribution, but the choice of channel can have an impact on what people believe about your brand. All the advertising in the world will not make a poorly distributed product successful. By the same token, a business can gain a decisive advantage over a competitor by opening up the right new channel of distribution, even with limited advertising.

One of our favorite stories—part fact and part legend—is the story of a pizza retailer in Tulsa, Oklahoma, called Ken's Pizza. In the late 1970s Ken's Pizza was a very successful pizza store in Tulsa, with several locations all over the city.

This is the story of what Ken's Pizza did when it heard that Domino's Pizza® was going to open its first store in Tulsa. At the time Ken's Pizza had very fine, clean stores, but it did not deliver. Ken knew that Domino's single advantage over his stores was that Domino's delivered its product to the consumer. Ken also knew Domino's had some natural limitations. First of all, a single Domino's cannot deliver to the entire city; instead, it delivers in the area that is closest to the store. He also knew that even if Domino's Pizza opened several stores in the city, each would likely have a different telephone number. After all, Domino's stores were independent of each other.

Ken looked at the marketing challenge from a distribution point of view. He made the strategic decision to take ownership of the pizza delivery domain in the minds of all the pizza eaters in Tulsa. And he decided to do it before Domino's even opened its doors.

First, Ken built a citywide network of little pizza-making operations, some based within existing stores, others in small storefronts without any customer seating. Then he established one easy-to-remember telephone number that customers could call from anywhere in the city. Their order would be routed to the pizza-making operation closest to their location so the pizza could be delivered hot. The final nail in the coffin was a thirty-minutes-or-it's-free delivery guarantee. Legend has it that Ken's new city-wide delivery operation was set up in thirty days! By the time Domino's opened the doors to its one location, there was no benefit to ordering pizza from Domino's. The Ken's Pizza campaign was a tremendous success, mostly led by the lightning-fast reinvention of its distribution.

In the context of Woodland Nurseries, you may remember that in chapter 4 we heard Sam, the owner of Woodland Nurseries, wish he could generate new revenue from the apartment complex that was recently built near Woodland's main location. Sam could decide to look at this particular opportunity from a distribution point of view and simply bring the product to the new consumer. One way to do it would be for Woodland Nurseries to open a pop-up store under a big tent across the street from the apartment complex and fill it up with all sorts of house plants in containers that would be appropriate for apartment dwellers. The only advertising required might be a flyer or a door hanger distributed specifically to the occupants of the apartment complex.

Distribution Questions

It is important that facilitators ask clients both what *are* and what *might be* their distribution channels for any particular product or service.

- Is there one (or more) distribution channel(s) the client wants to focus on for this project?

- Is the client satisfied with the current channels of distribution? Is the client searching for other ways to get the product in front of the customers?
- Is there anything special or different about the way the client is going to use the channels of distribution?
- Do the client's channels of distribution pose any unusual challenge or opportunity?

WOODLAND NURSERIES' CHANNELS OF DISTRIBUTION

Woodland Nurseries has three different locations through which it sells all its products directly to its customers. Although the landscape design and installation division does send staff people out to meet with prospects, their function is not connected to increasing sales of the product (perennials).

Alesia asks Sam point blank whether he sees an opportunity to expand to other channels of distribution beyond his three stores. After a very brief conversation about the benefits and difficulties of selling plants on the Internet, it is decided there will be no change in the distribution of Woodland Nurseries' plants.

Now that we know where the target consumer can purchase the product, let's find out how much it costs.

9. WHAT IS THE PRICE OF THE PRODUCT?

Clients have well-established methods for arriving at the prices they charge for their products. Even in the case of a new product introduction, clients arrive at an initial price after considering their costs as well as the prices of comparable products available in the market.

The facilitator will be interested in the price of the product insofar as it has an impact on the demand for the product. The facilitator will also want to explore whether the price might give the product a competitive advantage and whether the client has a mechanism to help the target consumer pay for the product or service. Finally, the facilitator will want to know whether the price of the item should be included in the advertising.

Questions about Price

- What is the price of the product?
- How does the price compare to that of other products in the same frame of reference?
- Is there anything the target consumer would find significant or noteworthy about the price of the product?
- Is the client contemplating a price reduction or some promotional price to increase the demand of this product?
- Do we know what plans the competition might have as it relates to price reductions?
- Are there any terms the client is willing to offer to help the target consumer pay for the product?

WOODLAND NURSERIES CONSIDERS PRICE

When Alesia asks the price questions above, she confirms what she already suspected: Woodland Nurseries will never win on price. Everyone knows—and most especially Woodland Nurseries' loyal customers know—that Sam has always had a "you get what you pay for" attitude toward his pricing.

It is very common for the plants at Woodland Nurseries to be 30 percent higher than one might pay at Whisper Hill and easily twice as high as the big box stores. Other than a couple of annual sales to get rid of some inventory, Sam does not reduce his prices, most especially the price of his perennials.

10. WHAT ARE THE PRODUCT'S SEASONS?

A season is a measure of time. It can be defined as broadly as a season of the year (next summer) or as narrow as a specific date (February 14). It can be a one-time event (the grand opening of a new football stadium) or a regular occurrence (every Saturday night). The intention of this question is to identify the natural time-anchored elements of the client's marketing plans: When do people *really* want breakfast? When do people *really* start working on their taxes? When do people *really* buy school supplies?

Clients can experience short-term and long-term benefits from busy seasons. In the short term, there are more target consumers shopping in the client's product category. In that case, the first challenge is to find ways to get more of the people who are entering the product category to choose the client's products over those of the competitor. In the long term, clients who are astute will benefit from doing things that are specifically designed to cause the newfound customers to become loyal customers. In that case, the objective that needs to be met is how to persuade the people who come in during the high season to come back on a regular basis.

The facilitator's job here is to help the client map the times of day, week, month, or year when the product is naturally in high demand as well as the times when this product is in low demand. Here are some examples of detours the facilitator might use to explore the seasons of a particular business.

- Let's look at the calendar for a typical year. Can you point to the months or weeks of the year that are typically busy and those that are usually slow?
- Let's do the same thing for a typical month. Are there weeks in the month in which business is busy or slow?
- What about in a typical week? Are there days that are busy and days that are slow?
- What do your busy and slow seasons tell you about what is happening in the life of your target consumer?

The two previous marketing analysis questions help the facilitator learn where the target consumer can purchase the product and how much she will have to pay for it. With this marketing analysis question, the facilitator learns when the target consumer is likely to buy the products. Let's see what Alesia discovered about the different seasons at Woodland Nurseries.

WOODLAND NURSERIES' SEASONS

Here Alesia confirms what she already knew from her experience as the manager of the landscape design and installation department. There are two major seasons for this business, although the first one dwarfs the second one. The first four weeks after April 10 is the key time. The overwhelming majority of the year's business happens at this time. There is a second season in the fall for people who want to plant trees, but that season does not compare to the spring.

SUMMARY OF THE WOODLAND NURSERIES MARKETING ANALYSIS FINDINGS

We have learned a lot in this chapter! It makes sense to summarize our key findings before we move on. But before we do, let's also take stock of all the work the facilitator has done in order to get the answers to the marketing analysis questions. As we predicted, in some cases the answer was readily available. In others, the facilitator helped the client arrive at an answer by making a list of options and then selecting the one answer he wanted to use for this project.

Here are the summary of findings from the marketing analysis Alesia conducted with Eric and Sam:

- Product: Perennial plants
- Target Consumer: Sandy—a forty-five-year-old woman who owns her own home and who loves to garden
- Trigger: Last frost—after April 10
- Purchasing Process (from the point of view of the target consumer):
- *Step 1*. I survey my garden.
- *Step 2*. I decide what colors I want to see in my yard and where.

- *Step 3*. I make a little rough drawing of each section of the garden, showing what plants I want to plant and more or less where I want them.
- *Step 4*. I create two shopping lists of the plants I need to purchase: one for annuals and one for perennials.
- *Step 5*. I visit three or four places during the first week. When I am buying flats of annuals, I am checking out everyone's prices. When I am buying perennials and nice plants, I am not as worried about price.
- *Step 6*. I ask for help only when I am looking at a perennial, especially something new or interesting. I like to get advice on that from the staff.
- *Step 7*. When I get to the nurseries, I am ready to shop. If there are no wagons outside, then I know the place is too crowded and I come back later or another day.
- *Step 8*. In the store, I find the plants, check for the happiest-looking ones, put them in my wagon, and check them off my list. I also browse for surprises.
- *Step 9*. I go to the cash register and pay with a credit card.
- Benefits Sought: Variety of plants; knowledgeable staff; healthy plants
- Competition: Whisper Hill
- Product Positioning: "Deep-Rooted Wisdom to Help You Grow Your Garden"
- Distribution: Three store locations
- Price of the Product: Generally higher than Whisper Hill by about 30 percent
- Season: April 10 through May 15

Armed with the information that has surfaced as a result of the marketing analysis, the facilitator is now ready to ask the resource group to make a list of marketing objectives. In the next chapter you will see how Alesia helps a resource group invent a list of marketing objectives from which Sam or Eric can choose the focus for this project.

6

THE MARKETING OBJECTIVE

The boss asks everyone to come in early and gather in the conference room. He's bought doughnuts. When everybody is settled, he thanks the group for coming and says, "Over the last few weeks I have been speaking to each of you individually about the fact that the summer is almost here and we need a big push to get more customers in the door. I thought it would be fun to get everybody together to see if we could brainstorm some ideas."

Upon hearing the topic of discussion, and particularly the fateful words "we need a big push," the employees—especially the veterans—roll their eyes back into their skulls. They've been in this meeting before. Over the years many of them have confided in us that they wanted to say, "Why don't you just print the list of ideas we came up with the last three times we did this meeting?" But—out of either politeness or fear—they don't.

So the boss grabs a marker and asks for ideas, and as he writes them on the whiteboard, he begins to recognize them. These are the same old ideas he has heard before. He's just as frustrated as his staff. These ideas, for the most part, are useless, but he writes them down again hoping that this time some of them will be different. He cannot put his finger on it, but there is something missing.

We know what the problem is. He is brainstorming a wish (like "increasing traffic"). This idea-generation session is missing a marketing objective.

WHAT IS A MARKETING OBJECTIVE?

A marketing objective is a succinct, focused statement that answers the question "What do we want to accomplish with this marketing project?"

The answers to the questions in the marketing analysis begin to generate facts that we can use to create marketing objectives. The good news is that marketing objectives have a consistent structure and contain specific ingredients, and once you learn what these are, it will become much easier for you to create them.

Before we discuss how to compose marketing objectives, let's look at the big picture of marketing communications.

GETTING TARGET CONSUMERS TO DO OR BELIEVE

You could take all the marketing communications that bombard us as consumers and divide them into three different buckets.

Brand

The first bucket contains what most marketers would probably describe as "brand campaigns." Brand campaigns are ultimately designed to get target consumers to believe something about a product or a service. The geeky-looking guy in the glasses who seemed to walk all over America asking the persistent question "Can you hear me now?" was invented to get consumers to believe that Verizon has the most reliable wireless network.

Effective brand campaigns don't beat around the bush. They do a great job of communicating the key benefit sought by the product's target consumer. They also find relevant and imaginative ways to give the target consumer reasons to believe the product delivers that key benefit.

Activation

In the second bucket we would put all the communication that most marketers would describe as "activation campaigns." These campaigns are ultimately designed to get a target consumer to do something with a product or a service.

All campaigns that use sales promotional tools go in the activation bucket. They include the restaurant that sends you a coupon in the form of a text message for a free dessert with the purchase of a meal, the soft drink that gives away tickets to a concert among the people who buy a six-pack, the pizza company that gives you two pizzas for the price of one, and the breakfast cereal that puts a toy in the box.

The great activation campaigns have a clear focus: to get a target consumer to try or buy a product or service. To this end, the messaging contains relevant and imaginative ways to give the target consumer reasons to do the things that the campaign wants him to do.

Another way to describe the difference between brand and activation communication is that a brand campaign answers the question "Why?"—for example, "Why should I buy a Ford F-150?" The activation campaign, on the other hand, answers the question "Why now?"—for example, "Why should I come in to Ferguson's Ford this Friday?"

Other or Nonfunctional

The third bucket of marketing communications is, alas, the largest bucket of all. It contains all the marketing communications that leave target consumers baffled, sometimes angry, and, perhaps worst of all, indifferent. It's the television commercial with the guy selling—we think—an air filter. We're not sure because he thought it would be cute to do the commercial with his drooling grandbaby on his lap. The baby was cute as a button; the product we can't remember. It's the interactive campaign that wanted full-grown adults to produce inane videos of themselves eating a candy bar. Two hundred and fifty so-called adults posted their videos to YouTube; the rest of us never saw them. It's the radio campaign in which the client wanted to communicate twenty different features and benefits about his store, and the newspaper ad with the message hidden in a riddle—as if anyone had the time or the interest to decipher it.

The most confusing part of the campaigns in this third bucket is that they are often designed and executed by very smart, well-paid executives, and yet they fail miserably to make any point at all to any target consumer.

ACTIVATION IS SHORT-TERM. BRAND IS FOREVER.

Effective activation campaigns give target consumers concrete reasons—even rewards—to take a short-term action, most often to try or buy a product or a service. Activation campaigns, therefore, are short term, lasting from as little as a few hours to as long as a few weeks.

Effective brand campaigns are designed to create and solidify a belief in the mind of the target consumer. The best brand campaigns give the target consumer relevant and persuasive reasons to believe the product delivers a key benefit. This requires a consistent long-term message. The "Please don't squeeze the Charmin®" campaign, which made Charmin the best-selling toilet paper in America, was on television for twenty-three years. If the Verizon people maintain their focus—and all indicators are that they will—that geeky guy with the glasses will have a job for life.

MARKETING OBJECTIVES HAVE TOPPS

Before one begins to make a list of marketing objectives, one must know what a marketing objective sounds like.

Earlier we said that marketing objectives are succinct statements. We want to add that they have ingredients that can be summarized with the acronym TOPPS. Because brand campaigns are forever, generally brand objectives need to contain only the first three ingredients. Activation campaigns, on the other hand, need more. Let's take a look at the elements of the TOPPS acronym.

Target

T is for *target consumer*. All marketing objectives are designed with a specific target consumer in mind. A target consumer is a person, not a demographic age range. (Has anyone met a woman who is twenty-five *and* fifty-four years old?) The target consumer (also known as the target) might be a twenty-eight-year-old single guy or a forty-five-year-old mom. In cases where the company has dedicated the time to create a persona of the target consumer, the target might be referred to as a person, like Max or Rachel.

Outcome

O is for *outcome*. What do you want the target consumer to do or believe? We recommend that the outcome be explicit and concrete. Avoid using euphemisms. For example, sampling a beverage product is vague; drinking it is concrete. Experiencing a shampoo is vague; washing your hair with it is concrete. Introducing the new almond chocolate bar is vague; getting the target to take a bite out of one is concrete. Earlier we mentioned the three buckets of marketing campaigns. We suspect that the campaigns in the third bucket began with vague outcomes.

The same need for concreteness exists on the brand side. For brands, the concreteness that is required—and so often missing—is the specificity of the key benefit. Getting the target consumer to believe that FedEx can absolutely, positively deliver a package the next day is concrete. You can visualize the package being delivered on time just as clearly as if you were watching a movie. However, getting a target consumer to believe that any given company provides "better service" or is a "different kind of company" is vague and can lead to generic, meandering messages.

Product or Service

P is for *product or service*. A marketing objective should mention the specific product or service in question. At first blush this requirement might seem like a no-brainer. However, mentioning a product by name will help prevent campaigns that are generic and end up promoting a product category rather than a specific brand.

Place

P is for *place*. Place can be as broad as a city or an entire region of the country. It can also be as narrow as a specific store and even a section of a store, for example, the automotive department at Wal-Mart.

Place can also refer to a specific channel of distribution, such as getting a target consumer to buy an iPod® from a vending machine at an airport.

Season

S is for *season*. As we explained in the marketing analysis, every product category has natural hot and cold seasons, sometimes referred to as spikes. The season can be as long as the summer or as short as a Friday night.

CONSTRUCTING MARKETING OBJECTIVES

It is important to remember that the facilitator's job is to make a list of marketing objectives from which the client will select just one on which to focus. It is also important to make sure that all the items on the list are marketing objectives, not wishes. It has been our experience that if a wish sneaks into the list of marketing objectives, it is invariably chosen by the client, and that puts you back into the troublesome position of having to generate ideas based on a wish—which, as we have already demonstrated, is a waste of time.

All the marketing objectives on the list should have TOPPS. The way to begin the list of marketing objectives is to analyze the facts we learned as a result of the marketing analysis.

Let's try one using the Woodland Nurseries example. We know that the target consumer is a forty-five-year-old female who owns her own house and who loves to garden. We also know that she usually begins to shop for plants the first week of April. So, using these facts, we can compose a marketing objective that reads like this:

1. To get a forty-five-year-old female homeowner who loves to garden to visit Woodland Nurseries the first week of April.

Does our first marketing objective have TOPPS? Let's see how we did. The target is a person, not a demographic group. The outcome is that we want her to visit the nursery. The product is Woodland Nurseries, which also serves as the place, and the season is the first week of April. Great! We have our first marketing objective and it has TOPPS. You may have also noticed that this first marketing objective will lead to an activation campaign, as it suggests that we want the target to *do* something in relation to Woodland Nurseries rather than *believe* something about Woodland Nurseries.

Let's try another objective:

2. To get Sandy (our forty-five-year-old female who owns her own house and who loves to garden) to believe that the plants at Woodland Nurseries are the healthiest plants she could buy.

Let's check our second marketing objective. Here we see how creating a persona can be a great time-saver. Our outcome is that we want her to believe that the plants are healthy. Our product is the plants at Woodland Nurseries. Our second marketing objective has a TOP. Notice that because it is a brand-oriented objective it only requires the first three elements (target, outcome, and product).

MAKING A LIST OF MARKETING OBJECTIVES

In the last few pages we have discussed how to compose the first couple of marketing objectives. The challenge, however, comes when, in the role of facilitator, you must help a client and a resource group generate a list of marketing objectives. Here we will discuss how this is done.

First, you remind the group that there are two types of marketing objectives. You might even write these two phrases on a flip chart.

- To get a target consumer to do something with a product, in a place, in a season.
- To get a target consumer to believe something about a product.

Most of the time, these visual cues will be enough to get the list started, especially when there are people in the resource group who have some experience in the process. In cases where the visual cues are not enough, you might need to show the group how to construct the first marketing objective. You might say, "How about if we get our forty-five-year-old gardener to come to Woodland Nurseries the first weekend in April?" Most of the time, an illustration such as this is enough of a prompt to get the group to understand how to play the game.

Again, you should always guard against putting wishes on your list, which can be a little tricky when you're creating a nonjudgmental environment. If one of the participants says, for example, "We need to reach twenty-five- to fifty-four-year-old women," you can say, "Help me turn that into a marketing objective. Who is that woman and what do we want her to do or believe?"

Getting a list of clear marketing objectives can be hard work, but it will pay off in spades when it comes time for the client to choose the marketing objective for the project.

So, the facilitator has done a good job of getting the resource group to make a list of marketing objectives. It looks like a pretty good list:

1. To get a forty-five-year-old female homeowner who loves to garden to visit Woodland Nurseries the first week in April.
2. To get Sandy (our forty-five-year-old female homeowner who loves to garden) to believe that the plants at Woodland Nurseries are the healthiest plants she could buy.
3. To get our forty-five-year-old gardener to come to Woodland Nurseries the first weekend in April.

4. To get a forty-five-year-old female gardener to believe that the staff at Woodland Nurseries has the training to offer her the best gardening advice.
5. To get Sandy to visit the Woodland Nurseries Web site before she begins to design her garden.
6. To get Sandy to bring a friend to Woodland Nurseries the first weekend in April.

Marketing objective #3 on the list shows how being more or less specific about any given element of the marketing objective can help make the list longer. This objective looks a lot like #1, but it is different. It is one thing to get the target to visit the nursery the first week of April. It is an entirely different thing to get the target to show up at the nursery during the first *weekend* in April.

Now imagine for a moment that the client chose marketing objective #4 on the list. You can already see that all the ideas that would be generated to accomplish this objective would focus on the expertise of the staff and the formal training they have received. For instance, one idea might be to publish an "Ask the Expert" blog on the Woodland Nurseries Web site. Another idea might be to run a series of television commercials that communicate the staff's vast knowledge and experience. Yet another idea might be to record a series of brief podcasts on which the Woodland Nurseries staff offer advice on topics of interest to the target consumer.

Now let's imagine that instead the client were to choose marketing objective #1. You can see how this might lead to several simple activation ideas, such as sending the customer database coupons for early-bird discounts and perhaps making those coupons available on the Web site. More complicated ideas could include doing a spring festival at the store during which all the gardeners in the city could come to enjoy the new plants at Woodland Nurseries.

The point is that these two marketing objectives are fundamentally different, and so they would lead to completely different idea-generation sessions. We make a list of different marketing objectives because we want the client to consider a variety of different paths before selecting one focus for his project.

The Imagination Ingredient

Did you notice anything different about the last marketing objective on the list?

> 6. To get Sandy to bring a friend to Woodland Nurseries the first weekend in April.

The first five marketing objectives on the list might be described as literal. They contain information gleaned from the marketing analysis and match the required TOPPS structure. The sixth marketing objective on the list still has the TOPPS structure: Sandy (T), bringing her friend (O), to Woodland (P, P), the first weekend in April (S). However, it breaks out of that literal mode by introducing a new element that did not appear in the facts we uncovered in the marketing analysis. Suddenly we have Sandy bringing a friend on her next visit to Woodland Nurseries. Where did that come from?

One of the most frequently asked questions in our facilitator workshops is: "Other than the ingredients in the TOPPS acronym, is there anything else that goes into a marketing objective?" The answer is yes. The secret ingredient is *imagination*.

As we begin to explore the notion of injecting imagination into the list of marketing objectives, you should bear in mind a couple of fundamentals we covered earlier. First, the job of the facilitator is to make sure that all lists contain a variety of items from which the client can choose. It is desirable for the list of marketing objectives to include items that extend beyond the literal and the obvious. Second, the client will always be your backstop. The list can include all kinds of unexpected and even risky items; the client will keep you honest when it is time to make a choice.

Let's take a look at one technique the facilitator can use to extend the list of marketing objectives beyond the obvious. This technique is referred to as *morphological analysis* because it is based on the technique of the same name devised by the physicist Fritz Zwicky in the 1950s.[1]

First, lay out the components of a marketing objective horizontally, as they would appear on the title row of a spreadsheet, as shown in figure 8.

To Get	Target	Do	Believe

Benefit	Product	Place	Season

Figure 8. Components of a Marketing Objective

Second, generate lists of alternate definitions for the words on the heading, as shown in figure 9. Remember—this is a detour, so it's okay to have fun with it.

You can probably see where this is going. All the facilitator needs to do now is ask the resource group to create new marketing objectives by combining words from each of the different columns. Some members of the resource group will play it safe, choosing words from the different columns to build fairly conventional marketing objectives, as shown in figure 10.

So now we have added another objective, #7, to our list. Most people would consider this a fairly safe objective:

7. To convince Sandy that the healthiest plants come from Woodland.

Other participants will take a bigger risk and come up with objectives that make new combinations, as shown in figure 11.

To Get	Target	Do	Believe
Inspire	Sandy	Run	Remember
Scare	Husband	Eat	Endorse
Convince	Neighbor	Sleep	Praise
Embarrass	Friend	Pay	Blog
Push	Kids	Plant	Advertise

Benefit	Product	Place	Season
Clean	Perennials	Backyard	Fridays
Healthy	Roses	Woodland	Weekends
Funny	Fertilizer	State Fair	Spring
Organized	Annuals	Parking Lot	After Work
Fresh	Trees	City Hall	Winter

Figure 9. Different Names for Category Headings

To Get	Target	Do	Believe
Inspire	✓ Sandy	Run	Remember
Scare	Husband	Eat	Endorse
✓ Convince	Neighbor	Sleep	Praise
Embarrass	Friend	Pay	Blog
Push	Kids	Plant	Advertise

Benefit	Product	Place	Season
Clean	Perennials	Backyard	Fridays
✓ Healthy	Roses	✓ Woodland	Weekends
Funny	Fertilizer	State Fair	Spring
Organized	Annuals	Parking Lot	After Work
Fresh	Trees	City Hall	Winter

Figure 10. Selecting Predictable Combinations

To Get	Target	Do	Believe
Inspire	Sandy	✓Run	Remember
Scare	Husband	Eat	Endorse
Convince	✓Neighbor	Sleep	Praise
✓Embarrass	Friend	Pay	Blog
Push	Kids	Plant	Advertise

Benefit	Product	Place	Season
Clean	Perennials	Backyard	Fridays
Healthy	Roses	✓Woodland	Weekends
Funny	Fertilizer	State Fair	Spring
Organized	Annuals	Parking Lot	✓After Work
Fresh	Trees	City Hall	Winter

Figure 11. Injecting Imagination into New Combinations

Here is a more daring objective, #8, that we can add to the list:

8. Let's embarrass Sandy's jealous neighbor into running to Woodland Nurseries after work.

The result is a fresh look at the marketing objectives with an injection of imagination. Once these imaginative objectives have been added to the list, the facilitator is ready to help the client make a choice.

CHOOSING A MARKETING OBJECTIVE FOR WOODLAND NURSERIES

Let's remember where we are in the process.

First, Alesia, our facilitator, helped Sam, her client, make a list of wishes and then choose one wish to work on first. Sam said he wished to have a successful spring season.

Next Alesia engaged Sam in a very thorough marketing analysis of the business, focusing specifically on the facts that pertained to having a successful spring season, which was Sam's wish.

The marketing analysis, which we covered in the last chapter, netted Alesia all kinds of valuable information that was then used to inspire the list of eight marketing objectives that appears on the last several pages.

The time has come for Sam to select the marketing objective he wants to work on first. To help him do that, Alesia will ask him to consider three criteria that you have seen before:

- *Importance.* We only want to work on challenges that are important. The definition of important could include profitable, and it could also mean providing leverage. In other words, we want the client to select a marketing objective that is likely to make him money, or a marketing objective that can give him leverage to solving other problems.

- *Ideas.* Second, we want the client to pick a marketing objective that requires an idea. Here we are trying to avoid having the client give us a challenge he has already solved or that doesn't really require a lot of new ideas because the solution is obvious. After all, this process is designed for the generation of cool, custom, and effective ideas, so he should choose a marketing objective for which he needs some new ideas.

- *Influence.* Finally, we want to make sure that the client chooses a marketing objective over which he has influence, in an area where he can actually take action on the idea. We don't want to solve someone else's problem today. We are interested in working on a challenge that is within the client's sphere of influence.

Sam, the owner of Woodland Nurseries, has reviewed the list of marketing objectives, and, having considered the three criteria above, selected this marketing objective as the focus for his project:

To get our forty-five-year-old gardener to come to Woodland Nurseries the first week in April.

Before the meeting concludes, however, Sam makes a slight adjustment to the statement. He says, "I want to be a little more specific in describing the target and even the dates. Is that okay?"

Alesia responds, "Absolutely! We want the statement to communicate exactly what you want to have happen."

"Well," says Sam, "I would rather you guys work on getting this forty-five-year-old female homeowner who loves to garden to visit Woodland Nurseries between April 10 and May 15."

"Perfect," says Alesia. "We have a marketing objective!"

Albert Einstein said that a problem well stated is half solved. Alesia has just completed what may be the most important step of the process. Her next task is to lead the resource group in generating a long list of ideas to accomplish Sam's chosen objective.

7

IDEA GENERATION

We have arrived at a crucial and exciting step in the process. All the work that has been done up to this point has helped the client zero in on the marketing objective he wants to accomplish first. Now the job of the facilitator is to lead the client, the agent, and the resource group in a productive idea-generation session. As the person responsible for the generation of ideas, the facilitator is looking for two things: quantity and variety. Let us show you what we mean.

THE WEDDING

Imagine you are at a friend's wedding. The ceremony was beautiful. You hop in your car and drive over to the reception. As you walk into the ball-room an obviously agitated bride suddenly grabs you and pulls you aside.

"Oh, I'm so glad you're here!" she says. "The photographer just left. He had a family emergency, and I need someone to take pictures at the reception. Do you have a camera?"

"Sure, I have a pretty good digital camera."

"Do you have it with you?"

"No. It's at home. But I can go get it and be back in no time."

"Great!"

"I'll be back in ten minutes. You relax and enjoy your party."

As you turn to run to your car, the bride grabs your arm and says, "I really appreciate you doing this for me. I could not trust just anyone to take pictures of my wedding reception."

You are now in your car driving home to pick up the camera. You are probably mentally reviewing a checklist of questions: "Do I have enough memory in the camera? Are the batteries charged?"

Allow us to ask you another question: "When you get back to the wedding reception, what is your job?"

Over the years we have run this scenario by thousands of students. We have consistently received two responses to our question.

1. My job is to take lots of pictures.
2. My job is to take pictures of everything.

It is fascinating to note that when people are presented with this scenario, they always go for quantity. When we tell the story we always add a little extra emphasis on the part where the bride, with tears in her eyes, says, "I could not trust just *anyone* to take pictures of my wedding reception." Everyone groans and cringes. It seems that it is precisely because the stakes are high that everyone feels the situation calls for taking a lot of pictures.

So we have established that the act of making a long list of options before making choices is a natural reaction to a situation in which the pressure is on and the stakes are high.

But if we look at the second response, there is something different going on. When our students tell us their job is to "take pictures of everything," they are suggesting something more than quantity.

Let us put you back at the wedding reception for another moment. You are walking around with your digital camera. You would probably want to make sure that you covered the event from all possible angles. "Have I taken enough pictures of the bride's family? What about the groom's family? Did I catch the first dance? What about the tossing of the bouquet?" Without any prompting at all, you would photograph the event from many different angles.

What you would experience if you were to find yourself in a situation such as this is a need for variety. Which is why the best facilitators know that helping the resource group generate lots of ideas is good; helping the resource group generate lots of *different* ideas is best.

This is probably a good place to stop long enough to define what we mean by an "idea." After all, if we are going to ask facilitators to help a resource group generate a lot of different ideas, we should probably make sure they know what they are looking for.

MARKETING IDEAS DEFINED

After facilitating thousands of idea-generation sessions, we have come to the conclusion that most people don't know what an idea is. People use the word *idea* to describe pretty much anything that comes out of their head. And although that may be fine in most situations, it is not enough in marketing.

In the first few pages of this book, we defined a marketing idea as the communication a target consumer experiences that causes him or her to do something or believe something about a product or service. In this chapter our mission is to show how a facilitator creates a list of ideas. To do this, we need to make that definition a little more concrete.

A Marketing Idea Is a One-Sentence Story

The facilitator's job is to make sure he generates a long list of different ideas from which the client can make choices. That assignment requires the facilitator to capture the ideas in a manner that allows the client to see each idea clearly in his head, and also to see the ideas as different from each other. The best way to do that is by capturing each idea as a one-sentence story. Here are three examples of ideas that might appear on an idea-generation list:

1. Every guy who buys one of our barbeque grills will be given a promotional code that he enters on our Web site to receive two free Omaha steaks of his choice in the mail.
2. Let's run a campaign in which we show a man and a woman who have the same name—like Kelly or Pat—who met for the first time on our dating Web site and ended up falling in love and getting married.
3. Let's show some sort of a factory with an assembly line that makes it look like our brightly colored computers are manufactured the same way brightly colored candy is made.

Even though you don't know the marketing objectives that motivated the three completely different ideas above or the brands being promoted, there is a good chance that when you read them you actually saw them happening in your mind. You saw the guy buying the grill. You probably also saw the steaks—maybe even on the grill! You saw the happy couple who met on the dating Web site. You probably began to imagine what they would be saying about the funny things that have happened as a result of the fact that they have the same first name. You might even have invented an assembly line in your head and maybe even heard the noises it made as it stamped out those brightly colored computers as if it was stamping out candy.

A story increases the likelihood that, if the client chooses it, the idea will become reality. That's what we mean when we say we want ideas that are specific and clear (Rule 5 of the Rules of Brainstorming). We want facilitators to capture ideas as very brief little stories because we want the client to see the idea in his head as clearly as if he was watching a movie of it.

We also said at the outset of this book that for an idea to earn the title of "marketing idea" it must meet three very specific standards. Let's review those three standards again.

Cool

A marketing idea has to be cool to the target consumer. Above all, cool means relevant. The idea has to completely fit the target consumer and her lifestyle. It's as if the company marketing the product was saying to the target consumer, "I know you well enough to do this cool thing for you."

Ideas don't have to be entirely new to be cool, but they do have to be current and fresh. Cool also means that the target consumer will see it as positive, valuable, and appealing. If two people who fit the description of the target consumer were having a conversation about the idea in question, there would be something novel, unique, unexpected, or entertaining that would cause both of them to describe the idea as "cool."

Custom

Custom means the program needs to look, sound, smell, and feel like the product or the service being promoted. The idea needs to be customized enough to the product or the service that it lets the target consumer know who is responsible for this cool idea. In many cases you remember a cool advertising campaign but you don't remember the name of the advertiser. That happens because the program did not have enough custom elements in it to connect the communication to the product or the brand being promoted.

If the brand is going to do something cool for the target consumer, it ought to receive full credit for it.

Effective

Let's remember that all marketing ideas are born with only one of two objectives in mind: To get a target consumer to believe something about a product or service (branding) or to get a target consumer to do something with a product or service (activation). Effective ideas lay out a clear path for the target consumer to follow as he engages with a given program.

A branding campaign will offer persuasive reasons to believe specific key benefits about a product or a service. An activation campaign will set clear expectations about what the target consumer should do with a product and offer specific reasons, even rewards, for the target consumer to try or buy the product being promoted.

To summarize, marketing ideas have to be cool or they will not be noticed by the target consumer; they have to be custom or no one will remember the product being promoted; and they have to be effective or nothing will happen as a result of the communication.

So far in this chapter we have discussed what an idea should sound like and we have discussed the three standards ideas must meet to be considered marketing ideas. The next thing we need to keep in mind is that marketing ideas have to be manifested somehow in order for the target consumer to experience them. That is to say, the idea quite literally needs to happen, to materialize, in order for the target consumer to experience it. Marketing ideas are manifested with the use of tools. Let's define what we mean by a tool.

TOOLS DEFINED

Anything that can be used to communicate a message to a target consumer is a tool. The most common communication tools are the major media, such as radio, television, newspaper, the Internet, and others. However, in a culture of integrated marketing communications, where the mission is to surround the target consumer with messaging, marketers are availing themselves of quite a varied menu of unexpected tools.

A bank advertises on the sides of airport sky bridges all over the world, while inside the airplane newly released movies are being advertised on air-sickness bags. A clothing manufacturer recarpets an entire department store with colors that are evocative of its brand of clothing, while a package delivery company "delivers" the green flag to start a car race at the Daytona International Speedway. These are all examples of tools used by marketers to communicate with their target consumers in ways that are cool, custom, and effective.

The inextricable connection between ideas and tools sometimes makes people think—erroneously—that the tool is the idea. An idea is a story that describes what the target consumer will experience. A tool, on the other hand, is the method, the technology, the medium that will be used to manifest the idea and deliver it to the target consumer.

Imagine that a composer has come up with a brilliant idea for a piece of music. No one else knows he has had that idea until he sits at the piano or grabs a guitar and plays it. But the piano or the guitar is not the idea. It is a tool the composer uses to express the idea.

It is not enough for us to imagine the sentence you are reading. If we want you to experience our ideas, we have to use a tool—a computer—to write it down and then use the much broader tool of the publishing industry to transform it into the book you are now holding in your hands. We could also have expressed our ideas in the form of a blog, a Sunday morning radio program, a mural on the side of a building, or even a message in a bottle!

The facilitator needs to be very aware of the special relationship that exists between tools and ideas. This awareness will be especially important during the idea-generation session, because that is where the facilitator will have to work hard to help the participants verbalize the entire idea and not just the tool that would be used to manifest that idea.

Now, before the idea-generation session gets under way, there are a couple of things a facilitator can do to help the resource group generate a higher quantity and variety of ideas during the session. First, the facilitator should make sure the marketing objective is stated correctly. Then the facilitator needs to help the resource group get ready to be creative by reminding them of the rules of the game they are about to play. We will show you both of these techniques next.

STATING A MARKETING OBJECTIVE

In the last chapter we discussed the ingredients that are required in order to write a focused marketing objective. In this chapter, we want to introduce a phrase that you should put at the beginning of every marketing objective to help the process of generating a long list of ideas. Perhaps the best way to illustrate this technique is to put it in the context of a marketing situation.

Let's say a facilitator who works for an advertising agency that represents a very large car dealership has been asked to facilitate a session to help the dealership increase sales of one of its brands. When the project was first explained to the facilitator, it was described as: "The client needs us to help him come up with ideas to sell more Jeeps." The facilitator followed the steps we outlined in chapters 4 through 6 and helped the client arrive at a much more focused marketing objective: "To get a twenty-eight-year-old guy to experience the rush of driving a Jeep Wrangler."

The simple act of making sure that the marketing objective has a TOP (a target who is a person, not a demographic group; an outcome of what we want the target consumer to do or believe; and a specific product or service) will go a long way to increase the likelihood that the resource group will produce lots of different ideas. Also, even before the facilitator takes a single detour, the stage will have been set for the ideas to be much more specific and actionable because the resource group can actually *see* the twenty-eight-year-old guy sitting in the Jeep Wrangler with a big smile on his face. Resource groups always find it much easier to come up with persuasive ideas when they can visualize the target consumer who needs to be convinced.

Now that we have a well-crafted marketing objective, there is still one more thing we want to add to it before the idea-generation session begins:

In what ways might we . . .

We recommend that this simple and powerful phrase be added to the beginning of all marketing objectives, as in:

In what ways might we get a twenty-eight-year-old guy to experience the rush of driving a Jeep Wrangler?

This phrase serves two purposes. First, the word *ways* reminds the resource group that we are looking for quantity. Second, the word *might* reminds the resource group we are looking for any possible way that we might accomplish the marketing objective and that we are not going to judge any of the ideas just yet.

And speaking of judgment, there is a potential problem we want to help the facilitator anticipate. It is very common for people who appear open-minded and enthusiastic under normal circumstances to adopt a surprisingly closed and reticent posture as soon as the idea-generation session begins. For instance, we saw how most of us, upon finding ourselves in the middle of a wedding reception with a camera in our hands, would naturally go for quantity and variety. However, that is not what most people really do in an idea-generation session—at least not initially. In fact, the first time the facilitator asks the resource group for ideas, the bewildering reaction can be exactly the opposite! This is why idea generation can be a tricky step to facilitate. You see, this is the spot where people suddenly decide they want to be "creative." We have observed that by "being creative" they usually mean they are going to put all sorts of pressure on themselves and not say a word until they come up with that one brilliant idea that blows everybody away.

LEARNING FROM CREATIVE PEOPLE

Since this is the place in the process where we often observe people adopting bizarre notions of what "being creative" is, we thought it might be good to take a look at what creative people really do. Figure 12 is a fun exercise you can use to illustrate creative people's love of quantity. The way to play the game is to match the numbers on the left with the creative people on the right. It should take just a couple of minutes to complete.

Creative People	
2121	The average number of shots taken by Michael Jordan in a single season.
192	The number of symphonies, operas, concertos, and other compositions written by Wolfgang Amadeus Mozart.
1668	Number of novels, novellas, short stories, screenplays, and articles written by Stephen King.
626	Number of patents held by Thomas Alva Edison.
1903	Number of paintings, sculptures, drawings, and other works by Pablo Picasso currently housed in the Musée Picasso in Paris.

Figure 12. Creative People

Let's see how you did. If you go to the National Basketball Association Web site, you can download the database of every statistic of every basketball player in the history of the game. I discovered that no basketball player has thrown the basketball at the basket more than Michael Jordan. Jordan took an average of 1,668 shots per season.

Wolfgang Amadeus Mozart wrote his first symphony when he was seven. (I don't know what took him so long!) He died at the age of thirty-five, and between the ages of seven and thirty-five, he wrote 626 pieces of music.

Stephen King published his first book in 1974. It was called *Carrie*. He threw the manuscript in the trash, but luckily his wife saved it and convinced him to keep writing; his fans are glad she did. Since that first effort in 1974, King has published almost two hundred novels, novellas, scripts, and articles.

Thomas Alva Edison had so many projects in the works at any given point in time that he often set them in motion and then handed them over to his employees to finish. To this day, no human being holds more patents than Edison; he has 1,903.

Pablo Picasso painted his first picture—a bullfighter—when he was eight years old, and he died at the age of ninety-one. Between the ages of eight and ninety-one, Picasso lived twenty-nine thousand days, and he has to his name more than twenty thousand pieces. This means that, on average, he created one piece of art every day and a half. In the wonderful book on Picasso's paintings called *The Ultimate Picasso*,[1] there is a section that contains thirteen paintings that are all dated on the same day!

There are so many things we can learn from the behavior of people who are naturally creative. First on the list is that creative people have a well-established habit of generating a quantity of output. Second is that creative people are ultimately nonjudgmental about any one effort.

It's as if when Michael Jordan threw the ball at the basket and it didn't go in, he said to himself, "No sweat, I'll be throwing it again in a second." And when Picasso completed a piece he wasn't quite satisfied with, he said something to the effect of, "No problem, I'll do another one in a minute."

Perhaps this is why Pablo Picasso has been quoted as saying that he never truly finished a piece.

Fortunately, the facilitator can turn to the Rules of Brainstorming to help her create an environment in which the resource group will emulate the behaviors of the most creative people.

REMINDING THE RESOURCE GROUP OF THE RULES OF BRAINSTORMING

Effective facilitators make sure to set expectations at the beginning of all idea-generation sessions. We recommend that facilitators read these Seven Rules of Brainstorming out loud to everyone present at the outset of all idea-generation sessions. Even when the facilitator is working with a team of experienced participants, we strongly recommend that the Seven Rules of Brainstorming are reviewed every time.

Rule #1: *During the list-making or idea-generation session, there will be no judgment of ideas, no evaluation, and no criticism.*

Rule #2: *Freewheeling is allowed and encouraged. Wild and outrageous ideas are welcome.*

Rule #3: *We are going to make a long list. Remember that we're striving for quantity rather than quality, because when making lists, quantity leads to quality.*

Rule #4: *We are going to take detours and make connections that create quantity, novelty, and relevance.*

Rule #5: *We need ideas to be specific and clear so that all participants can understand them.*

Rule #6: *All ideas must be written down.*

Rule #7: *Everybody participating in the list-making or idea-generation session is equal in rank. There are no bosses. There is no hierarchy.*

We have just shown you two things that the facilitator can do right before the session gets under way to generate a quantity and variety of ideas. Now we want to talk about what the facilitator can do during the idea-generation session to help the resource group express their ideas.

HOW TO ELICIT MARKETING IDEAS

Let's return to the Jeep Wrangler illustration to show you what facilitators need to do to obtain marketing ideas in an idea-generation session.

The resource group has been given this assignment:

> *In what ways might we get a twenty-eight-year-old guy to experience the rush of driving a Jeep Wrangler?*

The facilitator has reminded the group to follow the Rules of Brainstorming, and the session is ready to begin.

The job of eliciting marketing ideas from a resource group requires the facilitator to be very clear as to what she is listening for. First of all, the experienced facilitator is looking ahead to the next step. She knows that at some point a client will need to review the list of ideas and choose the ones he likes the best. She also knows that the client will simply skip over anything he cannot see clearly in his head. Clients also habitually skip over ideas that look similar to other ideas they may have seen earlier on the list. We have actually had clients who just cluster all the ideas that look alike into generic groups ("Put that one with all the other test-drives").

As you see, when the facilitator looks ahead to the client making choices off the list, her mission becomes clear: The facilitator needs to capture the ideas clearly enough so the client can see them like a movie in his head and with enough specificity that the client will see that they are all different from each other.

Secondly, the facilitator knows that ideas have to meet three specific standards (cool, custom, and effective). However—and this is important for the facilitator to keep in mind as the session gets under way—she is not expected to insist that the idea satisfy all three standards when they are verbalized during idea generation. A facilitator who insists on capturing only ideas that are, in her view, cool *and* custom *and* effective will simply bog down the idea-generation session, and the resource group will become frustrated. Our experience has taught us that it is sufficient for the facilitator to look to satisfy two of the three requirements as the ideas are being verbalized during the idea-generation session.

Any elements that are missing from an idea the client chooses will be satisfied during the process of development, which we will cover in chapter 10.

Finally, as if everything we have covered so far was not enough for the facilitator to think about, there is the issue of how people naturally express ideas. Let's look at that.

People Express Ideas the Way They Tell Jokes

"A guy walks into a bar . . ."

Even if you had never heard that famous setup before, you would know that it is just the beginning of a story. In marketing, ideas are stories. And, as with all stories, there is a natural progression in the way they are expressed.

Even when ideas are well formed in the person's mind, they are usually expressed in short bursts. The first burst is usually a tool, because the person communicating the idea wants to put you in a frame of reference. So the facilitator might hear something like, "Make it a video game!" The inexperienced facilitator will write down the words "video game" and move on to the next idea. That is how you end up with a list of tools instead of ideas. The experienced facilitator, however, knows that a video game is a tool and that there is a lot more to the idea. She just needs to give the participant time to finish the story.

Given the chance—and sometimes a little encouragement from the facilitator, like "Tell me more about this video game"—the participant finishes the story: "They could experience the rush of driving the Jeep Wrangler if we created a video game on our Web site with increasingly difficult levels. We could even call the highest level 'The Rush'!"

The facilitator's patience was rewarded with a one-sentence story. And, as we established earlier, the facilitator will be mentally checking to make sure the idea meets two of the three standards that marketing ideas should meet (cool, custom, and effective). In this case the idea has cool elements, since the target consumer loves video games, and it has custom elements because the vehicle in the video game would be a Jeep Wrangler. The only question at this point is effectiveness. The client actually wants the target consumer to drive the car. So this idea will need more work, but this could be fixed later if the client were to choose the idea. For now, the facilitator has added another idea to her list and she can move on to the next idea.

"It should be an extreme test-drive," says a participant in the back of the room.

Once again, the facilitator recognizes this is just the initial burst. She asks, "Tell me more."

"More like a rugged test-drive," says the participant.

The facilitator writes down "rugged test-drive," knowing she doesn't have everything he needs yet. She asks, "What do you see the target consumer doing in this rugged test-drive?"

"We build a rugged outdoor test-drive area, and these guys come out and experience driving the Jeep Wrangler through a natural obstacle course."

Over the years we have half-jokingly told our students that our job as teachers is to make the job of the facilitator look easy. In fact, it isn't always easy. Sometimes the facilitator has to work a little harder for an idea.

How Much Is Enough?

A moment ago we showed you that often the first burst of an idea is a tool. When a participant says, "Let's do a television commercial" or "I see an annual event," the facilitator knows those are tools and she needs to wait for the idea that will be manifested by the television commercial or the annual event.

However, other times the first burst of an idea is what might be described as an element or a fragment of an idea. When that happens, the facilitator needs to do two different things in no particular order. She needs to get the participant to finish the idea, and she needs to attach some sort of tool to it so the client can see not only what the idea is but at least a part of how it might be executed.

Back at the idea-generation session, a participant comes up with a slogan, "Strip down!" This contribution is met with laughter from the rest of the resource group.

The facilitator knows there is nothing to work with here yet. So she says, "Finish the story for me."

"Well, that's one of the cool things about the Wrangler; you can strip it down."

"Still not enough," thinks the facilitator. So she asks the participant to put it in the context of what we might get the target consumer to do.

Finally, a different participant offers to finish the story. "How about if we have these guys come down to the dealership? Everyone who test-drives the Jeep Wrangler can take part in a contest to see who can strip down a Wrangler the fastest. The winner of the contest wins Jeep merchandise." And another idea in the form of a one-line story makes it onto the list.

Another participant says, "They should experience the rush on YouTube."

The facilitator asks for more, knowing YouTube is a tool. "Can you tell me more about the rush on YouTube?"

"No!" says the participant, who gets applause from the rest of the group.

"Okay," says the facilitator, "Can someone help me finish this thought, please?"

A different participant then adds, "The guys who already own a Jeep Wrangler can just videotape their most rugged ride and post them on YouTube. The guys who don't yet own a Jeep Wrangler can come down to the dealership and do their test-drive with us. All they have to do is bring a buddy with a camera to film the ride. We will give an award to the best video."

How Much Is Too Much?

We have cautioned you to make sure to get enough of an idea so the client can clearly see it in his head and so he can see it as different from the other ideas on the list, and we have described a couple of techniques you might use to elicit enough detail for one idea.

Now we want to caution you that you can also end up with too much of a marketing idea. This can be an insidious problem, because it will make you think you have more ideas on your list than you actually have.

To illustrate this problem, we will continue with our session for Jeep Wrangler. The group is humming along, generating ideas to get that twenty-eight-year-old guy to experience the rush of driving a Jeep Wrangler. Suddenly a participant shouts, "Jeep music!"

The facilitator needs more. She has no idea what this is or what tool might be used to materialize the program. Fortunately, the participant does have an idea, so he says, "I think we need to schedule a concert series sponsored by Jeep. We would carefully select acts from a variety of music styles as long as they target these twenty-eight-year-old guys."

The facilitator captures the idea as #23 on the list. This idea inspires a slew of other ideas from the group. Here they are:

24. The concerts could be in small venues and the only people invited are people who either own or test-drive a Jeep Wrangler.
25. We could put a Jeep Wrangler on the stage.
26. We could have a red Jeep Wrangler signed by all the artists and then give it away at the end of the series.
27. Every person who test-drives a Jeep Wrangler could receive a CD of the next band to play in the concert series.

Do you see what is happening? Ideas 24, 25, 26, and 27 are not new ideas; they are developments of idea number 23. What has happened here is that the group has latched on to one idea that sounds kind of cool—and they don't want to let it go.

Remember learning about Isaac Newton's laws of motion in science class? His First Law of Motion, the Law of Inertia, says that an object at rest wants to stay at rest and an object in motion wants to stay in motion until an unbalanced force is applied. The thing about human beings is that for some reason we think we are exempt from the laws of physics. But of course we are not. We like to find a place of comfort and stay there.

The effective facilitator knows that members of the resource group will have a tendency to find an idea that sounds comfortable and fixate on that idea to the exclusion of any further new ideas. She needs to learn to recognize when the new ideas being generated are improving on an earlier idea rather than adding new possibilities to the list.

How do we correct this problem? Take a detour! The facilitator might say, "These ideas are great. Let me take you in a different direction to see if we can come up with new and different ways to achieve the marketing objective."

And that is the topic of our next chapter.

8

THE MAGIC OF DETOURS

In 1656 the Spanish painter Diego Velázquez created a painting he named *Las Meninas* (The Maids of Honor). Long recognized as one of the most important paintings of Western art, *Las Meninas* has been studied and analyzed for more than three hundred years. The fascination with the painting comes in part from the unusual nature of the multiple focal points in the piece. The first focal point is the daughter of King Philip IV of Spain, who is surrounded by her maids of honor. The second, in a sneaky self-portrait, is Velázquez, who depicts himself in the act of painting the king and queen of Spain. The third is a small mirror image of the king and queen, who are supposed to be the subject of the painting, which appears behind Velázquez.

Perhaps it is because of all the different levels of depth that can be discerned in the painting (experts count at least seven), or maybe it's because of the curious and daring strategy of not really showing his subject in the painting itself, but the fact remains that artists love this piece. One of them in particular, Pablo Picasso, loved it so much he painted fifty-eight different versions of it!

In 1961 a young jazz virtuoso named John Coltrane heard Julie Andrews sing "My Favorite Things," written by Richard Rodgers and

Oscar Hammerstein. Like Picasso's fascination with *Las Meninas*, Coltrane was so inspired by "My Favorite Things" that by the time he died six years later he had recorded fifteen different versions of it—as short as 5:22 and as long as 57:19.

We don't think Picasso ever made a list and then made choices. We doubt Coltrane was familiar with the Rules of Brainstorming. But somewhere along the line these two artists learned and mastered one of the most fundamental and powerful tools of the creative process, something we call the *detour*.

MAKING NEW CONNECTIONS

Back in chapter 1, when we first discussed detours, we described them as a question, a suggestion, or a piece of information that serves as a stimulus to increase the generation of ideas. We now want to add to this definition that a detour is also a tool a facilitator uses to deliberately force a resource group to make new connections.

Had we asked them, Picasso and Coltrane might have said they found inspiration in the work of other artists. In our language, *Las Meninas* was a detour, and Picasso's fifty-eight versions of it were his new connections. For Coltrane, Julie Andrews's original version of "My Favorite Things" was the detour. His new connections were the fifteen different versions he recorded.

When creative people talk about finding inspiration, they are actually taking detours. They don't use that terminology because they're not facilitators using the Creative Resources Process, but their process of making new connections is similar. When the well runs dry, they go out and read, watch, or get involved in something that will create inspiration.

In this chapter, we will spend time exploring how detours work and how the facilitator can use them to help a team of people come up with cool, custom, and effective marketing ideas. At the end of the chapter we will return to the Woodland Nurseries case study, where we will see how Alesia, the facilitator, uses detours to help the resource group generate a long list of ideas to accomplish her client's marketing objective.

HOW TO TAKE A DETOUR

Imagine you are driving down the road and are suddenly directed to follow detour signs. You would do this with the expectation that you were going to temporarily drive in a different direction, but one that still leads toward your intended destination. This is also how detours work in idea generation. The detour takes you in a new direction where you make new connections that might help you accomplish your marketing objective.

Detours have their different levels of complexity. At the simplest end, detours take the form of questions or prompts. The next level, which we might describe as intermediate, is the detour as a side list. At the complex end of the continuum are detours as full-fledged experiences. Let's examine these one at a time.

A Detour as a Question or a Prompt

The overwhelming majority of the detours in this book are detours as questions or as prompts. When Richard, the facilitator in the very first chapter, was helping his resource group make a list of names for dogs, he coaxed them into making the list longer by prompting them to think about a big dog, a little dog, or a family dog. Questions and prompts are the most widely used detours because they take very little time to execute and are very effective in changing the direction of an idea-generation session. Let's take a look at how they work.

In the last chapter we introduced you to a facilitator who works for an advertising agency and who has been asked to lead an idea-generation session for a major Jeep dealer. You may remember that the marketing objective chosen by the client was: *In what ways might we get a twenty-eight-year-old guy to experience the rush of driving a Jeep Wrangler?*

Now let's imagine the session is under way and the facilitator decides she wants ideas that have a direct connection to the summer. So she takes a detour in the form of a question, "What if we wanted this guy to drive the Jeep Wrangler right before the July 4th holiday?"

We already know that two things will happen right away. First, the quantity of ideas will increase quickly as the resource group responds to that question. Second, the list will begin to contain ideas that are obviously—and sometimes not so obviously—inspired by patriotic themes, like a Red, White, and Blue Jeep Wrangler sale, for every test-drive we send a calling card with a picture of a Jeep on it to troops stationed overseas, and maybe images of young men and women driving their Jeep Wranglers on the beach.

A couple of minutes later the idea-generation session slows down again and our facilitator decides to take another detour. This time she uses a prompt instead of a question: "Think about Christmas!" Again, there will be a surge in the number of ideas generated, and the list will begin to include ideas that probably feature Santa Claus distributing gifts in a red Jeep Wrangler instead of a sleigh and off-roading in the snow test-drives.

These examples illustrate detours as questions and as prompts. They are as powerful as they are simple.

A Detour as a Side List

The side list is a more involved way to take a detour. To illustrate it, let's continue our idea-generation session for Jeep Wrangler. Our resource group has already generated a dozen or so ideas and the facilitator feels it is time to take a detour.

"I need everyone to help me make a list of everything that comes to mind when I say the word 'outdoors.'"

As the resource group begins to make a list, the facilitator hangs a clean sheet of paper on a different wall and captures those items on the new sheet, entirely separate from the main list of ideas.

Once the facilitator has captured seven to ten items on the list, she turns to the group and says, "Now I am going to read the list back to you. I want you to let me know if any of these items inspires a new idea that will get a twenty-eight-year-old guy to experience the rush of driving a Jeep Wrangler." The facilitator then reads the new list back to the group:

1. Yellowstone
2. Dirt
3. Tents
4. Hunting
5. Fishing
6. Freedom
7. Off-roading
8. Climbing
9. Roughing it

One participant has an idea right away: "I think we could give away an outdoor adventure to one of the guys who test-drives the Jeep Wrangler. Maybe the winner chooses from among three different adventures on three different continents."

The facilitator just netted a new idea from this detour. She walks over to the main list of ideas and adds the outdoor adventures idea to the list.

Then she returns to the side list containing the words inspired by the outdoors and asks again, "Is there anything else on this list that might help us get a twenty-eight-year-old guy to experience the rush of test-driving a Jeep Wrangler?"

This time a young woman speaks up. "This idea has nothing to do with that list. Is that okay?"

"No problem!" says the facilitator. "We are looking for a long list."

"Well, I think we should give people, especially young guys, Jeep Wranglers as loaner cars. Anyone who brings in a car to be serviced at the dealership gets a brand-new Jeep Wrangler as a loaner."

As she listens to the idea, the facilitator walks over to the main list of ideas and captures the loaner car idea in a couple of lines.

She chooses one of the items on the side list and says, "I have a feeling we can come up with some ideas that are inspired by the word *dirt*! What connections can you guys make?"

There is a brief silence in the room and then one of the participants says, "Jeep Wranglers love to play in the dirt."

"Okay . . ." says the facilitator, waiting for more.

After a short silence, another participant finishes the thought, "Everyone who does a test-drive gets a special edition T-shirt that looks really dirty and it has that slogan on it."

Now the facilitator must decide whether to continue to push for ideas inspired by the word *dirt*, or to move on to a different item on the side list.

Let's pause for a moment and take a look at how the side list detour works.

First, the facilitator comes up with a topic (in this case, connections to the word *outdoors*) and asks the resource group to help her make a side list of items inspired by that topic. Notice that this is a side list, so it is not attached to the main list of ideas. When the facilitator has seven to ten ideas on the list, she reads the list back to the team and gives them a chance to make new connections with any of the items on the list.

Once the participants have made as many connections as they can see, the facilitator has the prerogative to choose any one item that she feels has additional potential. Then, by focusing the participants on that item, she coaxes them to make new connections and generate new ideas.

Over the years we have observed that there are some facilitators who are satisfied with whatever ideas the participants generate on their own, while others are skilled at forcing the resource group to make several new connections with each item on the detour list before moving on to the next one. There really is no right or wrong way to do it as long as the facilitator is generating a variety of ideas from which the client can make a choice.

A Detour as a Full-Fledged Experience

There is no end to the number of elaborate techniques facilitators can use with resource groups to make new connections. One facilitator may split the resource group into teams and have each team compose a poem or a song for the Jeep Wrangler. Another facilitator might have the resource group go off-roading in Jeep Wranglers, after which they all return to the conference room to explore their experiences in search of new ideas.

The only limitations to these detour experiences are the imagination of the facilitator, the stamina of the resource group, and the time allowed for the project. Regardless of the detour technique you choose, you need to keep sight of the purpose: helping the resource group create a variety of ideas by adding quantity, novelty, and relevance to the list.

We recommend that you get comfortable with detours as questions and prompts and detours as side lists before you attempt to get any fancier. Once you have mastered the fundamentals, you will know when and how to use the more complicated idea-generation techniques most effectively.

Now that we have a pretty good handle on how detours work, let's take a look at the impact that detours can have on an idea-generation session.

DETOURS CREATE QUANTITY

A productive idea-generation session sounds a lot like microwaving a bag of popcorn. It always begins slowly, with not much going on. Then you hear a couple of pops, followed by a sustained increase in pops. Then, within a few seconds, the popping slows down—and, finally, silence.

If we were to create a simple graph tracking the number of ideas generated per minute during a typical idea-generation session, the graph might look something like figure 13.

The challenge for effective facilitators is to keep the idea-generation session going. The problem is that repeating the phrase, "What else?" is not a productive way to keep things moving. As a matter of fact, we have seen it become counterproductive, because without the help of detours, the resource group gets fatigued very quickly.

Detours give the facilitator an effective way to keep the ideas coming. When the facilitator uses detours effectively, the idea-generation session should look more like figure 14.

The facilitator knows that, as the natural order of things, people will run out of ideas if they stay on one topic for too long. So she pays attention when the idea generation begins to die down, at which point she takes the resource group on a new detour. Well-timed detours are very effective ways of helping the resource group make the list longer than they ever thought they could.

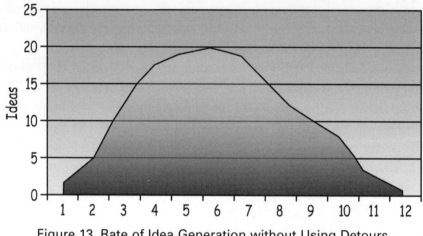

Figure 13. Rate of Idea Generation without Using Detours

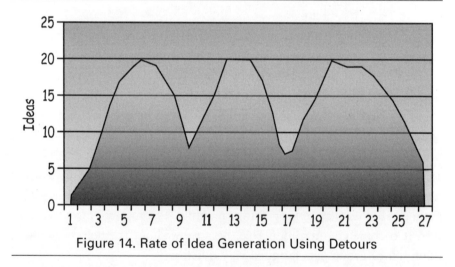

Figure 14. Rate of Idea Generation Using Detours

Generating a longer list of ideas is valuable, but it is not enough. In addition to quantity, we want our list of ideas to contain relevance and novelty. For those two ingredients, we turn to fact-based detours and novelty detours.

RELEVANCE: FACT-BASED DETOURS

Fact-based detours get their name because they are based on the facts of the situation. They are effective tools a facilitator can use to make sure that any list of ideas contains ideas that are relevant to the target consumer.

In chapter 4 we showed you for the first time how facts surrounding the clients can play a very important role in identifying marketing objectives. Now we want to show you how those same facts can also become powerful detours. Consider the following illustration.

Out to dinner with a group of friends from work, Tyler, who happens to be an experienced facilitator, decides to take advantage of the occasion to get help with a personal challenge he is facing. His sister Winnie is about to turn forty. Since everyone in his family knows he's the "idea guy," he has been appointed the person in charge of coming up with a really cool birthday celebration.

Most everyone has finished their meal when Tyler calls out, "Everybody," as he taps his wine glass with a fork. "You're probably wondering why I brought you here this evening." Undaunted by the boos, the groans, and the dinner roll launched in his direction, Tyler continues, "I need your help. My sister Winnie is turning forty and I need some ideas to make her birthday really special."

The group's immediate response is the predictable list of generic birthday suggestions: "Send her flowers . . . give her a day at a spa . . . buy her some nice jewelry."

We have given this scenario to our students as an exercise and have observed that in very short order, they become impatient with their own ideas. At first they don't even know what is bothering them until finally one of them asks, "Wait a minute! You need to tell us more about Winnie or we won't be able to come up with any cool ideas for her."

People are naturally hungry for relevance. They need information—facts—in order to come up with relevant ideas.

And that is exactly what happens to Tyler. One of his colleagues says, "These ideas are boring. You need to tell us more about Winnie. What does she like? What is she into?"

Tyler responds with a list:

1. She loves horses.
2. She has three cats.
3. She loves to go to the Caribbean.
4. She loves convertibles.
5. She loves to read murder mysteries.

The group seems to become reenergized by the list of things Winnie is interested in. "Why don't you throw a Caribbean-themed dinner party for her birthday?"

The other participants react to the Caribbean idea by offering their own connections.

"How about if you send her on a weekend getaway to the Caribbean?"

"I'll bet you can find some beautiful books full of photos from the Caribbean."

"See if you can get your hands on some of the photos she took during her Caribbean vacations and make her a framed collage or a scrapbook."

Tyler's detour seems to be working. After he told the group that Winnie loves the Caribbean, they were able to make the new connections listed above.

You probably recognized Tyler's detour as a side list detour. You saw how, having made a side list of facts about Winnie, he read it back to the group, allowing them to be inspired by any of the items on the list. Now he is going to choose one of the items on the list that looks promising to him. He will ask his friends to make new connections with that one item. He says, "You know what? I'm intrigued by this murder mystery thing. Winnie loves to read murder mysteries. There's got to be some ideas there!"

Now the group starts generating a new series of ideas based on the fact that Winnie likes to read murder mysteries: "Take her to an old castle in Scotland where they're doing one of those murder mystery parties, and she can take part in a murder mystery."

"Maybe you can get her an autographed first-edition copy of an important historical murder mystery."

Here you see the power of fact-based detours at work. The idea of taking Winnie all the way to an old Scottish castle to take part in a murder mystery party was definitely not on the list already, so Tyler got quantity out of his detour. And because the idea connects to the fact that she has an interest in murder mysteries, the same detour netted Tyler a relevant idea.

There are two important points to be made here. One is that the facilitator, as leader of the process, has the prerogative to explore as many facts in a situation as she thinks can lead to ideas that will be relevant to the target consumer. The other important point is one that we made in chapter 4 when we were trying to help a friend create traffic for his restaurant. Without exploring the facts of a situation, it is difficult—if not impossible—to generate ideas that will be relevant to the target consumer.

Just imagine that Tyler had asked his work buddies, "Hey, my sister Winnie is having her fortieth birthday and I was thinking of doing something cool for her." Not many people would raise their hands and say, "You know what you ought to do? You ought to fly her to Scotland where there's lots of old castles and I'll bet you there's a murder mystery party that you could take her to." This just goes to show how, in just a couple of minutes, that tiny little fact-based detour took you all the way to Scotland, which is something you wouldn't have done without the help of the detour.

Let's take a look at three fact-based detours. As we explore each one, remember that they can be delivered as questions ("What if I told you that the target consumer loves to play video games?") or as side lists ("Help me make a list of all the different ways in which the target consumer spends her disposable income.") The facilitator decides how simple or complicated to make the detour. The decision will probably be based on a variety of factors, such as the level of experience of the resource group, the quantity and variety of ideas that have already been generated, and the amount of time available for the session.

Fact-Based Detour #1: The Target Consumer

Our first fact-based detour requires the facilitator to bring into the idea-generation session as much information as possible about the target consumer.

The list of questions below is by no means exhaustive, but it can help a facilitator create a profile of a target consumer. We suggest that the answers to the questions below be posted all over the room, so the members of the resource group can consider them as they generate ideas.

1. What do we know about the target consumer as a person? Consider the target consumer's hobbies and interests. Consider all the different roles the target plays, such as parent, spouse, lover, employee, neighbor, etc.
2. What do you know about all the ways in which the target consumer interacts with products or services in this category?
3. How specifically is the target consumer's life improved by the purchase of this product or service?

In chapter 5, when we were going through the marketing analysis, we discussed the importance of having customer insights about the target consumer. We just saw a vivid example of how a fact-based detour that contains specific information about a target consumer can help a resource group generate very relevant, even charming, ideas for a person they have never met.

Fact-Based Detour #2: The Product

This fact-based detour consists of using all the senses to deconstruct and make a list of all the attributes of the product or service. Before you begin, however, consider that the senses can be literal as well as allegorical—for example, "feel" could refer to how the product feels to the touch, but it can also mean that it gives you a feeling of confidence.

Just as the facilitator asked a series of questions to explore the target consumer as a person in the first fact-based detour, now the facilitator will again ask a series of questions to explore the client's product or service. The answers to the questions below should be posted all over the room so that the members of the resource group can look at them as they generate ideas.

Sight

- What are all the product elements the target consumer can see?
- What visual elements grab the attention of the target consumer?

Sound

- What does the target consumer hear while experiencing the product or service?
- What does the target consumer hear that would make the experience memorable?

Smell

- What smells are associated with the use of the product?
- Are there any elements in this product or service that would "smell" to the target consumer (as in make the target consumer suspicious or cautious)?

Taste

- What might the target consumer taste?
- Are there any elements of this product or service that might leave a good or a bad taste in the target consumer's mouth?

Touch

- What parts of the product might the target consumer touch?
- How does the product or service make the target consumer feel?

Just as the first fact-based detour will increase the number of ideas relevant to the target consumer, this fact-based detour will increase the ideas that highlight the specific features of the client's product.

Fact-Based Detour #3: The Brand

Here, we are intentionally separating the product from the brand. The product is the physical item being marketed. The brand is much larger than any given product. The iPod Shuffle® is the product, while Apple is the brand. Yellow Tail® Sparkling White Wine is the product, while Yellow Tail is the brand. Even in cases where it could be argued that the product is iconic enough to have its own brand identity, like the Mustang® or the Corvette®, there is a difference between the features of the physical product, like the size of the engine or the number of cup holders it has, and the images of masculine freedom and independence that are associated with those brands.

As with the first two fact-based detours, the questions below can be answered before the idea-generation session begins and posted all over the room so the members of the resource group can see them as they generate ideas.

- What are the elements of the brand that are unique?
- What colors are associated with the brand?
- What words are associated with the brand?
- What are the key benefits that the target consumer associates with this brand?

We've seen how fact-based detours can increase the number of relevant ideas generated by a resource group. Next we will explore a type of detour whose job it is to create newness.

NOVELTY DETOURS

As its name implies, the novelty detour is a technique the facilitator can use to help the resource group generate ideas that are new. Novelty detours take the resource group far away from the facts of the situation, forcing them to exercise their imagination and then come back to the marketing objective with novel connections. The best way to get the most out of novelty detours is to use them as side lists. Let us illustrate.

You remember that Tyler was sitting with a group of friends from work who were helping him come up with ideas to celebrate his sister Winnie's fortieth birthday. There is no question that the group has already come up with some great ideas to make Winnie's birthday special. But Tyler doesn't feel the group has gotten "out of the box" yet. He decides to push a little bit harder: "I want to try something here. I want you guys to forget about Winnie's birthday for a moment and help me make a list of all the things that come to mind when I say the name Steven Spielberg."

As expected, it takes a couple of seconds for people to get into the new groove, but then the connections begin to flow quickly. The group comes up with this list:

1. *E.T.*
2. He makes movies
3. *Jaws*
4. He wears a beard
5. He wears glasses
6. *Jurassic Park*
7. He won an Academy Award

Tyler captures all the Steven Spielberg items on a paper napkin. After reading the list back to the group, he asks, "Can you guys make connections to any of the items on this list to help us make Winnie's fortieth birthday special?"

Someone yells, "Make a movie!"

Being an experienced facilitator, Tyler knows there is more to this idea, so he waits a couple of beats.

Another friend says, "I say we make a movie in which we interview her friends and ask each to tell us one cool story about her."

A different person says, "I made a different connection with the word *movies*. Let's create a page on Facebook and have her friends, no matter where they are, upload pictures and video clips with birthday salutes to Winnie."

Now Tyler looks down at his napkin and says, "I wonder if there is anything we can get from item 6. Can you make any connections with *Jurassic Park?*"

There is silence. Even Tyler looks a little unsure that the detour will work. At last a woman says, "She's going into a new world."

"Tell me more."

"What if we pretended that Winnie is going into the mysterious and dangerous world of being older than thirty-nine . . ."

"Okay."

A second colleague finishes the thought: ". . . and we all give her gifts that will prepare her for the journey. Almost as though forty is the beginning of a different world, and we want to give her the tools to make it out there among the old people."

The group bursts out laughing, but the idea inspires the group to start offering some of the items Winnie is likely to need on her voyage, such as an AARP card and a box of adult diapers.

And so another novelty detour has served its purpose of causing a resource group to stretch beyond the obvious and generate brand-new ideas.

When we choose a novelty detour, we introduce something into the dialogue that isn't connected to the conventional. We deliberately step away from thinking about relevance and get people to connect unrelated things to see what comes out. This increases the likelihood that the group will say something new because the facilitator compelled them to make a connection with something that is not directly related to the problem.

When using novelty detours, the facilitator needs to be prepared for silence. Typically, resource groups take longer to respond to novelty detours because novelty detours make them stretch beyond the obvious.

Let's take a look at four novelty detours that we use very successfully. These novelty detours were inspired by the Product Improvement Check List (PICL),[1] created by Arthur VanGundy, PhD. The four novelty detours we are about to explain will all generate more new ideas as if they are used as sources of side lists.

Novelty Detour #1: People

The basis for this detour is a list of characters. Table 1 illustrates a list of what we think are fairly recognizable characters. They are all famous enough and different enough from each other that every one of them is likely to take the idea generation in a different direction. Note that some of these are names of specific well-known people (like Steven Spielberg), while others might best be described as job descriptions (like a carpenter). We invite you to make the list longer by adding your own characters.

Table 1. Characters Who Can Be Used in Detours.

John McEnroe	Michael Jackson	Barack Obama
Ralph Nader	Hugh Hefner	Al Capone
George Patton	Hillary Clinton	Michael Jordan
Big Bird	Your Dad	Donald Duck
Stephen King	Lee Iacocca	Jane Fonda
Woody Allen	Santa Claus	Pablo Picasso
Bozo the Clown	Howard Stern	Gandhi
Bill Clinton	David Letterman	Jesse Jackson
Abe Lincoln	Rush Limbaugh	John F. Kennedy
Richard Nixon	A Carpenter	A Policeman
An Accountant	Pete Rose	A College Buddy
Mozart	Eminem	Britney Spears
A Taxi Driver	George W. Bush	A House Painter
Mother Teresa	The Pope	A Dentist
Your Pet	A Lion Tamer	Donald Trump
Oprah Winfrey	Groucho Marx	Lance Armstrong
Julius Caesar	Miles Davis	Paris Hilton

The detour Tyler took earlier—when he used Steven Spielberg to help his colleagues come up with cool birthday ideas for his sister Winnie—came from this list. First he made a side list of items connected to the Steven Spielberg name and then he asked his colleagues to make connections with the items on the list.

Novelty Detour #2: Things

Table 2 contains a long list of things. The facilitator can select one of the items on the list, for example, a shovel, and ask the group, "Make a list of everything that comes to mind when you think of a shovel." The resource group will probably generate a list that looks like this:

1. New construction
2. Horse manure
3. Digging a hole
4. Eating lots of food
5. A handle
6. Sharp edge
7. Calling a spade a spade

As with all side lists, the facilitator will first allow the resource group to look at the entire list and make new connections with any ideas they find inspiring. Then the facilitator can exercise her prerogative to select one of the items on the list and ask the resource group to make new connections with it.

Table 2. Things That Can Be Used in Detours.

A Bag	A Boat	A Book
A Box	A Bug	A Cage
A Chain	Dirt	Electricity
An Event	A Hat	A Finger
A Flat Tire	Food	A Fork
Glass	A Hand	A Hole
A Letter	Love	Motion
Music	A Nail	Numbers
A Party	A Pencil	A Pill
A Question	A Report Card	A Ring
A Ruler	An Application	A Shoe

A Sign	A Branch	A Star
A String	A Stamp	A System
A Telephone	A Telescope	A Kiss
Fire	A Toothpick	A Tree
A Trophy	A Wheel	A Whip
A Whisper	A Wild Animal	A Hammer

Novelty Detour #3: Attributes

Table 3 contains a list of attributes. The facilitator introduces this detour by asking the resource group to help him make a list of things that are large, small, red, fast—whatever the selected attribute is. She then lets the resource group consider the items on the side list and asks them to make new connections that will help them accomplish the marketing objective.

Finally, the facilitator can select any one of the items on the side list and force the resource group to make new connections to achieve the marketing objective.

Table 3. Attributes That Can Be Used in Detours.

Abstract	Adjustable	Bright
Bumpy	Calm	Clean
Clear	Cold	Colorful
Complex	Cuddly	Dangerous
Dark	Deep	Delicate
Delicious	Difficult	Disposable
Easy	Exciting	Final
Flexible	Fragrant	Frail
Funny	Green	Hateful
Hot	Huge	Icy
Impossible	Itchy	Joyous
Juicy	Portable	Red
Rough	Round	Scary

Shaky	Sharp	Silly
Simple	Slow	Smelly
Soft	Tall	Tense
Tiny	Unexpected	Vague

Novelty Detour #4: Actions

As with the previous three detours, the facilitator will ask the resource group to make a side list. This time the list should contain things that behave in ways suggested by the verb she chooses from table 4. For example, let's take a look at a list of things that shine:

1. The sun
2. A mirror
3. A lightbulb
4. A smart person
5. The moon
6. Diamonds
7. Eyes

You don't even need to know the marketing objective to recognize that each of the items on this list will take the idea-generation session in an entirely different direction.

Table 4. Detours Using Actions.

Amaze	Appear	Assemble
Balance	Bend	Blend
Bounce	Build	Chop
Climb	Compete	Count
Crush	Cut	Dig
Elevate	Fight	Fly
Fold	Freeze	Hang
Heat	Hurt	Increase

Inflate	Jiggle	Match
Melt	Predict	Pull
Pump	Push	Quit
Repeat	Ring	Roll
Rotate	Run	Screw
Slice	Smear	Snap
Spread	Sprout	Swim
Swing	Teach	Throw
Tighten	Turn Around	Win

Additional Novelty Detours

Since novelty detours are, by definition, not connected to the facts of the situation, you can base a detour on pretty much anything. Here are some other ideas:

- Hold up a photograph or a picture so that everybody can see it. Tell the group, "List everything you see, feel, and think about when you look at this picture." Once you've made a list of everybody's reactions, you can have the group make connections from that list and generate ideas that relate back to the marketing objective.
- Hold up three different pictures and invite the resource group to choose a picture that speaks to them. Give the group five minutes to write a five-sentence story about their picture, and then ask each person to read his story aloud. Tell the group to make a list of all of the elements in their stories, and then to make new connections from that list that are relevant to the marketing objective. Add their ideas to the list.
- Send the group on a ten-minute scavenger hunt to find five items. Make each item as generic as possible, such as "something with letters on it" or "something to prop the door open." Use the objects the group brings back as novelty detours, and use the new connections they make to generate ideas for the list.
- Novelty detours can also be sounds. Once we played fifteen- to

twenty-second portions from a variety of famous pieces of music (Rimsky-Korsakov's "Flight of the Bumblebee" and the guitar lick from Eric Clapton's "Layla") and allowed the resource group to generate ideas inspired by those pieces of music.

- Pick up any item you see in the meeting room, like a water bottle or a notebook. Have the resource group describe it in detail. For instance: "A water bottle is round and plastic. It has got a top. It has a weird shape. It is three-quarters full of water." Ask the resource group to make new connections to the marketing objective using the description of that object.

Helping Clients Get Comfortable with Novelty Detours

If you are finding yourself getting a little uncomfortable with novelty detours even as you read about them, welcome to the club. The fact is that some novelty detours can get pretty strange, which can make a resource group—and most especially the client—very uncomfortable.

During idea generation, the facilitator might use a novelty detour that sends the resource group in a direction the client is not comfortable with. The group starts generating ideas that involve a dinner with a supermodel, a trip to Europe, or a sweepstakes with a $100,000 grand prize, and the client is thinking to himself, "There's no way I can do any of these ideas." At this point the client starts worrying that the group is wasting his time, and he becomes frustrated with the process. Many clients will try to stop the session entirely, saying, "Wait a minute. This is going in the wrong direction." Clients who choose instead to be polite will often bite their tongue and stay quiet, but may be uncooperative for the rest of the meeting.

At this point, the facilitator needs to remind the client about the nature of the creative process and reassure him that the wild ideas being generated will be contained within a set period of time. The facilitator can say, "For the next ten minutes we're going to take a risk and be adventurous. I understand that you are concerned about time, but I promise we will put a ten-minute cap on this portion. Remember that idea generation is all about generating quantity, and the way you get quantity is by not judging ideas. It might be hard to not be critical of ideas you don't like, but let me just write them down, and then you will get to choose your favorite ideas later. If you don't like any of these ideas, you can skip this whole page; however, we are generating options you may not have considered that you may end up choosing later on."

Once the group has exhausted a particularly wild detour, the facilitator can bring the session back to more familiar territory by taking a fact-based detour about the target consumer or the client's product. This will further reassure the client that the group is attentive to relevance and will make him more willing to venture out on a limb the next time.

✺✺✺✺✺

Whether fact-based or novelty, detours are the facilitator's best friend. They help the facilitator perform her most important duty, which is to create a long list of different ideas from which the client can make choices.

Next we are going to take a look at how detours work in the real world.

WOODLAND NURSERIES NEEDS A MARKETING IDEA

We are about to embark on an idea-generation session for Woodland Nurseries, the privately owned high-end gardening supply store with three locations in the affluent suburbs of Atlanta.

Let's review the cast of characters as it was introduced earlier. You probably remember the client, Sam, is the founder and owner of Woodland Nurseries. Sam's right-hand man, Eric, who is in charge of sales and marketing for the company, is playing the role of the agent in this session.

Eric has put together a resource group of four women who are familiar with the Woodland Nurseries brand, own their own homes, and enjoy gardening. A couple of the members of the resource group were chosen based on their expertise in marketing. They live in the Atlanta area and have shopped for gardening supplies at Woodland as well as other garden centers in the Atlanta suburbs. The group is meeting in the conference room at the nursery's main store. Although Sam, the client, will not be in the room, Eric will represent him during the session.

You may remember that in chapter 6 we followed Alesia as she sat down with Sam and Eric and facilitated the process in which Sam identified his marketing objective for this particular project. Here is the marketing objective Sam chose:

> *In what ways might we get a forty-five-year-old female homeowner who loves to garden to visit Woodland Nurseries between April 10 and May 15?*

IDEA-GENERATION SESSION FOR WOODLAND NURSERIES

Eric, Alesia, and the resource group assemble in the company meeting room. There are two flip charts at the front of the room. Once everybody has settled, Alesia begins the introduction.

"Good afternoon, everyone, and thank you for coming to this meeting for Woodland Nurseries. We have asked you to join us today to help us come up with ideas that will get a forty-five-year-old female homeowner who loves to garden to visit Woodland Nurseries between April 10 and May 15."

Icebreaker

"We're going to review the Seven Rules of Brainstorming in just a minute," Alesia tells the group, "but before we do, I'd like to start us off with an icebreaker. This is to put you in the mind of the target consumer and to show you how I'll be managing our meeting today. Since it is always the season to give gifts, help me make a list of all of the presents that you might give a loved one."

The group seems eager to make a list.

"Diamonds."
"A massage."
"Skis."
"A trip to Paris."

Detour #1

Alesia introduces a detour: "What if it were his or her birthday?"
 The group responds again:
 "Headphones."
 "An iPod."
 "A drum set."
 "A puppy."

Detour #2

Alesia introduces another detour: "What if it were a Christmas present?"
 "A car."
 "A cappuccino machine."
 "A case of wine."

Detour #3

Alesia takes another detour: "What if it were a kid's birthday?"
 "A bike."
 "Tools."
 "Transformers®."
 "An annual pass to the aquarium."
 "A T-Rex."
 "A Radio Flyer® red wagon."

The Participants Introduce Themselves

Alesia says, "Thank you, resource group. In five minutes, we have generated seventeen great ideas about what presents we might give a loved one.

What I would like us to do is make choices from this list. I am going to read the list of presents back to you. I want you to choose from this list a gift that you would like to receive. In a moment, you are going to introduce yourselves by saying your first name and telling the group what gift you chose from the list."

Alesia reads the list, waits for everyone to choose, and then continues. "Okay, I will start. My name is Alesia, and if I could choose any gift for myself from this list it would be a bicycle."

Eric follows, "Hi, I'm Eric. I would choose a cappuccino machine."

"I'm Evelyn. I would definitely choose a trip to Paris."

"Mia. I want a puppy."

"I'm Katie, and I would love a massage."

Olivia finishes, "I'm Olivia, and I would like the diamonds, please."

As everyone speaks, Alesia puts a check mark next to the item each group member chooses. Then she says, "Take a look at this list. I want you to notice that people have chosen ideas from the beginning, middle, and end of the list. The reason we make a long list of ideas is that whenever we do this, we find that people make choices from deep inside the list. If we had gone with only the first few ideas that came to mind, the people who chose ideas eight, ten, and thirteen from the end of the list wouldn't be nearly as satisfied with their choices. The more quantity you have on a list, the better the quality."

Orienting the Resource Group

Alesia continues to explain to the resource group how she wants them to behave during the upcoming session. "So, how did we make our list in such a short period of time? We were able to suspend judgment. Everyone had a different idea of what gifts they'd like to give, but we didn't discuss or judge the ideas that went on the list. The rules of engagement were: You said it, and I wrote it down, so we made a long list of ideas.

"We also made our list longer by taking detours. As we were making the list about gifts we might give, I added a new way for you to look at making that list. For example, I asked you what might be a good birthday gift or a good Christmas gift. Those were ways to help you think about giving a gift in a different light. We call them detours. Throughout the session, I will ask you to join me in taking detours, and I want you all to play along.

"Today in our session, we have a cast of characters that I'd like to introduce to you. My name is Alesia, my day job is to manage the Landscape Services Division of Woodland Nurseries. During this meeting, however, I am playing the role of facilitator. I am here to manage the process and to help you make a long list of ideas for our client, the owner of Woodland Nurseries. You are the resource group. Your role is to help come up with a long list of ideas for Woodland Nurseries. You were selected based on your marketing expertise and your interest in gardening. Thank you for your help today.

"In our process we have someone called an agent, the person who has a vested interest in making sure we come up with ideas, and that is Eric. As you know, Eric is in charge of sales and marketing for Woodland Nurseries and needs our help to generate marketing ideas. The client, the owner of Woodland Nurseries, cannot be here for this meeting, so Eric will be representing him today. After this meeting Eric will be making some choices from the list that we will develop further in our next session. Olivia will be our scribe; it is her job to capture everything you say during idea generation.

"During this meeting our mission is to generate ideas, and to do this we use a process that begins with preparation. Before this meeting Eric and I gathered some information about Woodland Nurseries and our marketing situation. We also confirmed the marketing objective the client wants our help with. We passed the information along to you to help you prepare to come up with ideas.

"In this meeting, we're going to focus on generating ideas. After the meeting, Eric will review the list and choose the items he wants to show Sam, who is our client. I'm going to ask you to remember that the ideas we generate in this session need to remain confidential and should not be discussed outside this room. I think, unless anybody has any questions, we're ready to get started.

"Let me review the marketing objective: *In what ways might we get a forty-five-year-old female homeowner who loves to garden to visit Woodland Nurseries between April 10 and May 15?*"

The Seven Rules

"I know some of you have taken part in idea-generation sessions before, but we always like to remind everyone of the rules of brainstorming before we begin.

"Rule #1: During the idea-generation session, there will be no judgment of ideas; no evaluation or criticism will be allowed.

"Rule #2: Freewheeling is allowed and encouraged; wild and outrageous ideas are welcome.

"Rule #3: We will make a long list of ideas. Remember that we are striving for quantity here rather than quality; in idea generation, quantity produces quality.

"Rule #4: We will take detours, just like we did when we made the list of gifts. Detours are intended to help you add quantity, novelty, and relevance to the list of ideas.

"Rule #5: Your ideas should be specific and clear so that all the participants can understand them; specific ideas have a higher likelihood of becoming a reality. I want to remind you that if you give me a short phrase that isn't specific and clear, I will ask everybody in the room to help clarify the idea so that we can all see it in our minds.

"Rule #6: All ideas must be written down; choosing not to write down an idea would violate rule #1. Since Olivia is our scribe today, she will endeavor to write down every idea you say. If she doesn't, or if she doesn't understand your idea, or if idea generation is going so quickly she misses your idea, please stop her and repeat your idea, because I don't want to miss anything you've said.

"Finally, Rule #7: Every person taking part in this idea-generation session is equal in rank; there are no bosses, and no hierarchy."

Generic versus Custom Ideas

"I want to take a second to explain the difference between generic and custom ideas, and this connects to rule #5. Lots of times in a session like this, people will communicate in bursts of creativity, but not complete the thought. I'm looking for specificity. Rather than saying, 'Oooh, we could give away coupons,' we want to be specific about how those coupons might be given away, and even what the theme of the coupon might be. So please don't feel judged if I ask you for more specificity—or, Olivia, if you need more clarification, since you're scribing, please feel free to ask, because we want to be specific about the ideas we're writing on the list."

Generating Marketing Ideas

The group is ready to start generating marketing ideas. Alesia says, "Great. I think we are ready. Please help me make a list of all the ways we might get a forty-five-year-old female homeowner who loves to garden to visit Woodland Nurseries between April 10 and May 15."

Mia is the first to speak, "I would like to have them do a couple of things. The first one I thought of is to bring in a picture of their newly planted garden that year so that your garden can live on the Wall of Fame at Woodland Nurseries. The person with the winning picture, however that is chosen, wins a large gift certificate from Woodland Nurseries for her annuals and perennials for the next year."

Olivia offers an idea based on the magazines she enjoys reading. "I see a partnership with *Fine Gardening*. The *Fine Gardening* page, where they tell you what you need to grow now, what you need to plant now, could come as a joint e-mail from Woodland Nurseries and *Fine Gardening*. Every person who comes in after the last frost receives a free three- or six-month subscription to *Fine Gardening*."

Eric jumps in, "I see it as the Woodland Nurseries Early Bird Garden Tour, and from eight to ten o'clock on Saturday and Sunday mornings between April 10 and May 15, you come to the Woodland Nurseries

Early Bird Garden Tour, and you'll hear our plant specialists talking
about what you should be planting this spring, consulting with you
about your garden, and answering questions. It's for the serious gardener.
Maybe we cross-promote with Starbucks so they're serving coffee, and it's
the Early Morning Serious Gardeners Garden Tour."

Detour #1

Alesia interjects, "Let's think about the target consumer for Woodland
Nurseries. She is a forty-five-year-old female, a homeowner, and an avid
gardener. She has a decorator mentality. In other words, she views deco-
ration in her garden as an extension of her living room. She draws plans
for her yard. She strategizes about which colors she wants where and what
kind of feeling she wants to create in the garden. She's also willing to pay
a premium for perennials if they come with expert advice."

After listening to Alesia's description of the target consumer, Evelyn
starts. "I know that there are computer programs where she can be
encouraged to take a snapshot of her empty yard before the last frost is
over, bring it in, and scan it into a master gardener's computer. Then she
can work with a staff consultant to start dropping in plants and strate-
gizing how it would look best. The program provides her with a listing
of the plants she has chosen and what the costs are. Maybe there could be
a monthly purchase program so that her up-front investment isn't huge.
The computer program gives preorders to the greenhouse, and she can
choose to pay for it on a layaway basis."

Mia takes off on the consumer's love of advice. "What if she came in
and for a certain minimum purchase, she receives the help of someone at
the gardening store. There would have to be a minimum purchase—
you'd spend $100 and then you'd get a half hour of consultation to help
you lay out your garden at your home."

Alesia asks for clarification. "So a person comes to your house?"

"Right," Mia says. "A design consultant."

Olivia picks up on the idea. "On the flip side of that, what if there
was a design consultant person who would come by and evaluate your

property and show you where the most opportune place was to plant certain plants in your yard, and then there is some sort of certificate that you bring into the store to purchase those particular plants."

Eric chimes in: "You could even follow that up, to have the perfect Woodland Garden and cross promote with a professional photographer to go in and take shots of the most beautiful plants in the garden. It's almost like a garden portrait."

Mia interjects, "We could invite the target consumer to take videos of her garden and upload it to YouTube and then send the link to Woodland Nurseries, who posts it and reviews the garden. Then she makes a thirty-minute appointment for a garden consultant to brainstorm ideas for her garden for next year. So the master gardeners at Woodland get the video link, and they respond back and say, 'I'd love to meet with you from eight-thirty to nine o'clock on Tuesday morning. I have some neat new ideas for you to consider for this year's garden.' So it's by appointment and based on the look of their garden."

Evelyn speaks next. "Woodland could provide a soil analyst, and you bring in your soil right after the last frost and they test it for free. They evaluate the nutrients that your soil needs to have the optimum performing garden. This could become a new product we sell."

Katie chimes in, "Or you could have the Woodland Avid Gardener Club that once a month holds a garden party where you could have tea and snacks and 'ooh' and 'aah' over each other's garden pictures and talk about gardening. Getting back to that idea of having an expert there, maybe in the dead of winter you could take the avid gardeners by bus to the Atlanta Botanical Garden."

Eric says, "Since the research says these women draw a picture of their backyard as part of their process for designing their spring planting, let's invite them to participate on our Web site and post before-and-after inspirational pictures. So bring your designs, come on Saturday morning, we're going to help consult with you on the new trends and help you make choices on how you're going to plant your spring garden. We want to scan your sketch of your garden and then we want you to send us a picture two months later. We'll post the picture so we can see what the vision was, and later, when it's in full bloom, we make you part of teaching others how they, too, can be great gardeners."

Evelyn asks, "What if you designed your garden, purchased your gardening supplies from Woodland Nurseries right after the last frost, take a picture of the garden in bloom and e-mail it to us? Woodland could buy a full page in *Atlanta Homes and Life Style* to display the most beautiful garden and the plants that were used in the design."

Mia says, "What about a Last Frost Bash?"

Katie adds, "Let's run a contest for people to guess the exact day of the last frost. The winner becomes the Frost Queen. Or the Spring Queen, I suppose."

Olivia says, "You can bring the mayor in and have a party, because the last frost is done."

Eric continues, "What if we partnered with Wendy's? Everybody during the month of April has the whole month to bring in a picture of their garden, or you come in and purchase anything from Woodland and you get a free Frosty to celebrate."

Mia says, "You could focus on being a green gardener, low water, low maintenance, where you have experts who advise and demonstrate on a variety of topics such as rain barrels, how to recycle the water, composting, the right kind of mulch. You could invite people from the soil conservation service, the Georgia State Horticultural Society, or the department of horticulture at the University of Georgia, or even master gardeners from the area."

"How about recycling your garden gloves?" asks Katie. "For the first thirty days after the last frost, bring in your garden gloves from the previous year—your old, worn-out garden gloves—and we'll give you a new pair for this spring."

Olivia says, "Woodland white glove treatment—I would love to be treated as a white glove customer! Create a series of e-mails from Woodland Nurseries starting two weeks before April 10. Then I could receive updates on when the perennials are coming in. Perennials bloom at different times, and garden centers tend to carry them while they are blooming so they'll sell. Be the first to get the new perennials that are coming in. The first shipment arrives next Tuesday, and if you come in and buy yours on Tuesday, for every four perennials you buy, you get the fifth one free. Their e-mails would keep me coming back time and time again."

Evelyn continues the idea. "I could go online and register as a white glove customer, and I choose from a list of perennials, the ones I want to be notified about. That way, the garden store is showing that they are sensitive to the fact that I don't want fifty thousand bougainvillea e-mails if I don't want bougainvilleas. I only want to know about irises. So I get specific information just for me that I've chosen with the same deal: For every four I buy on a special, I get one free. It would be cool, too, if you closed the store, and you invited only members of the White Glove Club to come, and everybody that's working there that night is wearing white gloves in honor of their white glove customers and their white glove customer specials. Nobody else gets to shop then."

Olivia explains, "It would be neat to offer all sorts of exclusive events, maybe a gallery opening that shows horticultural paintings or landscapes. Perhaps it's a special tour of the Atlanta Botanical Garden. You receive personal invitations to these different kinds of events. And it would also be cool to appeal to her philanthropic side, because forty-five-year-old females who are going to buy perennials and invest this much in their garden want to see other people succeed at gardening. Maybe Woodland partners with a community youth or family shelter or a church that has some land, and for all of the sales on that particular day, the first day after the last frost, the garden company donates some seeds, fertilizer, and tools to a community garden."

Alesia, aware that the group is developing one of the ideas rather than generating new ones, is getting ready to jump in when Eric goes in a new direction, "What if Woodland Nurseries offered a master gardening certification of some sort? We have a database that we can use to e-mail all of our good customers starting in January, and launch the Woodland Nurseries Master Gardener Certification. We're looking for one hundred gardeners in our community who we're going to acknowledge as master gardeners, and we're going to have pictures of their gardens up in our stores, and we're going to donate to the Atlanta Botanical Garden in the names of our master gardeners. So come in. Let us help you with your garden this spring. Let us know when you're ready for us to come see your garden, and we're going to pick one hundred people, and then we're going to make a donation to the botanical gardens in your names and ours jointly."

Mia interjects, "I love to garden, but I can't think of anybody offhand. Maybe something on the DIY Network or HGTV. There has to be some sort of garden celebrity they can bring in after the last frost."

Olivia offers, "Martha Stewart."

Evelyn agrees, "Somebody like a Martha Stewart, and bring her in."

Eric adds, "She could be one of the celebrity judges."

Without any prompting from Alesia, Mia goes in a different direction and provides new momentum. "If this woman has a decorator mentality, then the inside of her house is probably beautiful. She could take a picture of her favorite room and bring it into Woodland Nurseries to get recommendations on what flowers would complement her indoors as well as outdoors. Woodland Nurseries' staff could suggest good flowers for cutting and display so she could make arrangements for her home."

Katie offers, "Maybe you could do a sweepstakes. Shop with us this spring, and enter to win a spring party. We'll provide the catering and music so you can celebrate how beautiful your garden is with your friends."

Olivia goes back to Mia's idea. "I'm thinking of the decorator mentality, doing something along the lines of bringing your inside outside. Maybe doing some kind of cross-promotion or partnership with a patio furniture store, so that the inside of the home could become an extension."

Evelyn jumps in, "You could do it with Frontgate."

Eric adds, "Right, and you could make a living space outside."

Olivia, who loves diamonds and extravagance, suggests, "You could partner with an outdoor kitchen company. Pop one of those outdoor kitchens right in the middle of your herb garden. How cool is that?"

Mia, who is more down to earth, adds, "Or an outdoor grill, or a fire pit. We'll provide the masonry to build an outdoor cooking area."

Evelyn continues, "Let's put an Italian wood-fired pizza oven in the backyard."

Detour #2

Alesia wants to get some fresh ideas, so she distributes some pictures of a beautiful country house surrounded by beds of beautiful flowering gardens. She says, "I want us to take a little visual tour of what we might experience if we were at one of the master gardeners' homes."

Alesia shows the front of the house with luxurious gardens planted all around and along the walk. Then she shows the back of the house with even more flowering plants and striking greenery, and says, "I'd like you to take a moment and look at these images and see if you might be able to make more connections to how we might get this female homeowner who loves to garden to visit Woodland between April 10 and May 15."

Katie adds, "For every $50 she spends, her name is put into a drawing to win a beautiful prearranged pot. She could have her choice of a pot for shade or sun."

Eric interjects, "I'm thinking she's going to need a manicure after she does all of this planting, so I'm going to give her a manicure for every $250 she spends."

Olivia, who has been doing a great job of scribing, turns from the flip chart to ask, "Is there something that we can do with her kids? She is forty-five; how old are her kids going to be?"

Evelyn replies, "Well, if you're me, they were seven and eight when I was forty-five."

"They could also be in their teens, right?" asks Alesia.

Mia adds a new idea to the list, "How about you make it a Sunday afternoon mother-daughter clinic to introduce your daughter to gardening. Bring her on Sunday afternoon and shop with us. We're holding short clinics for the youngsters to learn to garden."

Katie responds with, "I was also thinking about creating a kids' space at the store. Maybe when moms bring the kids to Woodland, they get a ten-cent packet of seeds. They do crafts to build a birdhouse or make a potted plant for mom for Mother's Day."

Olivia suggests, "Bring your children in to this youth project with all sorts of clinics: building a birdhouse, painting outdoor furniture, planting vegetable gardens, planting flower gardens."

Evelyn looks around at the others and says, "Well, I made a different connection with a honey-do/hero list, where the gardeners could create a wish list of things that they wish their kids or their significant others would help them do in the garden or buy for their garden, and Woodland could keep that for them."

Olivia suggests, "What if, on a Saturday after the last frost, moms come in with their kids, and it is a full-day camp for the kids to do all of those activities, whether it's painting a birdhouse or planting a pot, while the mom shops, picking all her perennials. Then she goes home to work in the garden without any distractions for four or five hours before returning to pick her kid up from the planting day camp."

Olivia continues, "And what if during the month of April, for every purchase you make, Woodland automatically registers your name and one person gets a week's salary or three days off of work to throw themselves into their garden and do the planting: 'Woodland will pay your salary.'"

Katie says, "Or you could take that backward and have a garden Santa. She has planned her garden and purchases all of her plants. We send her off in a limo for a manicure, a pedicure, a massage, a makeover—and while she's gone, the garden elves go in and plant everything. When she comes back, it's done."

"I have a different one," says Eric. "I just made connections to the pictures here of the front of the house, too. There's all sorts of stonework, pavers, and so on. So maybe we have a point system. For all of your purchases throughout the spring, from the first day after the last frost through whatever the last day of smart spring planting is, you're earning points, and those points go to the labor of having your patio laid or your sidewalks done, or any walls built, or landscaping. You may love to garden, but you may not love to lay stonework, and the points go toward the labor for or purchase of the stonework."

Detour #3

Alesia starts another detour based on the company's signature color. "Help me make a list of everything that's orange."

"Oranges."

"The sun."

"The University of Texas."

"Life preservers."

"Gerbera daisies."

"Home Depot."

"Orange manila folders."

"Cheddar cheese."

"A hunter's protective gear."

"Clemson Tigers."

"Markers."

"Candy corn."

"Pumpkins."

"Knock-knock. Who's there? Orange you glad I'm not bananas?"

"Fingernail polish."

"Hair."

"Some ladies in Miami, their hair is definitely orange."

"Clown pants."

"Kumquats."

Alesia says, "Let me read this detour list back to you, and let's try to make some more new connections to how we're going to get that forty-five-year-old woman to come into Woodland Nurseries."

Alesia reads the list, and then Olivia starts. "You could do local school days and feature specials on flowers that are in the school colors, particularly if they have high school kids. The high school in Buckhead would be green and white. For the Tucker Tigers, everything in maroon and orange would be on sale. This way, you could honor your high school. There could be a donations pool with some sort of kickback to the school for any of the school spirit colors and plants that were purchased."

Mia excitedly says, "I think of tulips, and if you go and purchase the featured tulips, you automatically have an opportunity to win seats at the Rolling Stones concert, with the big lips. Forty-five, man. She likes Mick. Tulips for Two Lips!"

Everyone laughs.

Evelyn suggests, "We could tie in with a custom door company. When you come in after the last frost, you enter to win a beautiful, custom front door or maybe a door to your garden so that you can see your garden more easily through the beautiful glass."

"You could also create the Happy Hubby Gift Registry," Mia says, "he can buy or order in advance for delivery for his gardener wife on special days—birthdays, Mother's Day, in honor of Valentine's Day, the first day of spring, May Day. With a registry he will buy garden supplies that she wants, and he can do so without fear of repercussion. He won't get chewed out for buying something she doesn't want. She chooses what she wants for her gardening, so it's guilt-free shopping for the husband. He sets up an online order form that automatically picks what she needs, sort of like the wine-of-the-month club."

Katie says, "It would be cool if you could do what they do with the airline, where you can pick your seat with the airplane, and it shows what's been already purchased and what's open. If we could do that on a diagram of her yard, as she purchases plants, the diagram of her yard shows them solid and fills in the diagram. It shows what is still open. So she can leave a note in her account to the effect, "I want to do something under that big tree in the back with all shade back there, and I need annuals for back in there, and I can look at what hasn't been purchased yet and help her fill it in."

Olivia interjects, "Let's have the Woodland Nurseries master gardeners create ten garden vignettes all in different kinds of light. One garden will be in total shade, one in morning sunlight, another will get the afternoon sunlight. The different gardens are planted at the store and you can tour them throughout the season. We're going to invite these forty-five-year-old consumers that are really into it to come tour these gardens and see how they are doing."

Alesia holds up her hand and says, "Let me take a quick pause here to check in with Eric."

Olivia says, "Oh, good! My hand needs a break."

Alesia continues, "Eric, let's check in with you. How are you feeling about the list of ideas?"

Eric responds, "I think there are some great ideas here!"

"Shall we take one more detour?"

"Sure, one more quick one."

Detour #4

Alesia starts the fourth detour to force connections. "Let's focus on cheddar cheese. What new connections can we make thinking about cheddar cheese?"

Eric asks, "You know how you put a stick in cheese with a little flag to tell people what kind of cheese it is? What if we give kids some of those Popsicle sticks and have them decorate them for their mom's garden and use that as a hook somehow? She could shop while her children decorate the little garden sticks that tell you what the flower or plant is."

Mia adds, "Woodland could cooperate with the art programs at elementary schools, and kids could take home the decorated garden sticks along with a coupon from Woodland."

Eric reiterates, "So Woodland goes to the elementary schools, and students decorate the sticks and then bring the sticks and a coupon home."

Katie responds, "Well, you could do it one of two ways. You could go to the school and say, 'We'll provide you with all the materials to decorate these garden sticks,' the kids can take them home, and they have some sort of a bounce back to Woodland; or they could provide the materials at Woodland and get them to come in that way."

Evelyn suggests, "Or if the school decorates the sticks, and you buy that plant with that school stick, then ten cents of every purchase goes as a fund-raiser for the school."

Katie agrees, "Right, or that school's nature center, or whatever, because most of them have some sort of experience with outdoor things, with the science program or the art program."

Olivia says, "We could hold a Celebrate Spring Party for our white glove customers on the evening before all our customers come to see the new spring flowers. Woodland opens from seven to ten o'clock in the evening, and they'll have a party with candlelight, wine, and cheese, and the white glove customers are allowed to shop."

Eric asks, "Like an evening garden party for the white glove customers?"

Katie replies, "Yes, before the products are put on sale to the general public, they get special treatment. Maybe they get special pricing."

"Are there some wine stores that have heart-healthy programs in Atlanta?" asks Olivia. "I knew of one in the last place I lived. You get a credit every time you buy red wine. I think it's a pretty cool gimmick. And you try to promote gardening as being healthy. You cross promote a wine and cheese store so that frequent customers get discounts at both. Could you have a wine, cheese, and garden card that was sponsored by both—a punch card? I think you get the gist of where I'm going."

Alesia looks at her watch and announces that the session must conclude. She asks, "Olivia, how many ideas did we generate?"

Olivia replies, "Forty-nine."

The group breaks out into spontaneous applause.

"That's excellent!" exclaims Eric, clapping his hands as well.

Alesia, "Well, I think that will about do it for today. Later on I am going to help Eric select the ideas he wants to pursue with Sam, but for now I just want to thank you so much for taking the time to meet with us and share all your wonderful ideas. Did you have fun?"

The women all responded positively, "Yes!"

Eric, with a smile on his face, says, "Yes. This has been better than I expected. Thank you everybody for your time, and thank you, Alesia, for being the facilitator."

Alesia replies, "You're welcome."

Alesia did a very nice job of getting her resource group involved in generating a long list of ideas. She also used several detours very effectively to add variety to the list. Now Alesia will meet with Eric to help him make choices from the list, as we will see in the next chapter.

9

MAKING CHOICES

In chapter 8 you witnessed an experienced facilitator in the act of leading an idea-generation session. She took fact-based detours and novelty detours and succeeded in helping the resource group generate a nice long list of different ideas—forty-nine of them, to be exact.

Perhaps the biggest difference between the Woodland Nurseries session and many of the idea-generation sessions we facilitate on a regular basis is the absence of a client in the Woodland Nurseries session. In chapter 2, when we discussed the cast of characters, you might remember that we described the client as the person whose interest and passion ultimately drive the creative process. That is why, in this chapter, we are going to work as if the client is in the room throughout the process of making choices. At the end of this chapter, when we return to the Woodland Nurseries case study, you will see Alesia, the facilitator, manage the process of making choices for Eric, who is playing the role of the agent.

There is no question that the presence of a client makes facilitating an idea-generation session much trickier than when there is no client. For instance, clients can become excited about a particular idea, which forces the facilitator to attempt to keep a much tighter rein on the session and even on the client himself. The facilitator typically will ask the client to sit tight and allow the idea generation to unfold before making a public commitment to one idea or another. Of course, even when the facilitator is a strong leader, clients will be clients. They continue to revisit their pet ideas—at least until they fall in love with the next cool idea they hear.

When it comes to the act of making choices, it is very common for clients, even who are clearly the ultimate decision-makers in their companies, to seek input—even validation—from the rest of the resource group before making choices. In our experience, this happens when the client is surrounded by his own management team and he wants their input before selecting a course of action. It also happens when the resource group is made up of people whom the client considers experts, so he wants to get their point of view before making a commitment.

After facilitating many choice-making situations like these, we decided to divide the act of making choices into three parts. The first two parts make it easier for a client to select the ideas that feel right, while the third piece helps the client make sure the idea is going to work.

BEWARE DISCUSSIONS

It is not uncommon for the client to indicate to the facilitator that he wants to hear what the members of the resource group think before he makes his final choices.

If we can warn you about only one pitfall of managing the creative process, allow us to warn you of the death-defying grip of discussions. Nothing is as insidious and as detrimental to the creative process as allowing discussions to creep into your sessions. They begin quite innocently, with the client asking all of the people around the table what they think. The facilitator, not wanting to be rude, allows the question to be answered. After all, the client is the ultimate decision maker and he just needs a little input. Thirty minutes later, three of the six members of the resource group have taken the time to expound their opinions on each of the ideas on the list, particularly the ideas that, in their view, will never work. Two of the participants who haven't said anything are waiting for their turn to get on their soapboxes and convince the client of opinions they held before they came into the meeting. One guy made a perfectly rational argument proposing that the group should have been working on an entirely different marketing objective. The client is utterly confused and the facilitator is standing there wondering where exactly she lost control of the session.

SOFT CHOICES

This nightmare scenario is easy to avoid with a simple technique. Instead of allowing the group members to voice their opinions about the ideas on the list, the facilitator should ask the members of the resource group to take out a piece of paper on which they can jot down the ideas they think have the most potential. The instructions are simple and straightforward.

The facilitator says, "The first thing I am going to do is remind everyone of our marketing objective." After reading it, she continues.

"Our client would like some input from you before choosing his favorite ideas from our list. I am going to give you the opportunity to, in essence, vote for your favorite ideas. Rather than engaging in a discussion, however, what I am going to do is hand you seven red dots and give you a chance to put one red dot next to each of your favorite seven ideas.

"Now I am going to read out loud every single idea on this list. I am going to read them slowly because I want to give you a moment to think about each one and decide whether you want to make it one of your seven favorite ideas.

"I would like you to do this exercise in silence because I don't want us to influence each other. As I read all the ideas on the list, when you hear an idea that you like and that in your view has the potential to accomplish the marketing objective, I want you to jot down the number of the idea on your piece of paper.

"I'm sure by the time I am done reading all the ideas, several of you will have already selected more than seven favorite ideas. That happens all the time. So before I give you your seven dots, I'm going to give you time to review your choices and narrow them down to the best seven."

If our experience has taught us anything, we already know that one of the participants—or, worse yet, the client—will want to ask a question or make a comment on a specific idea. This is one of those moments when the facilitator needs to gently but firmly ask the participants to please hold all questions until the soft choices have been made.

Next the facilitator reads the list of ideas aloud to the group and each participant jots down the numbers of the ones they think have potential. Once she is finished reading, the facilitator asks the team to please narrow down their lists of soft choices to the top seven. A couple of people will want to choose more ideas; the facilitator must politely remind them that the essence of focus is sacrifice.[1]

The next step is simple and crucial. The participants are given seven red dots each and are asked to write down the numbers they chose on the dots themselves. For example, if one member of the group selected idea number 17, he should write the number 17 on one of his dots.

When everyone is ready—and *only* when everyone is ready—the team members are allowed to go up to the wall to place their dots next to the correlating numbers. What follows is a mob of people up on their feet, putting dots on the sheets of paper that are hanging on the walls. When the dust settles and everyone sits back down, what you have is something that, in our opinion, is the closest you'll ever get to consensus.

Let's take a moment to mention that the act of voting for their favorite ideas is not a required step in the process, but it does give the client a very quick view of the opinions of the resource group. It also gives the participants a tremendous sense of accomplishment because they can see quite visibly that they came up with a lot of worthwhile ideas.

At the end of the day, however, the resource group makes only soft choices. The client is the one who makes hard choices.

HARD CHOICES

Once the soft choices are made, all the facilitator has is the opinion of the resource goup. She still needs to help the client make the hard choices.

The second step in the sequence of making choices will help a client—or the agent who represents him—narrow the list of ideas down to his favorite top five.

The facilitator will want to remind the client that by choosing the top five ideas he isn't giving up the remaining ideas on the list. All he is doing is selecting the five he wants to consider first.

The client should also be reminded that he is not bound to follow the advice or consensus of the team. In fact, the point needs to be made that the last step was called making "soft choices" because those choices are not binding on anyone, much less the client.

At this point, the client chooses his top five ideas. Some of them will have a whole cluster of red dots around them. Others may not have any dots on them at all. That's okay. It's the client's prerogative to choose the ideas that, at least initially, seem *to him* to hold the most promise.

There are at least two scenarios in which we will see an agent making choices off the list instead of the client. The first scenario is probably the most common. It is not unusual for a facilitator to be recruited by an agent who is representing a client. As in the case of Woodland Nurseries, the client may not be present in the idea-generation session, so the job falls on the shoulders of the agent to make the choices. Later in this chapter you will see how Eric, as the agent representing Sam, the owner of Woodland Nurseries, makes choices on Sam's behalf.

In such cases, the job of the facilitator does not change: The facilitator says and does the same things with the agent that would normally have been said to and done with the client. The presumption is that the agent will take responsibility for moving the process forward in collaboration with the client.

There is a second scenario in which we see agents making their own choices off the list. To illustrate this, let's return to the scene we just described, in which the client is in the room and the facilitator has just completed the process of having the resource group make soft choices. Let's also imagine that the person playing the role of agent is a salesperson for a media company or an account executive for an advertising agency— neither of which would be unusual in a marketing situation. There are seventy-six ideas on the wall, several of them illuminated by a cluster of red dots placed there by the members of the resource group when they made their soft choices.

Now let's imagine the client makes his choices and the facilitator circles five ideas on the sheets. It is a common practice that our agent, who has expertise in a specific medium, might interject, "I am going to take it upon myself to develop a couple of ideas the client did not choose among his top five. I know it's a little risky, but I think I see more potential there, and I'm going to flesh them out a little more."

Clients rarely have a problem with agents doing a little extra work for free, so there are never objections to such an offer. In most cases, the only change in the facilitator's behavior is to ask the agent for a deadline by which he will have developed those additional ideas and put that deadline directly on a timeline.

FROM TOP FIVE DOWN TO ONE

Whether the client chose his top five ideas based on his gut and experience or his choice was influenced by the soft choices made by the resource group, the client—or the agent representing him—now has a list of his top five ideas. Even if the client intended to put all five ideas into action, he would soon enough have to choose one to work on first. So the facilitator needs to be ready to help the client narrow his choice from his top five down to the one that the client wants to execute first.

In the real world, some time may pass between the choice of the top five and the choice of the first idea to execute. It may be, for instance, that the client wants to "sleep on it" before making a final choice. It could also be that there are stakeholders who need to be consulted and sources of funding that need to be checked. Another common scenario is one in which the agent wants to flesh out all of the top five ideas so the client can make a more informed decision when he makes his final choice. In any event, a very important job of the facilitator is to help the client, or the agent, choose the one idea that really makes sense and will truly help the client's company. The best way to make such a smart choice is to consider success criteria, and that is what we will cover next.

CONSIDERING SUCCESS CRITERIA

Every decision we make, personally or professionally, is based on a set of criteria. Whether we're choosing what shoes to wear, selecting a restaurant for dinner or buying a car, we all base our decisions on a variety of criteria. For instance, when buying a new car, people will consider their lifestyle, their budget, how their family will use the car, and so on. In much the same way, the facilitator needs to help the client consider a set of criteria before making a final choice.

The tricky part, of course, is that very often the client's criteria for success are unspoken. It's not that they are secret; more often it is because they are not discussed in the normal course of conversation within most businesses. That is why the first task of the facilitator is to explain to the client what is meant by the word *criteria*. The conversation might sound something like this.

"When you got up this morning, how did you decide which pair of shoes you were going to wear today?"

The client might respond, "I was going for comfort," or "They had to match my outfit," or "They had to be appropriate for the weather."

This gives the facilitator an opening to respond, "These are the criteria you use to select shoes. My job is to help you select the idea that makes the most sense for you to take action on. You've got five ideas that you like and I'm going to help you narrow them down to the one that best meets your criteria."

MAKING A LIST OF CRITERIA

The facilitator continues, "I want you to help me make a list of criteria that you might use to select the best idea from among your top five. Here's one way to think of it: Help me complete the following phrase: 'Whatever idea we execute needs to . . . blank.'"

It is worth pointing out here that the facilitator can invite the members of the resource group as well as the agent to help the client make the list of possible criteria longer.

Also, as in all other cases when a list is being made, the facilitator can take detours to make the list longer. The way to do that is with questions and prompts that will cause the resource group, the agent, and even the client to consider new criteria. Detours might include thoughts like these:

- Think of possible criteria related to the calendar or the timing of the project.
- Think of possible criteria related to resources like money, staff, supplies, and so on.
- Think of possible criteria from the point of view of any other stakeholders that need to be involved in the decision or the execution of the program you choose.

Of course, the criteria are always specific to the client, so it is difficult to make a list of generic criteria. However, the list will probably include items such as:

1. Whatever idea we execute needs to appeal to the target consumer.
2. Whatever idea we execute needs to match my brand.
3. Whatever idea we execute needs to be something I can do in all my stores.
4. Whatever idea we execute needs to meet a certain budget number.
5. Whatever idea we execute needs to get everyone on my staff excited.

As with all other lists we have made in the course of this book, the facilitator now needs to engage the client in selecting the top criteria he wants to use to identify the best idea to execute. We will turn to this next.

CHOOSING THE SUCCESS CRITERIA

The client is about to be asked to select his top success criteria for this project. The top success criteria will become absolute musts once the client chooses them. In other words, if the idea does not meet any of the criteria, it will not be chosen, much less acted upon.

The question the facilitator will ask the client is, "Please choose criteria that are non-negotiable. If the idea does not meet a specific criterion, it will not be chosen."

We recommend that the client choose no more than three or four success criteria. Of course, there are situations that will require more complicated decision matrixes to weigh long lists of criteria against each other, but those are few and far between. What the facilitator wants to do here is make sure that the client considers enough success criteria to avoid wasting time and energy on an idea that will not create any results in the end. Once the client has chosen the top three or four success criteria, the facilitator and the client—or the agent—have a tool they can use as a filter to select the best idea on which to take action.

USING CRITERIA TO MAKE A CHOICE

Now all the facilitator has to do is ask the client to evaluate every one of his top five ideas against his top criteria. To do this, we like to use a very simple scoring method. It works like this: The facilitator helps the client evaluate each idea against all the top criteria before moving on to evaluate the next idea. If the idea meets a specific criterion, the facilitator puts a plus sign (+) next to the idea; if it does not, the facilitator places a minus sign (–) next to the idea. If the client is not sure whether or not the idea meets the criterion, the facilitator writes a question mark (?) next to it.

In the end, the client is still expected to make the hard choice. However, he will have the option to make his choice based on some rational success criteria rather than just his gut.

Years ago, we were the facilitators for an idea-generation session for a client who fell in love with a handful of ideas on the list. There was one idea in particular that he was very excited about, and he decided then and there that this was the idea he was going to execute.

When the time came to make choices, it was a no-brainer that his favorite idea would be among his top five. Then we asked him to make a list of criteria and select his nonnegotiable ones from that list. Following our process, we helped him (we had to convince him) to evaluate each of the ideas against the criteria that he himself had set just a couple of minutes earlier.

Lo and behold, his favorite idea did not meet his own criteria! "You know what's amazing?" the client announced to the resource group. "You can get pretty excited about something that makes absolutely no sense." We couldn't have said it any better ourselves.

There is one final point we want to make regarding criteria. We think all businesses should share their criteria with their entire staff. Every company has a set of criteria with which they make marketing decisions, yet those criteria are rarely shared outside the inner sanctum of the leadership of the company.

We wonder, why shouldn't the receptionist know the company's criteria for success? If your staff knows your criteria for success, they can make better decisions. If you keep your criteria secret, you train them to keep coming to you for answers.

Now we are going to return to the Woodland Nurseries case study. Alesia is getting ready to help Eric make choices from the list of ideas.

WOODLAND NURSERIES NEEDS A MARKETING IDEA

Alesia has just disbanded the resource group after a very productive idea-generation session. As an experienced facilitator, she knows that someone—either the client or the agent—needs to make choices from the list of ideas while the ideas are still fresh in their mind.

The Agent Chooses His Top Five Ideas

Alesia had already contracted with Eric that he would stay behind after the idea-generation session to make choices off the list of ideas.

They both agreed to take a fifteen-minute break, after which they would get back together in the conference room.

Eric took many notes during the idea-generation session and has already zeroed in on a few ideas he liked. Still, Alesia read the entire list of ideas back to him before he chose his top five.

"Eric," says Alesia, "I'm going to read the list of ideas back to you, and I want you to say 'Check' when you hear an idea you really like. I'm willing to go through the list a couple of times if necessary, as long as we eventually narrow down to no more than five top ideas."

One review through the list is enough for Eric. As he chooses his favorite ideas, he groups some of the ideas he thinks naturally go together.

Below are the four ideas Eric thinks have the most potential to accomplish the marketing objective he and Sam, the owner of Woodland Nurseries, had agreed upon.

1. White Glove Club. Take a photo of your yard empty, scan it into Woodland Nurseries program, click and drag plants to build your own garden. Member benefits include monthly planting guide; pay on layaway; bring in old gloves, get new ones free; advance notice on arrival of perennials chosen for their garden.
2. Series of parties between April 10 and May 15 when the store is closed except to these customers. Atmosphere and themes include soft lighting, wine and cheese party, and special spring plant previews as new plants arrive.
3. Master gardening certification of honor. Database e-mail to customers launches certification. Looking for one hundred master gardeners to acknowledge in-store. Donations made to botanical gardens in their name.
4. Create ten garden vignettes. Ten different gardens on the property: all shade, full sun, afternoon lighting, and so on. Woodland will plant and customers can tour throughout the season. Open for four weekends for touring.

Alesia then says, "Great. We have a narrow list of ideas. The next thing we need to do is get back together, develop a list of success criteria, and choose the idea you want to present to Sam."

Alesia and Eric agree to meet in a few days and, with fresh minds, they will then narrow the list down to one idea.

The Agent Identifies Success Criteria

After a couple of days have passed, Alesia and Eric get back together to select one idea that Eric will present to Sam. Alesia gets right down to business, "Let's reiterate the marketing objective: *In what ways might we get a forty-five-year-old female homeowner who loves to garden to visit Woodland Nurseries between April 10 and May 15?*"

Eric confirms, "Yes. That is still our focus."

Alesia continues, "Great. As you know, we now need to create a list of success criteria to help you select the idea that makes the most sense. So how did you decide on those duck things you are wearing on your feet?"

Eric smiles. They've played this game before, but he doesn't object to the reminder. "Well, look at it out there! It's rainy and cold today in Atlanta. I wanted shoes that were warm, waterproof, and comfortable. Oh, and quite fashionable, I might add!"

Alesia smiles in return, continuing, "All the things that you just described were criteria you used to select the best pair of shoes for you today. What I'm going to ask you to do now, Eric, is to make a similar list of criteria, except this time we want criteria to help you choose the best solution to achieve your marketing objective. We're going to use this list of criteria to measure the four ideas you selected so that we can choose which one solution we're going to focus on today. So help me make a list of criteria."

Eric says, "Well, I didn't want to go much further without involving Sam in the process, so I had a conversation with him prior to this meeting. I told him we'd done the idea-generation session, that we had a bunch of cool ideas, and that I needed his input before I selected one idea to recommend to him. Here is what I learned. Whatever idea we bring to him has to appeal to a woman who loves to garden. Springtime is an important time for that woman who does a lot of gardening and buys a lot of gardening products. It has to make sense for the springtime, and the timing of this is critical. From my perspective—and I know this is important to Sam as well—whatever idea we choose has to match and enhance our brand. It has to have the look and feel of a Woodland Nurseries program. Those are the main criteria.

"Now, we also talked about not wanting it to be operationally too intense because this is such a busy time of the year. So whatever idea we pick can't require the retail staff or the gardening staff to do too much over and above what they currently will be doing."

Alesia asks, "Are there any kinds of financial criteria involved?"

Eric replies, "Yes. We have an $80,000 budget for the media, and we also have some operational money. So I think we have to stay within the ballpark of about a $100,000 program."

Alesia asks, "So it should not cost more than $100,000?"

Eric replies, "Yes. For the total program, we need to think in that range. If we buy gifts or hold parties or whatever, it has to all work within that budget."

Alesia asks, "Are there any other success criteria that come to mind?"

Eric says, "Well, I know that Sam wants to tap into the Web site and the customer database more than we have up to this point, so it would be a home run if we found ways to build relationships with these customers through some of the tools that we haven't quite maximized."

Alesia says, "So build relationships with customers specifically through the Web site? Am I capturing what you want?"

Eric replies, "Yes, we want to use and take advantage of the various tools that we already have."

Alesia says, "Great. Now, as you well know, whenever we make a list, we always make a choice. Eric, I'm going to read this list of criteria back to you, and what I'm asking you to do is to choose the criteria that are nonnegotiable for you. You can select as many as you would like, and then we'll evaluate your ideas against the criteria. So let me read the criteria back to you.

"1. It must appeal to a woman who loves to garden.

"2. It must make sense for spring.

"3. It must enhance the Woodland brand."

Eric interjects, "These are all important so far. Check each one."

Alesia continues, "4. It cannot require the staff to do a lot of work over and above their normal responsibilities or to be distracted, since it's a busy time."

Eric says, "Check."

Alesia says, "5. It has to come in for $100,000 or less."

Eric says, "Let's not check that. I don't want to let finances limit us, because we might be able to bring some co-op dollars from some of the vendors. Let's not let the money get in our way."

Alesia says, "6. It has to take advantage of tools and assets available."

Eric says, "That's an 'it would be nice,' but it's not a 'have to.'"

Applying Success Criteria

Alesia says, "Okay, great. I'm going to read back the list of top ideas to you, and I'm going to use a simple scoring system. If the idea meets the criterion, I will write a plus sign next to it; if it doesn't, it will get a minus; and if we don't know, it will get a question mark. We are going to use the same scoring system to evaluate all the ideas against your most important criteria. Ready?"

"Ready!"

"The first idea is a White Glove Club: Take a photo tour of your empty yard, scan it into the Woodland Nurseries program, click and drag plants to build your own garden. It would also include member benefits such as a monthly planting guide, pay on layaway, bring in your old gloves and get new ones free, advance notice on arrival of perennials chosen for the garden—the ones they chose from their photos that they would get advance notice of."

Eric asks, "In other words, all these benefits could be part of belonging to this club?"

Alesia replies, "Yes. We put the ideas together that you chose to be a part of this club: So do you feel that this is going to appeal to a woman who loves to garden?"

Eric answers, "Yes."

Alesia asks, "Does it make sense for spring?"

Eric replies, "Yes, if you get to them soon enough so that their gardens are still empty."

Alesia asks, "Do you feel like it will enhance the Woodland brand?"

Eric replies, "Yes. I'm not sure I like the title 'White Glove,' but I like the idea of some sort of club."

Alesia says, "Well, we're all about invention, so we can certainly change the name if that's the one you ultimately want us to focus on."

Alesia continues applying the criteria, "Do you feel that the White Glove Club would distract the staff?"

Eric says, "No, I think we could do that without taking staff away."

Alesia replies, "So that's another plus."

Every time Eric gave a positive evaluation to the idea, Alesia put a plus sign next to it. The White Glove Club received four plus signs.

"Okay, idea number two: A series of parties between April 10 and May 15 where the store is closed except for these customers. Soft lighting, wine and cheese parties, special spring plant previews as new plants arrive—those are some of the party themes. It would be a series of parties between April 10 and May 15. Do you feel that this would appeal to women who love to garden?"

Eric replies, "I'm not so sure. Maybe. Give it a question mark."

Alesia asks, "Does it make sense for spring?"

Eric replies, "Sure. Give it a plus."

Alesia asks, "And do you feel that it will enhance the Woodland brand?"

Eric says, "I'm not sure."

Alesia asks, "And do you feel that it would require staff to be distracted and have to go over and above in this busy time?"

Eric says, "Yes, that might be too much."

Alesia summarizes Eric's evaluation, "This idea, number two, got two question marks, a plus, and a minus. All right, let's move on to idea number three: Master gardening certification. A database e-mail to customers launching the certification program. Looking for one hundred master gardeners to acknowledge in-store. A donation would be made to the Atlanta Botanical Garden in the master gardeners' names. Do you feel that would appeal to women who love to garden?"

Eric asks, "Is this the one where we pick them as master gardeners based on their gardens?"

Alesia replies, "Yes."

Eric says, "I think it might appeal to them, but I'm not sure it's going to accomplish the marketing objective of getting them into the store."

Alesia asks, "So is that a question mark?"

Eric replies, "Yes, it's a question mark."

Alesia asks, "Does it make sense for spring?"

Eric says, "Yes, it makes sense for spring."

Alesia asks, "Does it enhance the Woodland brand?"

Eric says, "Yes, I think that would."

Alesia asks, "Would that require staff to work over and above during this busy time?"

Eric replies, "Not necessarily. I'm not sure that it's going to bring people into the store in the spring, so I'm not sure it accomplishes the marketing objective."

Alesia says, "Okay, let's move on to idea number four: Create ten garden vignettes. Ten different gardens on the property: all shade, full sun, afternoon lighting, and so on. Woodland will plant these different gardens, and customers can tour throughout the season. Do you feel that would appeal to women who love to garden?"

Eric says, "Yes. That would go with the house tours and home decorator tours."

Alesia asks, "Does it make sense for spring?"

Eric says, "Yes."

Alesia asks, "Does it enhance the Woodland brand?"

Eric says, "Yes."

Alesia says, "Does it require staff to work too much more? Do you think it would distract the staff?"

Eric says, "I don't think so. I think the gardens could be planted on off hours, and it's just one of the reasons why people would come there in the spring."

Alesia says, "Okay, let's take a look at what we have. It looks like we've knocked number three off the list, because we didn't feel that it would accomplish the objective."

Eric says, "I'm not sure I want to do number two, either. I think the choice is between creating a White Glove Club or doing these spring garden vignettes. I don't know if it's ten, but the various versions of gardens done by professionals would give these ladies new ideas."

Choosing the One Marketing Idea

Alesia asks, "Which one of these solutions do you feel make the most sense? Remember the marketing objective. We're trying to get a forty-five-year-old female homeowner who loves to garden to visit Woodland Nurseries between April 10 and May 15. Inherent in that is we want them to come into the store."

Eric says, "I think number one. You can help me come up with a name, right?"

Alesia says, "Absolutely!"

Eric says, "Yes, number one."

Alesia says, "Okay, this is very exciting! We have the idea that we are going to turn into a full-on solution."

In this chapter we discussed how to help a client choose a marketing idea. We illustrated it as Alesia helped Eric choose a marketing idea by narrowing the long list down to a short list, then to the one choice that met his criteria.

The next step is to develop the idea chosen by the client. In the next chapter we will see how a fairly simple idea is transformed into a full marketing program.

DEVELOPING THE IDEA

G reat ideas are the result of two idea-generation sessions, not just one. In chapters 7 and 8 we saw how the first idea-generation session is conducted. In chapter 9 we saw how a facilitator helps a client or his agent select the idea that makes the most sense. So we know which idea the client wants to make happen. Now we need to make that idea as cool and custom and effective as it can be. It's time for the second idea-generation session. We call this *development*.

WHAT IS DEVELOPMENT?

Development is the process of taking an idea that a client or an agent wants to execute—usually expressed in a sentence or two—and developing that idea into a complete marketing program. Development happens in three phases:

1. In phase 1, the job of the facilitator is to help the client flesh out the program with as much detail as possible. The program will take the shape of a story with a beginning, a middle, and an end.

215

2. In phase 2, the job of the facilitator is to help the client create the communication plan for the program. The client will select the communication tools he wants to use and the most effective way to use them.
3. In phase 3, the job of the facilitator is to help the client create the messaging—sometimes referred to as the *creative*—for the program.

As each phase is completed, the program is developed in greater and greater detail.

Development is like every other idea-generation session you have seen so far in this book in that the facilitator will ask the resource group for a long list of ideas. Development, however, is different from the typical idea-generation session in that the facilitator wants a long list of ways to execute the one idea that has already been chosen by a client or an agent. The purpose of a development session is to take the client's chosen idea and make it as cool, as custom, and as effective as it can be, so that when the target consumer experiences it, it will accomplish the client's marketing objective.

Perhaps the best way to illustrate what we mean by development is to return to the Woodland Nurseries example.

At the end of chapter 8, Alesia, the facilitator of the Woodland Nurseries project, led the resource group in generating forty-nine ideas in a little over an hour. The focus of that idea-generation session was the client's marketing objective: *To get a forty-five-year-old female homeowner who loves to garden to visit Woodland Nurseries between April 10 and May 15.*

In chapter 9, Eric, the agent, narrowed the forty-nine ideas on the list down to his four favorites. After considering a set of success criteria, Eric chose the one idea he wanted to bring to Sam, the owner of Woodland Nurseries.

It is important to note here that all Eric has at this point is a name (the White Glove Club) and probably some initial ideas of what it might be and how it might work. What Eric needs now—and what Alesia will facilitate for him—is a development session where he can consider a variety of ways of carrying out a White Glove Club at Woodland Nurseries.

In a moment you will see Alesia facilitate this development session. You will see her ask the resource group to make a long list of ideas, except in this case the ideas will represent ways to carry out the White Glove Club.

COOL, CUSTOM, EFFECTIVE

The price of admission to a development session is having a marketing idea the client wants to execute to achieve his marketing objective. Effective facilitators know that the work is not done just because the client has selected the idea he wants to execute. The idea still needs development and troubleshooting before it is ready for prime time. In addition, only by creating a timeline with commitments and deadlines can the facilitator ensure that the marketing idea becomes an executable program.

Armed with the one idea the client wants to execute, the facilitator leads the resource group to make a list of ways to make the idea cool for the target consumer, custom to the client's brand, and effective in accomplishing the marketing objective. This is where a resource group can breathe life into the client's favorite idea by identifying the who, what, when, where, and how of the marketing program.

DEVELOPING THE WOODLAND NURSERIES WHITE GLOVE CLUB

At the end of chapter 9, Eric arrived at an idea he wanted to develop further before showing it to Sam, the owner of Woodland Nurseries. The idea was described like this: *White Glove Club. Take a photo of your yard empty, scan it into Woodland Nurseries' program, click and drag plants to build your own garden. Member benefits include monthly planting guide; pay on layaway; bring in old gloves, get new ones free; advance notice on arrival of perennials chosen for their garden.*

As we said at the outset of this chapter, development is the idea-generation session where an idea becomes a full-fledged program. And because it is an idea-generation session, the facilitator needs to treat it as such. In the case of Woodland Nurseries, about a week has passed since the original idea-generation session. Alesia, the facilitator, and Eric, the agent, have gathered a slightly different resource group in the same con-, ference room where the first meeting took place. Because the process of developing an idea assumes that whatever idea is developed is actually going to happen, Alesia and Eric have agreed they should invite a couple of new people—Max and Rachel—to the session. Eric invited them to the development session because they work for Woodland Nurseries' advertising agency and they will most likely be called upon to help with the execution of the program.

As the session begins, Alesia follows the same sequence of steps that she used to open the idea-generation session in chapter 7. She first engages the resource group in an icebreaker exercise. The point of the exercise is to get the resource group reacquainted with the behaviors of making lists and making choices. Alesia always begins her sessions with a lists-and-choices icebreaker to remind participants of the way the idea-generation game is played.

Alesia reads the Rules of Brainstorming to the resource group to remind them to suspend judgment and to follow her lead when she asks them to take a detour.

Finally, Alesia introduces them to the development step: "Okay, let me explain how our development session will unfold today. It will take place in two phases. Just as I have done up to this point, I will be managing the meeting by making a series of lists and then asking Eric to make choices. The first phase is for us to invent the idea as though we were telling a story. We will generate a list of ideas that will flesh out the details of what will make this idea cool to our forty-five-year-old woman who loves to garden, custom to the Woodland Nurseries brand, and effective in accomplishing the marketing objective that has been assigned to us by Eric. Then, in phase 2, we will make a long list of ways to communicate the program.

"There is a third phase of development, which we will not do today. It entails writing the creative message for the campaign. We are going to assign that to our advertising agency and to our media partners to work out. I would, of course, be happy to facilitate that creative session, but we will not be doing that today."

DEVELOPMENT DETOURS

All idea generation requires detours to add quantity, relevance, and novelty to the list of ideas. Development is no exception. We are now going to show you the development detours we recommend. To show you each detour, we will use this sequence: First we will describe the detour and explain how a facilitator can use it; then we will show you how Alesia uses it as she facilitates the Woodland Nurseries development session.

We are going to show you the list of ideas the resource group is generating as if you were seeing the scribe capture it on the flip chart. Rather than sharing with you all the dialogue that takes place during the session, as we've done in other parts of the book, we will just show you the list of ideas the group generates. Every time Alesia takes a detour, you will see the side list in bullet points. The ideas being generated will be displayed as a numbered list.

We are changing the way we display the ideas being generated because we want you to pay close attention to something that is true for all idea generation. For each phase of development, the main list of ideas is one continuously numbered list. When the facilitator takes a detour the resource group adds to the main—and only the main—list of ideas.

Development Detour #1: Appealing to All the Senses

As its title implies, this first development detour leads the resource group to invent ways in which the idea being developed will appeal to all of the target consumer's senses.

Here is how it works: First, the facilitator asks the resource group to adopt the point of view of the target consumer ("Imagine you are Sandy, our forty-five-year-old homeowner who loves to garden"). Then the facilitator asks the resource group to imagine themselves taking part in the program. Next she asks them to imagine what they might see, hear, smell, taste, and touch as they take part in the program.

Below is a list of questions and prompts organized by sense. The facilitator uses these to coax the resource group into generating ideas to develop the program. The facilitator has the prerogative to decide how many of these detours to use.

Sight

- What are all the elements the target consumer can see?
- Are there any visual elements that are particularly noteworthy or appealing?
- What can the target consumer read?
- How might we use the different colors on the product and what they signify?
- What visual elements are connected to the key benefits the target consumer receives from the product?

Sound

- What sounds will the target consumer hear?
- What other sounds are associated with the product?
- What sound does the target consumer make as he uses the product?
- What sounds would the product make if it could make sounds?
- What music would the product make if it could play music?
- What words would the product say if it could speak?

Smell

- What smells are associated with the product itself?
- What smells are associated with the use of the product?
- Are there things about the product or the product category that "smell bad" to the consumer—as in, they don't trust it or consider it distasteful?
- What parts of the product would smell particularly good to the target consumer?

Taste

- What words would the target consumer use to describe how the product tastes?
- What is noteworthy or memorable about the taste of the product?
- What other tastes are associated with the use of the product?
- How might the program appeal to target consumers who think they have good taste?
- In what ways might a target consumer get a taste of the product or service as part of the program?

Touch

- What will the target consumer touch?
- What are the parts of the product that are meant to be touched?
- How do people touch the product or service?
- What are the parts of the product that are not meant to be touched?
- How does the product make the target consumer feel?
- What might the target consumer hold or carry in his hand?

We get the best results from this detour when we use it right at the beginning of the development session. Let's take a look at how Alesia uses the senses detour.

Facilitating Development Detour #1: Appealing to All the Senses

As soon as Alesia finishes the introduction to the development session she posts a clean sheet of flip chart paper on the wall for everyone to see. On the sheet she writes five words in big block letters: *SEE, HEAR, SMELL, TASTE, FEEL*. Alesia uses this sheet as a visual reminder to the resource group of all the senses to which the program should appeal.

Now Alesia addresses the resource group: "I want you to close your eyes for a moment and imagine Sandy, our forty-five-year-old target consumer, as she interacts with the Woodland Nurseries White Glove Club program."

Alesia asks the resource group to use their imagination and begin to visualize how the White Glove Club program could contain elements that would appeal to all of Sandy's senses. Alesia will scan the list of detours we showed you above and select at least a couple of detours for each of the senses. For every sense, she always asks the first question to make it clear which sense she is going to explore, for example, "I want you to imagine all the things Sandy might see as she takes part in the program." Then, to encourage further ideas, she reads one or two other detours associated with the sense. For instance, to help the resource group explore the sense of sight, Alesia asks, "What might Sandy see as a result of being in the White Glove Club?" and then, "What can Sandy see when she walks through one of our stores that will cause her to notice the program?"

Once Alesia has explored all the different senses, she asks the resource group to open their eyes and help her make a list of ideas. "Okay, you have just spent a few minutes imagining Sandy as she takes part in the White Glove Club program. You saw many things she might see, you heard the sounds she might hear, you came up with smells and tastes she would associate with the program. You imagined how participating in the program would make her feel. Now, whenever you are ready, I would like you to help me make a list of all those ideas that just popped into your heads."

Here is the list of ideas:

1. Part-time valets in tuxedos parking cars.
2. A string quartet playing inside the greenhouse.
3. A series of e-mails, starting in January, to the Woodland Nurseries customer database outlining the benefits of the club and inviting them to join the club.
4. Extra parking along the driveway lined with plants. Plant names are posted.
5. Send an e-mail to everyone in the customer database around March 15. The e-mail contains a diagram tool so the customer can sketch out a design for her yard, and she can bring it to the nursery when she is ready to shop for her plants.

6. The diagramming program also provides a shopping list of all the items chosen.
7. Receive a special discount on select flowers and plants for being a member of the club.
8. The yard design program will allow you to drag and drop different flowers on the diagram, then the program generates a list of the flowers chosen.
9. Give the members a coupon book with discounts on flowers.
10. Use e-mail to notify club members when new perennials will arrive. Club members can be the first to know about the new perennials.
11. Signage at checkout counters or elsewhere in the store encouraging people to join the club a couple of months before the last frost.
12. Call it the Dirty Glove Club instead. You opt in to the club by bringing in your dirty gloves. Fill out a form to join and get new gloves.
13. Opt in online and get a reminder to bring in dirty gloves—get new ones.
14. Give an incentive to sign up for membership.
15. Have employees wear a button that looks like an old, well-used, crinkled-up glove that says "Join the Dirty Glove Club."
16. Give employees an incentive by creating an internal sales contest. The employee who signs up the most customers for the club each month gets some sort of prize.
17. Use e-mail to invite women to the Web site. Series of video podcasts could be hosted on YouTube. Things you need to do to be ready for spring planting. List of tips and reminders.
18. The "getting ready for spring" list can be printed from Web site. Mulch your roses, put in peony cages, empty compost bins, etc.
19. Members can nominate their yards by posting pictures of their garden to the Web site for a contest or they can bring pictures to the store to be posted on the Web site.
20. Use media to promote the club: radio or television, lifestyle magazines in town.

21. Come in to one of our stores and register to become part of the Dirty Glove Club. Receive a pair of nice gardening gloves on the spot.

22. Bring your old gardening gloves when you come in and we will take your picture wearing your dirty gloves. The picture will go up on our wall at the store and also on our fan page on Facebook.

23. All club members will be entitled to early-bird sales. Four times per year we have special sales. Every time we have a sale, we will open the store bright and early—7 a.m., so that the club members can make early-bird purchases before the store opens at 10 a.m. New members can sign up on the spot.

24. Publish at least four coupon books with deep discounts that they can redeem at our stores.

25. At least once per year we will have a celebrity of some sort—maybe an author or a famous gardener, like people on television, making an appearance at one of our stores. Probably the main store because it is larger.

26. We will invite students from the Masters Landscape Design program at the University of Georgia to take part in a competition. We will give them three different small areas of land on the grounds of our nurseries and have them create designs for those areas. Club members could judge them.

27. I see pictures of our staff on the Web site wearing white gloves.

28. We need to have our customers appear on our television, radio, and Web ads.

29. What about a widget that the members could have on their computer screen. Maybe it's a little weather widget that shows the temperature and weather forecast. If they click the widget, it will take them to our Web site.

30. Put links on our Web site to other sites of interest to gardeners.

31. Annual survey of the membership. We can ask them how we are doing.

32. A surprise of the season. Or Sam's Surprises. Sam sends club members an e-mail or a newsletter once a quarter with information about the plants he is looking at.

Development Detour #2: Fact-Based Detour—The Target Consumer

As in all idea generation, the facilitator can take fact-based detours during development to get the resource group to make a longer list of ideas.

Alesia is about to take her resource group on a detour about the target consumer, which is one of the three detours we introduced in chapter 8 (the other two were product and brand). The target consumer detour is the one Tyler used to get his colleagues to help him come up with ideas to celebrate his sister Winnie's fortieth birthday. You probably remember that the quality of the ideas increased dramatically once the resource group was given some information about Winnie.

Focusing a portion of the development session on the target consumer is always a good idea. All programs should be designed to get the target consumer to do things and believe things about products and services.

Here is how the target consumer detour works: The facilitator first posts a side list of facts about the target consumer on the wall. Then the facilitator asks the resource group to explore the items on the side list in search of any items that will inspire a new idea. The facilitator then captures the resource group's ideas on the main list of ideas. It is then entirely up to the facilitator's discretion as to whether she wants the resource group to generate another handful of ideas in response to an item on the side list that she finds promising.

The first time you saw this detour, it was used to generate ideas to accomplish a marketing objective. Now we are using it to develop one specific idea, the White Glove Club. But before we return to the Woodland Nurseries development session, let us remind you that there are several different fact-based detours a facilitator can use in any idea-generation session. The easiest way to find topics for fact-based detours is the marketing objective. For instance, a facilitator could put up a side list based on the place (describe everything you see at Woodland Nurseries stores) and the season (let's make a list of everything you think about in connection with the months of April and May).

Let's return to the Woodland Nurseries illustration to see how Alesia manages a fact-based detour.

Facilitating Development Detour #2:
Fact-Based Detour—The Target Consumer

Alesia introduces a fact-based detour to get the resource group to generate ideas that will be cool to the target consumer. She says, "Help me make a list of everything we know about our target consumer." The detour nets the information below:

- Homeowner.
- Busy with two kids.
- Has a pool.
- Likes to decorate.
- Looks at the garden as an extension of the interior design.
- Wants to be served quickly.
- Wants to be "in the know" about everything new for the garden.
- Likes to be pampered.

Alesia rereads the list that the resource group just generated out loud and then asks, "What new connections can we generate to make this program cool for her?" Here is the list the resource group comes up with:

33. The town's recognition. Gardeners get "Yard of the Month" signs in their yards.
34. Give members points for purchases. Points accumulate and can be used to buy outdoor patio furniture.
35. Points for purchases could go toward tickets to concerts.
36. Issue an affinity card or a credit card and the store tracks their points.
37. A kickoff with a garden celebrity, like Martha Stewart, or an organic cook from the Food Network.
38. Bring the author of a new gardening book to do a book signing.
39. Only members of the club are invited.
40. Allow members to order plants ahead of time.
41. E-mail in their order. When plants arrive they're notified. Plants are boxed and ready to load when they get to the store.

42. Use points toward purchase or win other offers from different companies. They provide product in exchange for involvement in emails. Third party tie-ins in e-mail notices.

43. Tie in with other companies, like patio furniture, pool services, anything for the yard.

44. During the program each member gets a gift pack supported by Woodland Nurseries' vendors. Miracle-Gro® sample packs. Woodland can charge their vendors to be involved.

45. Get manufacturers to give club members coupons.

46. Provide incentive for members based on their spending.

47. Give them prizes based on the points they accumulate.

48. At the store have a greeter who identifies Dirty Glove Club members and gives them a button to wear to identify them as a member.

49. Use outdoor displays at the store to highlight members chosen for "Most Beautiful Garden." It could have their names and say, "I get my gloves dirty at Woodland Nurseries."

50. Have a picture of their garden.

51. Have them in the picture.

52. Wearing their dirty gloves!

53. Extend the recognition into *Atlanta Homes and Life Style* magazine and specific Web sites.

54. Host a networking event at the nursery. A breakfast where members can network.

Development Detour #3: Novelty Detour—A Nail

The job of the facilitator is to create a variety of ideas from which the client can select the ideas he wants to execute. To get a variety of ideas, facilitators can take fact-based detours, as Alesia did a moment ago, and they can also take novelty detours.

As we said in chapter 8 when we introduced them for the first time, novelty detours do not have to have any connection to the facts of the situation. Their single purpose is to add novelty to the list of ideas.

Alesia is about to take a novelty detour based on the word *nail*, which she chose at random. Just as she did when she took a fact-based detour, she will first ask the resource group to make a side list based on the word *nail*. Once she has seven to ten ideas on the list, she will ask the resource group to look at the entire list and allow any of the items on the list to inspire new ideas. Alesia will encourage the resource group to come up with a number of ideas in response to the entire list. Then, she can decide to ask the resource group to make connections with one or more of the items on the list that appear promising to her. Let's see how she does it.

Facilitating Development Detour #3: Novelty Detour—A Nail

As the idea generation progresses, Alesia says, "Okay, everybody I am going to ask you to forget about the White Glove Club for a moment. I want you to help me make a side list of all the words that come to mind when I say the word *nail*."

One member of the resource group wants clarification, "What kind of nail?"

Another member of the group, who has played this game many times, jumps right in, "Whatever kind of nail pops into your head!"

Here is the resulting list:

- Red
- Hammer
- Hangnail
- Galvanized
- Rusty
- Picture
- Clippers
- Repair

Now that Alesia has seven to ten ideas on the list, she continues, "Okay, now I need you to make some new connections here. Please look through this list and give me any ideas you come up with."

The resource group generates this list of ideas in response to the novelty detour:

55. Staff pictures on the Web site wearing white gloves.
56. Take pictures of the club members and hang on the wall at the store.
57. Make the Web site look like a picture gallery of all the club members.
58. Give club members green toolboxes full of garden tools.
59. Have members upload pictures of their gardens.

Once Alesia has heard a pretty good list of ideas, she decides to push a little harder. "I've been looking at a word here at the bottom of the list. The word is *repair*. What connections can you make with that word that will help us make the White Glove Club really cool, custom, and effective?"

A few more ideas are added to the list:

60. If a club member has a garden that needs repair, she can e-mail a picture to one of our experts and get advice over the phone.
61. The club will take on city parks and gardens and repair them.
62. Call for best practices. Every month send an e-mail to the members describing a garden that needs some sort of repair. Post all member responses on a comment wall on the Web site.

Alesia's novelty detour pays off with new ideas for Eric to consider for the White Glove Club. In phase 1 of the development session Alesia has led her resource group to generate sixty-two ideas. It's time for Eric to select the ideas he wants to include in the program.

MAKING CHOICES TO TELL THE PROGRAM STORY

Just as she did at the end of the idea-generation session in chapters 7 and 8, the facilitator will ask the client to review the entire list of development ideas and choose his favorites. However, in this case, the facilitator must make it clear to the client that he is choosing things that need to make sense together because they are going to become part of a program that is going to happen.

The point of this decision-making exercise is to arrive at a cohesive program that the facilitator can describe as a story with a beginning, a middle, and an end. On the one hand, the client can choose as many items as he wants or can afford. On the other hand, these items need to begin to come together into a rational, cohesive program.

It is common for an effective facilitator to wait until the client has finished making choices and then review any items that appear to be in conflict. One example might be if one idea must happen in January, while another suggests the program will happen in the summer. The facilitator should point out the apparent conflict and give the client a chance to clarify which items he really wants to be part of the program.

AND THEN WHAT?

The job of the facilitator is to help the client organize all the program elements he chose from the list into a sequence of events, like a story. Naturally, all stories have to begin somewhere. So the facilitator will ask the client, "How do you see this program starting?" The client will likely select one or two elements he feels need to happen at the beginning of the program. The facilitator will then continue to ask the same persistent question until the story of the program has been worked out: "And then what?" At the end of the exercise, the client or his agent will have clarity about which elements will be present in the program and how they follow each other in a sequence.

One of the best examples of how a well-developed program should read like a story is a program done by those virtuosos of development, the Walt Disney Company.

A few years ago, Disney invited a number of media executives to an anniversary celebration of the Epcot® theme park in Orlando, Florida. The executives, mostly high-level managers in radio and television, were flown from several major cities in the United States to Orlando.

One of our friends, who lived in Los Angeles at the time, was among those invited to the festivities. He was picked up in a limo and driven to the airport, where he boarded the chartered airplane that was to transport him and a group of colleagues across the country. In addition to the crew and flight attendants, there were Disney cast members who provided entertainment.

Now, most of us would have been happy to be picked up in a limo and flown for free to a party at Epcot. But that was not enough for Disney. After all, what sort of a story would that be? So as the airplane made its way from California to Florida, every time it entered the airspace of a different state, the cast members appeared and descended upon their guests dressed in costumes that were evocative of the state over which they were flying. The music and food also changed to match each particular state. This entire production began again every time the plane entered another state.

The plane arrived in Orlando fairly early in the morning. Anyone other than Disney would have been happy to quietly put us on a bus to the resort. But again, that would not be the Disney way. As the executives disembarked the airplane, they stepped onto a red carpet. Disney cast members, playing the roles of photographers, reporters, and fans, treated the executives as if they were movie stars. They took photographs, interviewed them, and asked for their autographs.

Listening to that story, it is easy to imagine the facilitator at the development session persistently asking, "And then what?" Now you see why it makes sense that it was the Disney Studios that invented the practice of storyboarding animated movies before producing them. Storyboards are a series of drawings that illustrate a story in sequence from beginning to end, which is exactly what we want in phase 1 of development.

The Elements of the Story

Alesia says to Eric, "Let's take a step back from this list. The first phase of development is about the 'what' of the solution. Here's what I mean by this: The choices you are about to make off the list of ideas should tell the story of a cohesive program that our target consumer will experience. You can include as many elements as you would like. We'll get specific about the tools we'll use and the message in a moment. Looking at this list, do you feel you're ready to make some choices about what the program will include?"

Eric reflects upon the list and then replies, "Yes. I'm ready to make choices. I love the name Dirty Glove Club!"

Alesia gives the resource group a quick break while she and Eric review the list of development ideas. Eric reviews the list and makes his choices in the absence of the resource group. When everyone is back in the conference room, Alesia brings them up to speed by summarizing the program based on Eric's choices.

"The program, as we see it today, will be called the Dirty Glove Club instead of the White Glove Club. It's an affinity program for people who are avid gardeners and customers of Woodland Nurseries. The club will be announced sometime before April 10. Let's imagine Sandy, our target consumer. She will hear about the club because she will receive a letter or an e-mail from Sam, inviting her to join. The letter will tell her about the benefits she will receive when she joins the Dirty Glove Club. We launch the program in the stores in April, as the busy season gets under way. So, if we are following Sandy, she is going to go to the Web site and join the club or simply come down to her favorite location. At this point there are three concrete benefits Eric sees for the club. First, the Dirty Glove Club entitles the members to a pair of gardening gloves every year. There are some cute possibilities with a glove exchange program of some sort in the spring. Eric also likes the idea of giving the target consumers a coupon book as an added incentive to join the club. The third benefit Eric sees is early access to the store, especially when we are holding a sale. Members would get to shop for a couple of hours before the rest of the customers come in.

"Eric has also selected an annual event for members only. Woodland Nurseries will bring in a person of national stature—it could be an expert, or an author, or even a celebrity like Martha Stewart—to speak as well as mingle with club members.

"So is that the program as you see it today?"

Eric says, "I love it!"

With a smile on her face, Alesia confirms, "Is that a yes?"

Eric confirms, "Yes!"

When phase 1 is complete, in most cases the result is a fairly detailed story of the program from beginning to end. Now phase 2 can begin. Here, the facilitator will help the client choose which communication tools to use for the program and come up with a variety of ways to use those tools most effectively.

As we get into phase 2 of development, you can see why it was important to wait until the story of the program was clear before generating ways to communicate the program. The significant change in the name of the program from White Glove Club to Dirty Glove Club is likely to have an important impact on the ideas generated for the communication plan.

MAXIMIZING COMMUNICATION TOOLS

In chapter 7 we showed you the difference between an idea and a tool, illustrating that an idea is what needs to be communicated in order to get a target consumer to do or believe something, whereas a tool is the mechanism, the technology, or the medium used to manifest the idea. Let's revisit our discussion of tools because they are a very important part of idea development. Understanding the part tools play in this next phase of development will help you create a program that fully engages the target consumer with the client's product.

Tools include, but are not limited to, what has traditionally been called media. The word *media* describes big media outlets such as newspapers, radio, and television. When it comes to developing a marketing communication program, the more relevant word is *tools*. This is more than just a matter of semantics: The word *media* puts you in a more traditional mindset, whereas the word *tools* opens you up to consider anything and everything you might possibly use to communicate with your target consumer.

For instance, many people would probably not include powerful social networks like Facebook, Twitter, and LinkedIn under the heading "media," at least not as of this writing. Yet all these are very powerful tools marketers should consider as they design their marketing plans.

Tools Detours

Now we are going to show you three different detours designed to get the greatest impact out of the tools available to any given client. The first detour is fairly simple, while the other two are a little more involved.

Tools Detour #1: Consider All the Tools Available to the Client

To use this detour most effectively, the facilitator must make a list of all the tools that are available to the client. Some of the tools on the list will be the property of the client (like Woodland Nurseries' database of customers, its Web site, and even the uniforms worn by its staff). Other tools belong to the client's media partners; for instance, Woodland Nurseries might advertise on a television station, a radio station, or in a magazine. The list of tools would include the tools owned by those companies (television, radio, or magazine) because they are available to Woodland Nurseries. An example might be a special gardening section in the magazine, a weekend radio program on gardening, or a big home show event held every year that is sponsored by a television station. All those tools belong on the list.

Woodland Nurseries Tools

Web site
Staff uniforms
Window signs
Brochures
Signage in stores
Signage on trucks and vans

Partner Tools

Television commercials
Radio commercials
Annual GreenFest event held by radio station
Atlanta Home and Life Style gardening section
Atlanta Home and Life Style gardening Web site
Television station Web site
Radio station Web site

Having created the above list of tools, the facilitator shows the list to the resource group, saying, "These are all the tools we have at our disposal. I need you to look at it and see if you can come up with any ideas that will help us increase the ways we communicate the program to the target consumer."

The facilitator then asks the resource group to behave as if all the tools are the property of the client. Even the tools that technically belong to other vendors should be treated in the idea-generation session as if they were completely under the control of the client. We have found that taking this approach frees the resource group to generate more ideas because they don't wonder whether or not they need permission to do any of the ideas.

Facilitating Tools Detour #1

Alesia says to the resource group, "Okay everybody, now we go into phase 2. Let me ask you to take a detour that will focus on the communication tools that we might use to make the program successful. In telling the story of the idea, we've already heard some tools Eric would like to use. Let's make a list of all the communications tools that are available to us."

The resource group chimes in with different tools that could be used for the program:

- Woodland's database
- Woodland's Web site

- *Atlanta Homes and Life Style*
- Radio
- Television
- Newspaper
- Woodland's expert staff
- Newsletter
- Vendors
- Checkout area
- Facebook
- Public address system
- On-site events
- Lawn signs

Alesia then leads the group to make new connections. "I am going to ask you to focus your attention on one particular item on the side list we just created. Let's work with the Woodland Nurseries database and Web site. What connections can we make that will engage our target consumer with the Web site?" The resource group responds:

1. Have members use Twitter to let everyone know when they are planning their gardens, purchasing what they need, and planting. They could include when they visit gardens owned by other Dirty Glove Club members.
2. Have the professional staff of Woodland Nurseries on Twitter. They let Dirty Glove Club members know when different plants come in and recommend what to buy.
3. Use that, too, with e-mail messages Woodland Nurseries sends out.
4. In addition to the Woodland Nurseries logo, we create a little icon that says Dirty Glove Club, a garden glove in the shape of a hand. That's the icon for the club.
5. Buy the domain name dirtygloveclub.com.
6. You enter your password and click on the glove icon.
7. Give members of the club a chance to have a column in a newsletter. They can be guest writers.

8. Membership has its privileges. You can only get into the club link on the Web site and receive the newsletter if you are a Dirty Glove Club member.

By now you should be familiar with detours and how they work, so for the next two detours we want to show you, we will dispense with the Woodland Nurseries illustration. Suffice it to say, just as you saw with the first tools detour above, any detour Alesia takes will create a longer list from which Eric can make choices. You just need to remember as we show you these next two detours that they are designed to use all the tools available to the client in the most effective way possible.

In the last detour we showed you how a facilitator can create a side list of tools and lead a resource group to make new connections with that list. Perhaps more importantly, you saw that we want a resource group to behave as if the client owned all the tools at his disposal, even those tools technically owned by others. Now we are going to take another detour. This one will take us one level deeper than the first.

Tools Detour #2: Deconstructing a Tool

We developed this detour because we have worked with too many clients who underutilize the tools at their disposal. This squandering of a communication resource is especially evident when the tool in question is technically owned by somebody else. For instance, clients will sponsor an event, hang their name on a banner outside the event, and display their logo on the event poster, all the while missing a dozen opportunities before, during, and after the event to get their message to their target consumers who are attending the event!

Our diagnosis is that clients miss opportunities because they look superficially at the tools. The way to correct this problem is to break the tool down into its components (that's what we mean when we say "deconstructing a tool") and come up with ideas to use each one in the communication of the program.

Here is how it works. The facilitator begins by making a list that should look just like the list created in the last detour. It should include all the communication tools available to the client—whether or not he technically owns them. Let's use an example to clarify.

Let's imagine the facilitator asked the client to select a tool he wants to use. For the purpose of this illustration, we'll say the client chose the radio station's annual GreenFest event that appears on the Partner Tools List in the last detour.

The facilitator next asks the resource group to deconstruct the event into all its different parts. Here's the list:

- Pre-promotion announcements
- Announcements on stage
- Parking lot
- Seats
- Venue staff
- Venue floors
- Concession stands
- Signage, venue signage
- Bands performing
- Merchandise sales
- Speeches on stage
- Distribution of literature

The facilitator can now treat this detailed side list just as she would any other side list. She asks the resource group to consider all the different elements on the list and then help her add to the list of development ideas. And she can always choose one specific item from the list and have the resource group make new connections.

It is worth noting that this side list could have been made before the session began; alternatively, the facilitator could ask the members of the resource group to create the list during the session.

Tools Detour #3: The New Customer Expectations

There is one more detour to consider as we explore ways to maximize communications tools.

The speed with which new digital tools are being introduced and, perhaps most importantly, adopted by target consumers of all ages is truly mind-boggling. We believe the power consumers have received from all the new technology has spilled over into other areas of their lives.

Let's use the customer's ability to time-shift as just one example of what we observe to be going on all over the culture. We are using the expression "time-shifting" to mean that consumers have become completely used to controlling the time they receive any content (like a television program), shifting it from the time it was originally broadcast to the time it becomes convenient for them to receive it. A television network might broadcast the show at 10 p.m., but consumers—even avid fans of the program—know they can watch it whenever they feel like it.

Because time-shifting has become such a clear expectation among consumers, we believe marketers need to ask themselves the question: "How do we make *all* our services time-shiftable?"

The same goes for every one of the other topics covered in this tools detour. Every cluster of questions is designed to help a marketer think of ways that *all* his marketing communications programs can meet the expectations of modern consumers.

The tools detour you are going to see below is probably best used as a question or prompt detour rather than a side list detour. As you read each of the clusters of questions below, imagine what ideas you would generate for the Woodland Nurseries Dirty Glove Club if you were part of the resource group.

It is up to the facilitator to decide whether to ask one, several, or all of the questions contained in this very comprehensive detour. Because this is phase 2 of development, the facilitator needs to make sure all the ideas generated contain a tool the client can use to enhance the way the program is communicated to the target consumer.

Reflecting the Target Consumer

- How might the target consumer see himself, literally and figuratively, in this program?

- What mechanisms might the program include to gather information about the target consumer?

Compelling Content

- What elements might the program include that the target consumer would consider entertaining?
- What elements might the program contain that would get the target consumer to play a game?
- What elements might this program contain from which the target consumer can learn? What is going on in this program that will prompt the target to say, "I didn't know that!"
- How might we give the target consumer a chance to generate some or all of the content/education/entertainment in this program?

Dialogue

- How is this program set up to respond to the target consumer quickly?
- What specific elements might allow the target consumer to express herself and be heard?
- In what ways might this program establish two-way communication with the target consumer?

Empowerment

- What elements might be included in the program to give the target consumer control over *what* content he receives?
- What elements might be included in the program to give the target consumer control over *how* and by *what method* he receives the content?
- What elements might be included in the program to give the target consumer control over *when* he gets the content he wants?

Habit

- What program elements might get the target consumer to make a habit out of participating in this program?

Levels of Involvement

- What might the program make available to the target consumer absolutely free of charge?
- What different levels might the program contain?
- What different benefits might the target consumer receive at each additional level?
- What might be required of the target consumer in exchange for being able to take part in each additional level?

Community

- How might the program encourage and make it easy for the target consumer to share the program with friends and associates?
- How might the program encourage and make it easy for the target consumer to share the result of her own involvement with the program with friends and associates?
- How might the program encourage and make it easy for the target consumer to join a community?

Partners

- What other vendors' brands that focus on the same target consumer might benefit from being involved in this program?

Metrics

- In what ways might this program make it easy to measure outcomes created by the program?

Length

- What might happen before the program to entice the target consumer to engage with the program earlier?
- What might happen during the program to help the target consumer stay engaged with the program longer?
- What might happen after the program to extend the engagement with the target consumers who took part in the program?

Integration

- Are all the tools delivering a similar message?
- In what ways might the tools used for the program complement each other?

Choosing Elements of the Communication Plan

If the facilitator uses just a few of the detours described above, she will have succeeded in creating a very long list of ideas from which her client can choose the elements of the communication plan. When the client or the agent makes his choices off the list, he will have a much more complete plan, especially as it pertains to how the program will be communicated to the target consumer. The only work remaining to be done is the development of the message, which is what happens in phase 3.

DEVELOPING THE MARKETING MESSAGE

The third phase of development consists of creating the messaging for the campaign.

It is a common practice to schedule the session to develop the message at a different time and place from the rest of the development process. Our experience is that the creation of the message is a more solitary endeavor, and even when it is a team effort, the team is usually made up of people other than the ones who participated in the first two phases of development. But the message needs to be written after the first two phases, because messages need to be written in the language of each specific tool. The way you deliver the message in a television spot will be different from the way the message is delivered in a radio spot, and both will be different from what you might put on a Web site.

In this section we will discuss ways you can use the idea-generation techniques we've described thus far to help tie together the messages you develop, so they complement the marketing campaign.

You might remember from chapter 6 that all the marketing programs in the world can be separated into three different buckets: brand campaigns, which get target consumers to believe something about a product or a service; activation campaigns, which get a target consumer to try or buy a product or a service; and "other" campaigns, those that fail to get the target consumer to do or believe anything. We are going to explore in greater detail the ingredients any given message should contain in order to be assigned to one of those three buckets.

Brand Messages Must Contain Reasons to Believe

Brand messages need to give the target consumer reasons to believe that the brand indeed delivers the key benefit the target consumer seeks. Generally, brand messages take on three different forms: proof, illustration of product features, and illustration of customer benefits. Let's take a look at each.

Proof

One commercial reveals the results of an independent study that proves that people who ate a certain cereal lowered their cholesterol by 10 percent. A second commercial shows how coffee grounds were poured on carpeting and this amazing vacuum cleaner removed them all. In a third commercial a woman puts a birthday cake on a glass plate in a dishwasher and turns it on. When the dishwasher stops, the glass plate comes out clean; the cake is gone. These are messages designed to prove a claim.

In an idea-generation session to invent proof messages, the facilitator might ask: "Can you help me make a list of ways to prove this product delivers this key benefit more effectively than its competition?" or "What are all the different ways to substantiate our claim that this product delivers this particular key benefit more effectively than its competition?"

Illustrations of Product Features

Product features are physical parts of the product, such as a handle, an ingredient, or a scent. The Lexus® television commercial showing the car parking itself is a good example of a message that illustrates a product feature.

To generate ideas like these, the facilitator might ask: "Can you help me make a list of specific product features and how they make this product superior to its competitors?"

Illustrations of Customer Benefits

The poor Maytag repairman just sat around all day to illustrate the product benefit that when you buy a Maytag®, you have purchased a product that won't break down. The Verizon Wireless® test guy walked all over the country asking the persistent question: "Can you hear me now?" to illustrate that you can get Verizon's signal everywhere.

Facilitators who want messaging ideas that illustrate product benefits might ask: "Can you help me make a list of ways to illustrate how the target consumer benefits when he uses this product?"

Illustrations of customer benefits also come from the point of view of the customer who made the mistake of purchasing the competing product. The guy who got fired for purchasing the wrong business software and the woman who is shunned by her cat for purchasing the wrong cat litter are just two common examples.

Facilitators who want to explore this point of view might ask for "a list of ways to illustrate what could happen if you choose a competing product instead of ours."

Activation Messages Must Contain Reasons to Do Something

Activation campaigns are specifically designed to get a target consumer to do something with a product or a service. Generally, marketers launch activation campaigns when they want a target consumer to try or buy a product. Activation campaigns are designed to create short-term results rather than the slow build required by campaigns that create long-term brand equity.

To the facilitator engaged in helping a team or an individual design an activation campaign, we offer this reminder: All target consumers do things in their own best interest. Generally, we can break this down into four subcategories:

1. *People do things because they are cool, fun, exciting, and entertaining.* There are ideas that are fun and entertaining enough that they draw a crowd on their own. Give most people a chance to meet one of their favorite recording artists and they will make the time to get there. Moms and dads take their kids to project classes at their local building supply store because the classes are fun for the kids, and the classes also keep the kids busy while their parents shop. The facilitator might ask: "What might we do or say in the message to communicate that the program is cool, fun, exciting, and entertaining?"

2. *People do things to avoid pain and discomfort.* This natural aversion to pain and discomfort is the essence of most advertising for companies that prepare people's taxes. The facilitator might suggest: "Help me make a list of ways to illustrate that taking the action we want the target consumer to take will help him avoid pain and discomfort." A different question might be: "How might we scare the target consumer into using or learning more about this product?"

3. *People do things in exchange for a relevant and valuable reward.* Here we have another topic that has been widely covered and taught in innumerable books. Commonly referred to as a sales promotion,

there are a dozen or so effective reward schemes such as gift with purchase, sweepstakes, and coupons that a marketer can use to cause a short-term result.

Since the different sales promotion tactics are readily available in many books, we won't cover them further here. We will, however, suggest that a facilitator could use the tools detours described earlier in this chapter and use the sales promotion as the topic of the side list instead of the tool. That way, the resource group can come up with ideas to create a short-term response from the target consumer.

4. *People do things they believe are required to improve their chances of participating in something that is cool and entertaining or to receive a relevant and valuable reward.* This point is best illustrated when a person is required to sign up or provide information in order to participate in a program she is interested in. She is much more willing to give real answers about herself if she feels providing such information might lead to a valuable benefit or reward. Here the facilitator might suggest: "Help me make a list of ways to illustrate how providing information about himself will give the target consumer a leg-up to receive either a benefit or a reward."

Weak Messages

Over the years, we have compiled a list of message nonstarters that we have seen or heard from marketers who should know better. We offer them here to help clients, agents, resource group members, and facilitators everywhere recognize when a message is in need of reinvention.

A facilitator who encounters one of the messages below knows right away the message belongs in the third bucket. The problem is they do not communicate anything concrete about the product or service they intend to promote. It is not clear what they want the target consumer to do. It is not clear what they want the target consumer to believe. It is not clear what key benefit the product or service provides to the target consumer.

1. You should buy our products because our children (or our pets) are really cute.
2. You should buy our products because we care about our families.
3. You should buy our products because there is someone famous in our commercial.
4. You should buy our products because we really understand the problem or the situation you are facing.
5. You should buy our products because we know customers like you.
6. You should buy our products because we really appreciate your business.
7. You should buy our products because our grandparents started this business.
8. You should buy our products because we are locally owned.
9. You should buy our products because our commercials are really funny.
10. You should buy our products because we can do the same thing our competitors can do.
11. You should buy our products because we give money to charity.
12. You should buy our products because our messages are laden with meaningful platitudes like "success" and "perseverance."
13. You should buy our products because we put our company's name on a really big building.
14. You should buy our products because we can satisfy all your (fill in the blank) needs.

There are many books in the market that offer very good advice on how to write the messaging or creative copy for a campaign. We recommend *Made to Stick: Why Some Ideas Survive and Others Die*, by Chip and Dan Heath.[1] Facilitators will recognize that much of the excellent advice in *Made to Stick* can take the form of detours that can be used to generate a long list of messages for any given campaign.

SUMMARIZING THE DIRTY GLOVE CLUB PROGRAM

As the development session comes to a close, Alesia is eager to summarize the program for Eric and the resource group. She knows everyone who has participated in this effort will feel great satisfaction in seeing how the program has evolved. "Eric, before we adjourn today, allow me to walk you through the Dirty Glove Club program as it stands today to make sure I haven't overlooked anything."

"Ready!"

"We are going to create a Woodland Nurseries Dirty Glove Club. Our objective is to get Sandy, our forty-five-year-old homeowner who loves to garden, to visit our stores between April 10 and May 15. The Dirty Glove Club will offer Sandy the following list of benefits." Alesia reviews the program:

"The membership benefits for this first year of the program include a pair of nice gardening gloves, which the target consumer would get as soon as she signs up, plus $100 worth of coupons. We also see what we described as early-bird access to the stores whenever we are having a sale, and an annual event where the members of the club can listen to and meet a famous author or celebrity that has expertise in gardening or landscape design.

"We see the program being carried out in phases. Phase 1 is what might be described as 'getting the word out,' during which we will advertise on radio and television. We are also going to reach out to our own customers with a direct mail piece and an e-mail. All the messaging for the radio, television, direct mail, and e-mail will be created in a different meeting in a few weeks.

"Phase 2 is between April 10 and May 15, which is when we expect most customers to join the club. During that phase we have talked about making the Dirty Glove Club a big part of the look of the stores. For instance, we have decided to put up a big dirty glove above the information desk, which is where people would sign up for the club. Also, we are going to have the staff at all the stores wearing buttons that look like a dirty glove.

"On the Web site, we have decided we are going to have all the photos of the staff retaken so we all appear wearing dirty gloves. We also see a dirty glove page where people can register for the club. We have a cool idea that we need to investigate further, which is to change the appearance of the cursor on the Web site to look like a dirty glove.

"But the big thing we are going to have on the Web site is a feature the members can put in the layout of their own gardens and then drag and drop images of plants into their layouts. They can then print those plans and bring them to Woodland to purchase the plants.

"In phase 2 we are going to continue to advertise on radio and television, except the creative will change to show actual members of the Dirty Glove Club talking about why they joined the club. Also, we are going to set up a full page on Facebook where members of the Dirty Glove Club can display photos of their gardens. Every activity we do at the nurseries, whether it is a quarterly workshop or the annual event with a celebrity, will be videotaped and put up on our Web site and on Facebook.

"Finally, you selected a number of ideas you are not sure can be ready for this first year. You said you wanted to explore them and look at them again for next year. Those ideas include a Dirty Glove Club affinity credit card, a yard-of-the-month contest in which members would submit before and after pictures of their gardens and the most beautiful ones would appear in *Atlanta Homes and Life Style* magazine, and a design contest among master's-level students at the University of Georgia's School of Landscape Design."

Once the marketing program is developed, the facilitator needs to help the client anticipate and solve any problems that might limit the success of the program. This step, called troubleshooting, happens next.

11

TROUBLESHOOTING

W hat some people call Murphy's Law, we call *troubleshooting*. The fact is that every idea, regardless of how well thought-out and airtight it seems, is always in danger of failing for one unexpected reason or another.

WHAT IS TROUBLESHOOTING?

As its name implies, troubleshooting is the part of the process in which the facilitator helps the client consider all the problems that might arise with the program and either prevent them or get ready to fix them as soon as they happen. In troubleshooting, the facilitator makes a list and makes choices twice. The first list is to find trouble in the program. The second list is to prevent it from happening or to fix it. An important point we want to make here, which we will reiterate later, is that everything the facilitator does in this step is in the interest of increasing the program's chances of succeeding.

Summarizing the Program

Before troubleshooting can begin, the facilitator needs to describe the program as it has been developed up to this point. After all, the client and the members of the resource group need something concrete to troubleshoot.

It is very common for the facilitator to ask the client and the agent to help in the description of the program as either one of them—or both of them—see the program unfolding.

Identifying Trouble Spots

Once the program has been described, the facilitator makes this request of the client, the agent, and the members of the resource group: "Help me make a list of everything that might go wrong with the plan as it has been developed to this point."

One detour we use quite often in troubleshooting is to ask the resource group to visualize the program going wrong. It sounds something like this:

"I want you to close your eyes. Imagine that we are halfway through the program. But instead of feeling good, you are frustrated and embarrassed.

"Imagine the target consumer is upset or indifferent toward the program. Now visualize why this is happening.

"Imagine the client himself is upset about the program. Now visualize why this is happening.

"Now, open your eyes and help me make a list of all the things that happened in your mind that got in the way of the success of the program."

Our experience is that the scribe who is keeping track of the ideas will need to write pretty quickly because the resource group is usually ready with a long list of all sorts of problems they visualized happening to the program. Having seen quite a few troubleshooting lists, we know the list will include everything that might go wrong—all the concerns: legal, logistical, budgetary, and so on.

We also know that not all of the items will be real concerns for the client. For this reason, the facilitator asks the client to make choices off the list, like this: "Now I know there are a lot of things on the list that the resource group just imagined could go wrong with the program. But I also know that not all of them are concerns for you. So I want you to look at this list and help me select the items you are really concerned about. Please choose the problems you think realistically could get in the way of the success of the program."

Once the client makes choices off the list, the facilitator is ready to take the next step, which is to engage the resource group in preventing or preparing to fix the problems before they happen.

Preventing or Fixing the Problems That Might Arise

The facilitator focuses on each of the problems the client selected one at a time. His objective is to get the client, the agent, and the resource group to come up with two kinds of ideas. First the facilitator wants ideas to prevent the problems; then she wants ideas to fix the problems if they were to happen. Each problem that the client has indicated he is truly concerned about gets its own idea-generation session to prevent and fix the problem if it were to happen.

For every one of the problems the client has selected, the facilitator first says, "Help me make a list of all the things we might do to prevent this particular problem from happening." The facilitator is keeping an eye on the client or the agent at this point to make sure he is seeing ideas on the list that he feels are addressing his concern. It is very typical for the facilitator at this point to ask the client or the agent, "Are you seeing ideas on this list that you think are good ways to prevent this problem from happening?" If the client says "Yes," the facilitator knows she can go on to the next question.

The facilitator next asks the client, the agent, and the resource group for ideas to fix or solve the problem if it were to happen anyway: "Imagine that we were not able to prevent the problem from happening. Help me make a list of all the different ways we might overcome the problem or reduce its negative consequences."

The ideas are captured on a flip chart, and again the facilitator checks in with the client to make sure that he is hearing ideas that he feels can fix the problem if it were to happen.

Once that list has been made, the facilitator asks the client to select the ideas he feels have the best chance of preventing or fixing the problem if it were to arise.

Adding the Ideas to the Development of the Program

All the ideas that are generated in troubleshooting have the potential to become part of the developed program, making it stronger than it was before troubleshooting. A common example might be an event that was originally planned to be held outdoors. Thanks to troubleshooting, the client could decide to bring it indoors or to schedule a rain date in case of bad weather.

The facilitator next asks the client which of the ideas that were just generated he wants to make part of the program as it has been developed up to this point. The solutions chosen are then added to the developed idea.

FINAL THOUGHTS ON TROUBLESHOOTING

There are two important points about troubleshooting that we want to underscore.

1. *Troubleshooting is about helping, not hurting, the program.* We have been in troubleshooting sessions in which the members of the resource group have misinterpreted their assignment. The facilitator is not looking to trash the program and create doubt in the mind of the client. The real point of the exercise is exactly the opposite: The facilitator wants to make the client more confident by demonstrating that potential problems can be prevented and the program can move forward.
2. *Troubleshooting can fundamentally change the program.* One of the big benefits of troubleshooting is that it is a very effective precau-

tionary step to prevent a real disaster. For instance, we have participated in sessions in which troubleshooting helped the clients realize they were about to sign up for a program that would have been ridiculously expensive. Other programs contained elements that could have damaged well-established brands.

The facilitator cannot lose sight of the fact that this is an optimistic process, and most of the problems any program is likely to encounter can be anticipated and solved either right before or right after they happen.

We are now going to return to the Woodland Nurseries case study, where Alesia is about to facilitate a troubleshooting session for Eric.

TROUBLESHOOTING THE DIRTY GLOVE CLUB PROGRAM

Alesia is facilitating the troubleshooting session in the event application of the process. Let us remind you that Alesia, with Eric's help, has recruited a slightly different resource group from the one they had used in the original idea-generation session. The two additions, Max and Rachel, are on the staff of Woodland Nurseries' advertising agency. The holdovers from the original idea-generation session are Mia, Evelyn, and Olivia, who is still helping Alesia as the scribe for the session.

We resume our case study in the conference room at Woodland Nurseries. On the flip chart at the head of the room is the list of ideas Eric has chosen from their development idea-generation session. Alesia begins the process of troubleshooting the Dirty Glove Club.

"Eric, we just reviewed the Dirty Glove Club program with as much detail as we have at this point. Is there anything you feel needs to be added to the program before we trash it completely?"

Eric chuckles and says, "No. It's a pretty good program, I'd say."

Creating the List of Concerns

Addressing the resource group, Alesia says, "Let me tell you about the next part of our session. I'm going to ask you to help me make a list of all of the things you are concerned about when you think of the program that I just described to you. Once you make that list, we're going to ask you to choose the things you're really concerned about, and then we are going to generate ideas that could fix those troubles and add those elements to your program. To begin, I would like you all to close your eyes and imagine you are at Woodland Nurseries. We are two weeks into the Dirty Glove Club program, and instead of feeling good, you are feeling frustrated. Imagine the customers who were supposed to think the program was kind of cool but are disappointed in it. The staff is feeling frustrated with the program. Even Sam feels like the program has not met its expectations. Now, open your eyes and tell me what the sources of your frustration are."

Eric says, "I'm worried that even though I think the Dirty Glove Club name is cute, it is hard to say, and when I step away a little bit from the idea generation that we did, I get worried that, standing alone, it isn't a very positive name. So I'm a little worried about that name. It might need to be tweaked."

Mia says, "I'm not sure we at Woodland have the capabilities to have a custom garden design and drag-and-drop program for the Web site."

Rachel asks, "Where's our brand? I mean, our position is that we have the wisdom to help you grow your garden, but I'm not sure I see it in this program."

Evelyn says, "This whole thing sounds expensive. Can we do all this within our budget?"

Mia calls out, "What about the staff? One concern might be they are busy enough as it is during the spring."

Alesia asks, "Is there any other kind of trouble the resource group might want to add to the list?"

The resource group is silent.

Narrowing the List of Concerns

Alesia continues, "Eric, I am going to read back this list of concerns. I would like for you to check the ones that you want us to work on. For everything you tell me is a real concern, we will generate ideas to fix that problem. So let me read the list back, and then I'd like you to choose what you're really concerned about. The first one is that you're worried about the Dirty Glove Club name."

Eric says, "Yes, that's one concern. I'd love you guys to play with a different club name for a minute."

Alesia says, "The next concern is about the garden design program."

Eric says, "Check that."

Alesia continues reading, "Concern about the Dirty Glove Club not reflecting the Woodland Nurseries brand."

Eric says, "Check!"

Alesia then reads, "Concern about the budget."

Eric looks at Evelyn. "Evelyn, we spend about $150,000 a year in advertising. I think we can pay for this program with a little over half of that."

Alesia continues, "And finally, there is concern about the staff."

Eric shakes his head, "I don't see this program really adding to the staff's responsibilities."

Alesia says, "All right, resource group—let me remind you that what we are going to do now is generate some ideas to fix these concerns. Eric, is there one that you want to work on first?"

Eric says, "The name."

Making a List of Ideas to Fix the Name

Alesia says, "I want you all to imagine the name Dirty Glove Club was not available to us. Help me make a list of other names we might give the club."

Eric says, "What about the Green Glove Club?"

Max says, "Flowering Finger Club."

Mia says, "It could just be Glove Club."

Evelyn says, "Preferred Gardener's Club."

Olivia says, "Green Roots. Good Soil Club."

Rachel says, "The Blooming Daisy Club."

Mia says, "Fertile Ground."

Evelyn says, "How about the Woodland Bloomers?"

"The Masters Club."

"Make it a mascot of the nursery."

"The Master Gardener Club."

"The Woodland Women."

Rachel says, "Woodland's Perfect Perennials. The Perfect Perennial Club."

Eric says, "The Pretty as a Picture Club."

Evelyn says, "Perennial Favorites."

Eric asks, "The Green Thumb Club. Is that too common? Is that too street? The Green Thumb Club? The Greenhouse Society?"

Olivia says, "The Society of Avid Gardeners."

Rachel says, "SAG. The SAG Club."

Max says, "The Petal Pushers. What are other things that are green?"

"Trees."

"Leaves."

Detour #1: Fact-Based Detour

Alesia says, "Let's take a detour. Let's describe everything you see in a nursery. I will write them as a side list."

"Poppies. Impatiens. Carts. Dirt."

"Fertilizers."

"Planters."

"Garden gnomes."

"Water fountains."

"Sprinklers. Hoses."

"Hanging baskets."

"Shrubbery."

"Annuals."

"You have those little sticks that go in the pot that describe the plant and give the instructions."

"Pots, potting soil and shovels and spades."

"Stones."

"Trellises."

"Mulch. Manure."

"Compost."

"Bark."

"Moss."

"Pine straw."

"Bulbs."

"Fertilizer."

Alesia says, "Okay, I'm going to read this detour list back to you, and let's see what new names we can come up with." As soon as she is done reading the list back, the ideas pour out.

Eric says, "The Blooming Bulb Club. The Green Bulb Club. The Bulb Babes."

Olivia says, "The Green Gnome Club. The Green Garden Gnomes."

Mia says, "The Perennial Society. The Woodlands Perennial Society."

Eric suggests, "Let's review the list of names. I've heard a few I like."

Alesia asks Eric to check off any that he likes as she reads the club names. "We started off with Dirty Glove Club."

Eric says, "Check."

Alesia says, "And we have added the Green Glove Club."

Eric says, "Check Green Glove Club."

Alesia says, "Okay, Flowering Finger Club, just Glove Club, Green Thumb Club."

Eric says, "Check Green Thumb Club."

Alesia says, "Preferred Gardener's Club, Good Soil Club, Blooming Daisy Club, Woodland Bloomers."

Eric says, "Check that one, Woodland Bloomers."

Alesia says, "The Masters Club, Master Gardener Club, Woodland Women, Petal Pushers."

Eric says, "I like that one, Petal Pushers."

Alesia says, "Green Gnome Club, Green Garden Club, Woodland Society."

Eric says, "Okay. Review the ones I checked."

Alesia says, "Green Glove Club, Green Thumb Club, Woodland Bloomers, Petal Pushers."

Eric says, "What could it be other than club? So Green Glove . . . ?"

Rachel says, "Society, Association."

Eric says, "What about The Green Glovers? The Glove Club is where the tongue tie is."

Olivia says, "Club, society, association, group, sorority."

Eric says, "The Petal Pushers. With the Petal Pushers, you don't need a club; you're the Petal Pushers."

Choosing the Name

Eric says, "I would like to hear what everyone thinks. Which of the new names do you like?"

Alesia interjects, "Let me repeat the names for you. We have Dirty Glove Club, Green Glove Club, Green Thumb Club, Woodland Bloomers, and Petal Pushers."

Mia says, "I vote for the Petal Pushers."

Rachel says, "Two for Petal Pushers."

Eric asks, "Would my gardening friend, Sandy, want to be a Petal Pusher?"

Olivia says, "I'm thinking number three. Woodland Bloomers."

Max says, "I vote for Woodland Bloomers, too."

Evelyn says, "Woodland Bloomers is what I vote for, too."

Eric says, "While I like Woodland Bloomers, I still like the Dirty Glove Club the best. Thank you for your suggestions. Hearing the other possibilities you came up with helped me make that decision, so thank you for your help."

Alesia says, "All right, so we're sticking with the Dirty Glove Club as the name of our program."

Fixing Concern #2

Alesia says, "You were also concerned about the garden design software."

Eric says, "Let me save us a bunch of time here. I don't think we need that element. I know there are a lot of Web sites out there where you can get premade garden designs. So let's just take that element out of the program."

Alesia says, "Does that mean, Eric, that you want to remove that particular element off the plan as it stands today?"

Eric says, "Yes. I wish we had the time and the resources to look into creating something like that on our own, but I know we don't. Plus, quite frankly, I don't think we need it. I think the program is very strong without it."

Alesia walks over to the flip chart page that contains the summary of the program and crosses out the description of the software that would have allowed the customers to design their own gardens on the Woodland Nurseries Web site.

Once that is done, Alesia addresses the group again, "Okay, the third and final concern you checked is the issue of the Woodland Nurseries brand."

Eric says, "Yes, I'm really glad Rachel brought that up."

Fixing Concern #3

"Let me frame this particular challenge," Alesia says. "Woodland Nurseries is going to launch a Dirty Glove Club for our target consumers. How might we use this program to support the perception that Woodland Nurseries has the deep-rooted wisdom to help avid gardeners like Sandy grow their gardens?"

There is silence in the room, which causes Alesia to remind them, "Whenever you are ready, guys. I need a list of ideas."

Rachel is the first to speak up. "We need to see the staff at Woodland Nurseries teaching. So one idea is to have them teach workshops or classes that the Dirty Glove Club members can attend."

Evelyn adds, "I propose a monthly workshop taught by one master-level horticulturist at Woodland Nurseries."

Max says, "And the workshops need to be recorded and put on the Web site and on the Facebook page."

"I think we need an owl," says Mia.

"An owl?" asks Olivia, who is still scribing.

"Yes, an owl. We create a gardening book for kids with a mascot called the Woodland Nurseries Owl. The owl can answer questions posed by the kids."

Alesia interjects, "Let's take a detour. I want you to help me make a list of things you would expect from an expert." The group responds with a quick list.

- Write a book.
- Have a PhD.
- Teach a college class.
- Write a blog.
- Get quoted in the newspaper.
- Get quoted in news stories.
- Get calls from famous people.
- Get quoted by other experts.

"That's a pretty good list," says Alesia. "You know what we need to do now! Help me make a list of ways to use the Dirty Glove Club to enhance our target consumer's perception that Woodland Nurseries has the deep-rooted wisdom to help them grow their garden."

"What about a book?" asks Mia.

Alesia knows there is more there. A book is just a tool. "What can you tell me about the book, Mia?"

"It's called *Garden Wisdom.*"

Mia continues, "Every one of our staff experts, and we have at least ten of them, will write a chapter on things they have learned over the years to make a garden beautiful. The book could have information about common gardening mistakes and tricks of the trade that our experts have learned along the way."

Eric adds, "You know what else it could have? It could have questions asked by the members of the Dirty Glove Club."

Rachel says, "I think the book could be composed of all the blog entries written by our experts. If we can get the staff to write one blog entry every other week, for instance, we could just create a book out of it once we have enough material."

"We should put Sam on the radio," says Evelyn. "He should have a weekly radio show where gardeners can call in and he would answer their questions."

Alesia sees there are quite a few ideas on the list. "Eric, are you hearing ideas that would satisfy the issue of the Dirty Glove Club enhancing the Woodland Nurseries brand?"

"Oh, yeah! Let's go over the list."

As Alesia reads the list back to Eric, he puts a checkmark next to:

- Workshops taught by the Woodland Nurseries staff.
- Recording of the workshops put on Web site and Facebook.
- Blog.
- *Garden Wisdom* book.

Alesia wants to know how many of the ideas Eric checked are actually going to become part of the final program. "Eric, you've selected four new ideas we did not have before we did this troubleshooting session. Which of these ideas do you want to incorporate into the plan for the Dirty Glove Club?"

"I think initially a monthly workshop is going to be too much," Eric responds. "But I am confident we could offer a quarterly workshop on topics that are of interest to the members of the club. This idea, though, has sparked another idea that we won't have time to do this year, but we can definitely do in future years."

"What's that?" Alesia asks.

"We know this avid gardener works out a design for her garden sometime during the month of March. I think we need to offer a series of chats to help with designing. Sam and his team could cover topics like which plants go well with each other or the blooming season of plants so she will have continuous color in the garden all season long. Topics directly related to what Sandy, our target consumer, is thinking about as she is designing her garden."

"I also want to add the blogs," Eric continues. "We could easily come up with one blog entry every other week. I really like the idea of turning the blog entries into a book, and, Mia, I especially like the title *Garden Wisdom*."

Mia responds, "Okay, since you like my *Garden Wisdom* idea, I'll forgive you for ignoring my owl idea."

Alesia jumps in, "All right, so we have come up with a couple of improvements to the Dirty Glove Club program. Our agent seems to be happy with this name. Our next step is to create a timeline.

With all the major concerns articulated and taken care of, the only tasks left to do are to create a timeline and assign responsibilities to make sure the Dirty Glove Club becomes a reality.

12

CREATING A TIMELINE

e said at the beginning of this book that it is the job of the facilitator to do whatever is possible to ensure that the ideas generated actually happen. The timeline is the facilitator's most powerful tool
for making sure that ideas are acted upon. The timeline displays *who* has
made a commitment to do *what* and by *when*.

As we begin to discuss the process of creating a timeline for a project,
we want to point out that the facilitator is attempting to accomplish two
things at the same time. First and foremost, the facilitator has a vested
interest in making sure that the program is executed successfully, so she
needs to create a concrete plan of action with specific deadlines. Second,
the facilitator needs to make sure the ownership of the program gets trans-
ferred to the responsible parties, most especially to the client or to the
agent if there is one involved in the project. Even the simplest marketing
programs are usually executed by more than one person. There are vendors
to contact, copy to write, and legal requirements to be met. Every one of
these responsibilities could potentially fall upon different shoulders.

We see the job of the facilitator as coming to an end once the timeline has been created. Of course, it could happen—and it often does—
that the facilitator works in the same company, even the same depart-

ment, as the client. In those cases, it is reasonable to expect that the facilitator could end up being responsible for executing some portion of the project. When that happens, the responsibility to carry out a portion of the program is separate and distinct from the responsibility to facilitate the session that is about to conclude. We want the facilitator to treat that portion of the project for which she will be responsible as if it were being assigned to a different person.

To be very clear: The function of facilitating an idea-generation session should remain separate from whatever other job the person playing the role of facilitator performs in the company. If every time a person facilitates a session, she ends up getting saddled with the job of executing whatever ideas are generated at the session, the number of sessions that she facilitates in the company will drop.

So the timeline becomes the tool with which the facilitator will hand the project over to the people, such as the client and the agent, who will be responsible for executing it. Sometimes the handoff to the agent can be especially delicate. We will discuss this issue more fully later in this chapter.

It should be noted that very often the facilitator reduces the number of people involved in creating a timeline by thanking and excusing the resource group. This makes sense when the members of the resource group are not expected to take responsibility for executing the program. When the resource group does have a stake in the project and will be responsible for its execution, they should stay in the room until the timeline has been completed.

REVIEWING THE PROGRAM

The first step is to review the program with the resource group. As the facilitator gets ready to start the review, she sets the expectation: "I am going to review this program with as much detail as we have. As I review the program we have developed, I would like you to begin to think about—and maybe even capture on paper—all the things that you feel need to be done in order to get this program in motion. When I'm finished with the review, I'm going to ask you to help me make a list of things we want to put on the timeline."

The review begins by reiterating the marketing objective. The facilitator then reviews the program.

CAPTURING THE TO-DO LIST

As the facilitator describes the program, the members of the resource group begin to jot down on their own pads of paper the tasks they feel need to be performed to make the program a success. As soon as the facilitator finishes the review, she asks the resource group to help her make a list of all the things that need to be done.

The facilitator captures the list on the first of three columns that appear on a flip chart or whiteboard, as shown in figure 15.

Timeline		
What?	Who?	When?

Figure 15. Capturing the To-Do List.

For now, the job of the facilitator should capture *everything* the resource group feels needs to be done. The tasks will pour out of the group in no particular order, and that is okay. When the list slows down, as we know it will, the facilitator should use detours to explore areas the group may not be considering. The facilitator can take the resource group on detours that explore the details of the program, the people who will be responsible for moving the program forward, and the resources they will need to do it. Here are three examples:

- Think about each of the phases of the program we have developed. Are there any tasks that need to be carried out to move the project forward from phase to phase?
- What about the people who need to be involved to move the project from launch to conclusion—what tasks do they need to perform?
- What about the resources that will be required to move this process forward—what tasks need to be performed to secure those resources?

CHOOSING *WHAT* AND ASSIGNING *WHO* AND BY *WHEN*

Now that the resource group has created a long list of tasks, the facilitator knows that choices need to be made. The trick is how to make them.

There will always be a temptation to put a name next to every single task on the list and assign a deadline to each. However, we've found it's more realistic to identify the first handful of things that need to be done in order to get the program moving.

The facilitator should ask the client and the agent, "What do you see on this list that needs to be done to get this program moving?" The client and the agent will choose the four or five items they think need to be handled first.

Speaking directly to the client and the agent, the facilitator asks each of them, "Which of the tasks on the list can you be responsible for, and by when do you think they can be accomplished?"

If the resource group is still in the room, the facilitator may give them an opportunity to choose and own some of the items on the list: "I would like to know if any of the members of the resource group see any items on the list for which they want to take responsibility."

Whenever anyone takes responsibility for an item on the list, the facilitator must make sure it is clear who is responsible for it and by when it will be accomplished.

Making One Immediate Commitment

One best practice we recommend is for the facilitator to suggest to the client and to the agent that they commit to completing some task from the timeline in the next twenty-four hours.

She may ask, "What can you take care of in the next twenty-four hours that will begin to move this project forward?" In cases where there is an agent in the room, the last question is a powerful way to cement the handoff from facilitator to agent.

Earlier we said that the act of handing the project over from the facilitator to the agent can be a little tricky. After all, up to this point the facilitator has demonstrated all sorts of leadership qualities and it is very common for a client, especially an inexperienced one, to want to continue working with the facilitator as the program unfolds.

One way to overcome this sort of bonding that happens between a client and a facilitator is to have the facilitator rehearse the handoff with the agent. By this we literally mean that before the session begins, there should be a conversation between the facilitator and the agent in which they agree on who is going to say what to make sure the project is visibly put in the hands of the agent.

When the facilitator gets to this point in the session, she might address the agent, saying, "Eric, I wonder if there is anything you could be doing in the next twenty-four hours to help move this project forward." At which point, right on cue, Eric—or whoever is in the role of the agent for the project—can look at the client and say, "Why don't you and I stay behind for a few minutes after the session and figure out when we should meet again?"

Let's take a look at how Alesia creates a timeline for Woodland Nurseries.

CREATING THE TIMELINE TO CARRY OUT THE DIRTY GLOVE CLUB

Alesia is still in the conference room at Woodland Nurseries with Eric and a resource group made up of Mia, Evelyn, Olivia, Max, and Rachel.

Alesia is ready to facilitate the last step of the process, which is to create a timeline so the project can begin to move forward.

Alesia reviews the details of the program while the members of the resource group jot down the tasks they feel need to be taken care of. Then Alesia says, "What I'd like to do now is make a list of all the things that need to happen to get this program rolling so that it can become a reality. What we're going to do is make a list of the 'what,' and then we'll fill in the 'who' and finally the 'when.'"

Eric jumps in right away, "Well, we know we will run television and radio commercials to launch the program. And we know we are going to be sending out a letter and an e-mail to our customers."

Max reacts to Eric's comment, "It's going to take at least a month to produce all that. I would put on the timeline that we need to write and produce the copy for television, for radio, and for the direct mail and e-mail campaign."

Rachel asks, "Is there anything legal that we need to check out?"

Alesia says, "Is the name trademarked or anything like that?"

Eric says, "That's a good idea to do a search on Dirty Glove Club. I also need to meet with Sam to share the whole program as we have developed it."

Alesia says, "I would also say that you need all of this information back in writing." She adds to the list, "Session notes to Eric."

Eric says, "Definitely. Also, we'll need to collaborate with our Webmaster to understand all the things we could do on our Web site. He may need outside help on that."

Mia suggests, "We know the program needs to start on April 10, which means all the promotion should begin three weeks before that."

Eric then says, "That's a good point. I also think we should set a date to recap the program. Maybe June 30, after the busy spring season."

A few other members of the resource group suggest other tasks for the list.

Finally, Alesia says, "Okay, now that we've got the what, we need to fill in who's going to do it, and by when. So let me read the list back to you and we'll see who's going to do it, and by when they can get it done."

Alesia continues, "It looks like there is copy that will need to be written to help us get the word out about the Dirty Glove Club. Who can take that one?"

Eric says, "I think we need to schedule an idea-generation session for that. How about if Max, Rachel, and I coordinate that session. Put us down for February 28. When can I get these notes back?"

Alesia says, "Olivia and I can get the notes back to you by the close of business on Monday."

Eric says, "That would be great, because then I'm going to need to work on putting this all together for Sam. My deadline for presenting the plan to Sam is February 1."

Alesia says, "Eric, what can be accomplished in the next twenty-four hours to keep this program moving forward? The name search for Dirty Glove Club—is there someone who can help you with that?"

Eric says, "Rachel could help me with that."

Alesia says, "Rachel. Can you get that done in the next twenty-four hours?"

Rachel says, "I can do that today."

Eric says, "Thank you."

Alesia asks, "So do you feel this gets you started?"

Eric says, "It does. Absolutely."

Alesia says, "Great." She sighs, and the resource group, knowing they have come to the end of the process, burst into spontaneous applause.

Alesia says, "Thank you so much, everyone. I am excited about the program we have developed. I've really enjoyed working with all of you on the development of this program. If you have any projects for me to facilitate in the future, don't hesitate to ask."

Eric says, "Yes. This is great. Thank you, guys. I really appreciate everybody's input, time, and creative ideas. And what about Alesia? She was great!"

Alesia says, "Thanks, guys!"

Figure 16 shows the timeline created by Alesia containing the initial commitments made by Eric as well as some of the members of the resource group.

Timeline		
What?	**Who?**	**When?**
Search for Dirty Glove Club.	Rachel	Immediately
Session notes to Eric.	Alesia & Olivia	COB Monday
Presentation to Sam.	Eric	Feb 1
Write and produce copy for television and radio. Also direct mail and e-mail campaign.	Eric, Max & Rachel	Feb 28
Phase 1 begins: Television and Radio commercials begin. Direct Mail and Email sent.	Eric, Max & Rachel	March 20
Phase 2 begins: Program begins.		April 10 – May 15
Recap of the program to date.	Eric	June 30

Figure 16. Timeline for Woodland Nurseries' Dirty Glove Club

After the troubleshooting and the timeline were completed, Eric sat down by himself and fleshed out all the elements of the program before presenting the plan to Sam. This is the program he presented.

THE WOODLAND NURSERIES DIRTY GLOVE CLUB

The Dirty Glove Club is an affinity program for people who are committed to making their gardens beautiful with the help of Woodland Nurseries. The program will include:

Year One Member Benefits

This is the list of benefits for the first year of the Dirty Glove Club. There are more benefits contemplated for future years, but they have not yet been finalized.

1. One pair of high-quality gardening gloves when they join the club and once every spring thereafter.
2. Upon joining the club, they would receive a coupon book worth a minimum of $100 in savings on products like plants, fertilizer, and other products available at Woodland Nurseries.
3. Early bird access during Woodland Nurseries' four annual sales. Members of the Dirty Glove Club will be allowed in the stores at 7:30 a.m., while the doors open at 10 a.m. for everyone else. (Of course, all a target consumer has to do to be allowed in at 7:30 a.m. on sale days is sign up on the spot!)
4. Free attendance to one workshop every quarter. The topics to be covered in the workshops will vary according to season and also according to the desires of the club members. Members will receive a quarterly survey with a list of topics as well as possible guest speakers. The members will get to vote on which workshop will be held each quarter. Refreshments will be served at the special workshops, which could be scheduled during week nights or maybe during Saturday or Sunday afternoons.
5. Monthly blog written by the Woodland Nurseries staff e-mailed to all the members. All blog entries will contain at least three practical tips for gardeners.
6. A minimum of once per year, Woodland Nurseries will bring in a well-known author, designer, or celebrity with some connection to gardening for a members-only event. The event will include a presentation by the guest of honor and an opportunity for the members to meet him or her.

Phase 1: Getting the Word Out—March 20–April 10

The first phase consists of inviting the target consumers to come visit either the Woodland Nurseries stores or the Web site to register for the Woodland Nurseries Dirty Glove Club. During this three-week campaign to get the word out, Woodland Nurseries will use:

- Radio and television commercials.
- Direct mail to the database of customers.
- E-mail to the database of customers.
- The message for Phase I, which has yet to be written, will display Woodland Nurseries staff inviting avid gardeners to join the club and mentioning the benefits it offers members.
- Web site—The Woodland Nurseries staff will appear on the Web site wearing dirty gloves. The Web site will display an icon in the shape of a dirty glove, which the target consumers can click and they will be taken to a Dirty Glove Club page where they can learn about the benefits of joining the club and register to join the club. When anyone visits the Woodland Nurseries Web site, the cursor will take the shape of a dirty glove.
- Sam and his team of horticulturists will offer a series of chats on some of the fundamentals of establishing a beautiful garden. The topics might include what plants to use in sunny versus shady areas and which plants go together with each other. All chats will be videotaped and posted on the Woodland Nurseries Web site.
- Store signage will include a big sign in the form of a dirty glove over the information desk. The staff will be wearing Dirty Glove Club buttons.

Phase 2: The Membership Drive—April 10–May 15

- Radio and television continues, except the message will change to begin to include members of the Dirty Glove Club appearing in the commercials.

- Launch of a Woodland Nurseries Dirty Glove Club fan page on Facebook.

Planning for Phase 3

By June 15 we will establish a Dirty Glove Club Advisory Group composed of a dozen members. We will invite them to an informal discussion and idea-generation session to improve the Dirty Glove Club.

By June 30 we will hold a staff meeting at Woodland Nurseries to take stock of the progress made to date, consider the ideas generated by the advisory group, and decide what to do with the Dirty Glove Club for the balance of the year.

Possible Benefits for Year Two

1. The chats by Sam and his team of horticulturists will become an annual program always held in March, which is when the target consumer is beginning to plan her garden for the year.
2. We are considering offering an affinity credit card that will earn the cardholder points she can redeem for Woodland Nurseries merchandise.
3. We are also considering a yard-of-the-month program in which the members of the Dirty Glove Club would submit before and after pictures of their yards and the most beautiful yard transformations could appear in a full-page ad that Woodland Nurseries would purchase from *Atlanta Homes and Life Style* magazine.
4. The University of Georgia has a master's program in landscape design. We will select three different sites on the grounds of each Woodland Nurseries location and have the students compete to create the best design for each of the three sites. The winning designs would be carried out using Woodland Nurseries plants, and the students would give chats to explain their design to the members of the Dirty Glove Club. All presentations would be videotaped and posted on the Dirty Glove Club fan page on Facebook.

❋❋❋❋❋

You have seen how an effective facilitator can manage a client, an agent, and a resource group through the Creative Resources Process. What began as a vague wish to have a successful spring season has become a full-fledged cool, custom, and effective marketing program that will accomplish the client's marketing objective. Next, we want to take a look at how a facilitator prepares to manage this process.

13

PREPARATION

was once called to facilitate a session for a major-market radio station, specifically involving the morning broadcast team. The goal of the idea-generation session was to come up with what morning teams call benchmarks. A benchmark is a recurring bit that always happens on the same day of the week at the same time during a show. For example, David Letterman's Top-Ten List is a benchmark, and so are Jay Leno's Jaywalking and Stump the Band. Benchmarks are a way for people to make mental appointments to view or listen to the show and—when they are good— they create water cooler talk: "Did you hear David Letterman's top-ten list last night?" It helps people remember your show.

The outcome of the session is that we came up with fifty-nine different benchmark ideas. The morning team was very happy because they had lots of ideas to choose from. Eventually, they chose the ones that made the most sense and put them on the air. This, however, is a story about how I prepared for the meeting, which is a very important step that all facilitators need to take before they begin an idea-generation session.

It would be reasonable to expect you to be wondering, "If preparation happens before the facilitator begins the process, why are we just now, in chapter 13, covering preparation?" The reason is we wanted you to have seen the process in its entirety so you had a good idea of what you were preparing for.

HOLD THE MEETING-BEFORE-THE-MEETING

When I spoke with the members of the morning team the week before the meeting, one of them was very suspicious. He was probably thinking, "Who is this Gerry Tabío, and what's he doing in my soup?"

It was a good thing I made that phone call the week before our session so I could hear his expectations before—rather than during—the meeting. I was able to say, "My job is to help you guys generate a wide variety of twenty-five to thirty benchmark ideas, and then, once we have a lot of possibilities up on the board, to help you make choices. So you guys will choose which ones to work on. I'm not going to tell you what to do, but I am going to collaborate and help you guys through the process."

After I explained my role as the facilitator of the idea-generation process, he said, "So you're the process guy. Great!" Having that conversation before the meeting calmed him down. When the meeting began, he knew what we were doing. He knew how the meeting would end. He was completely relaxed.

ANTICIPATING PATHS AND OUTCOMES

"Do the meeting-before-the-meeting" is not just a phrase. It's about playing the meeting in your mind before it happens, and, to the extent possible, identifying what the likely outcomes will be. Picture yourself starting the meeting with everybody in the room. What questions do you need to ask? What do you see? Are we going to be able to hear the guy calling in on a conference phone? Is he going to be able to hear us?

Preparation is painting a picture. There are different paths you can follow as you lead a session, and a variety of outcomes the meeting might reach. The client will need to make some choices about the results he wants to achieve, so even before you get in the meeting you will need to collaborate on that. You can preview the meeting with your client: "We're going to go through the process of making a list, and then it will be time for you to make choices. I'm going to give you a variety of options and say, 'We can do this, or we can do that. What do you want to do?'"

Preparation is also about anticipating what might happen and trying to figure out how to manage for it. Preparation will always make for better results, because when you prepare, you control the outcome of the session.

Contracting Expectations

A big part of preparation is setting the right expectations for everybody who will have an impact in the meeting. This can be done in person or in writing. When you set expectations, you establish a verbal contract with each of the players. You explain what the facilitator does, you tell the group members their roles, and you contract for time, for responsibilities, and for who makes the hard choices. Setting these expectations helps to ensure that:

- Everyone is prepared for what will happen.
- Disappointment and false expectations are avoided.
- Everyone knows your role and their roles.

Most of the lessons in this chapter are a result of mistakes we made in our early years. Working with people, you face an infinite range of unpredictable assumptions and behaviors. In some cases, we've had to learn the hard way just how important it is to put sufficient time into preparation. Setting expectations is just one of the many ways to prepare. In the sections that follow, we will give you a preview of some other important areas in which proper preparation is crucial. At the end of the chapter we have included preparation checklists we use to help us remember the different aspects of preparation.

PREPARING THE AGENT

As the facilitator, one of your most important jobs is preparing the agent. The power of facilitation is an amazing phenomenon to behold. If you're not careful, the clients you facilitate for will want you forevermore. You're the one standing at the head of the room, taking the client through the process; you show him that you're savvy and that you know how to solve a problem. As a result, the client falls in love with you and wants to break up with the agent.

This is a problem, because the agent is the one with an ongoing interest in seeing the project succeed. You need to make it clear to the client that, even when you work down the hall, your involvement with the project is only temporary, while the agent's involvement with the project continues.

And so preparation of the agent becomes very important. You need to tell the agent how to introduce the session to the client so he knows the agent is the one who has brought you in as a resource to facilitate the session. You also need to prepare the agent for his part in making sure the idea that comes out of the session actually happens. At the end of the session, when you are developing a timeline for action, the agent will need to be prepared to take assignments that will keep the project moving forward.

It is at this point that the agent begins to take ownership back from the facilitator as he says to the client, "Let's get together on Wednesday and discuss making these ideas we've developed a reality." The agent excuses the resource group because he doesn't need them anymore. And before you know it, the facilitator is also done with his part in the process. The agent might even excuse the facilitator from the room so he can talk with the client in private.

To reiterate, the facilitator needs to prepare the agent for what's going to happen in the room and for the role he is going to play in the process. The agent needs to be able to take over from the facilitator when it's time to take ownership of the timeline. This allows the agent to stay in control of his relationship with the client.

PREPARING THE CLIENT

Preparing the client is like telling him the rules of the game you're about to play. If you don't prepare the client, it's like sitting him down in front of a Monopoly® board with no instructions and expecting him to know what to do. When he doesn't know how to play, he will start going in the wrong direction, and you will have to teach him the rules mid-session. This will make him embarrassed and frustrated, and he will be less likely to cooperate with the process.

Preparing the client is especially important when there is an obvious difference in rank between the client and the facilitator. Many of the clients for whom you will facilitate will be decision makers—people who are used to being in control. When you can help them see clearly what to expect, and you can show them that there is a framework to the process you are going to follow, they will become more relaxed and more willing to follow directions.

You can use the following sample conversation to help prepare a client. You might want to include the agent in this conversation, if you are working with one on the project.

Introductions and Objectives of the Discussion

"Hello, and thank you for taking a few minutes to meet with me. My name is Stephanie, I am a facilitator and Greg has asked me to facilitate your meeting next week. The purpose for my call today is to help us prepare."

Process Overview

"I would like to start by giving you a little overview of the Creative Resources Process so that you know what to expect during the meeting on Tuesday.

"I have learned to facilitate a very powerful process that has been developed over the last twenty years and is used every day to generate custom marketing ideas for clients.

"Greg and I have already begun to prepare. He has helped me become familiar with the current marketing situation."

Meeting Objectives and Expectations

"When we meet, we will begin by doing some fact-finding to help us identify your marketing objective. Once we understand your objective, we will generate a long list of ideas. If you can imagine it, the room will be covered with flip chart paper filled with dozens of different ideas. I'll be using different techniques to help the resource group generate a large quantity of novel and relevant ideas, and we're going to write all those options up on the board without judging them. We're going to use a variety of techniques to think about the problem from many different perspectives before we get into a discussion about which ideas make the most sense.

"For you as the client, it may sometimes feel as though everyone is telling you what you should be doing with your business, but it is important to suspend judgment. Later we'll apply your criteria to make decisions.

"Once we have a long list, I am going to ask you to select your top five.

"Next, we will collaborate with you to select the solution that makes the most sense and develop a plan of action and a timeline so everyone knows who needs to do what and by when."

Post-Meeting Activities

"After the meeting, Greg will work with you to execute the plan of action."

Cast of Characters

"Let me tell you about the people who will be in the meeting.

"We have invited nine people from different departments to be part of the resource group. The resource group's role in the meeting will be to help us generate ideas.

"My role is to facilitate the meeting. That means I'm responsible for helping you and the resource group stay on task.

"Now let's talk about your role. First, this meeting is for you, so nothing will happen unless you want it to. We will encourage you to help us generate ideas, and when it comes to making choices, that will be your job. So once we have a list of options, I'm going to turn to you and ask you to make choices."

Contract for Time

"The meeting is scheduled for ten o'clock Tuesday morning. Is that still good for you? Great. We will be out no later than noon."

Ensure Confidentiality

"As I mentioned, we will start the meeting by fact-finding to identify your marketing objective. During this part of the meeting, the resource group is going to be asking you questions to help clarify your marketing situation. I mention this now for two reasons. First, it might frustrate you a little to hear people asking you questions to which you think they should already know the answers. Even people in your own department will be encouraged to ask you some basic fact-finding questions. Second, it could feel a little bit as though the people in the resource group are prying into your business. But this process is 'garbage in, garbage out.' A good outcome depends on the resource group having good information. The better we understand your situation, the better the ideas will be. I also want to assure you that everyone invited to this meeting understands the importance of confidentiality. Everything that happens in that room will stay in that room."

Questions

"What questions do you have about our process or the meeting next week?"

The students we have trained who have used the sample script you have just seen report a dramatic drop in cancellations and a dramatic increase in the number of clients who arrive at the session ready to get to work.

PREPARING THE RESOURCE GROUP

Preparing the resource group is essential to the success of the idea-generation session, for two reasons.

1. The resource group members have to know their role and how you want them to behave in the meeting.
2. The resource group members need to understand enough about the project they have been asked to participate in to be effective in their role.

Preparation can be as simple as asking the resource group to read a piece of research about the target consumer or to shop in the client's store before they arrive at the meeting. A while back, I did an idea-generation session for a national chain of coffee shops. As my resource group preparation, I mailed everybody a gift card. Each member of the group was required to go to the nearest coffee shop in the national chain, look around, experience it as a customer, and use their card to make a purchase. By the time they showed up, they had all kinds of notes. They knew what they liked. They knew what they didn't like. And they were ready to come up with ideas.

Making sure the resource group has enough information about the target consumer and the company is important because resource groups who are unprepared quickly become bored and uninterested.

In one of the most successful sessions I've led—my client was targeting thirty-year-old women—we prepared the resource group by instructing them to read two issues of *Cosmopolitan* magazine cover to cover—every word. When the resource group showed up, the members weren't necessarily in the target—one was a forty-year-old guy—but it didn't matter, because they had the target consumer in mind and they understood the topics we were addressing. We were even able to reuse the magazine as a detour! The resource group did an excellent job because they had mentally prepared and had internalized the target consumer.

The resource group also needs to know how to behave. They need to know the Seven Rules of Brainstorming introduced in chapter 1, and how they should respond and follow the instructions of the facilitator.

PLANNING THE INTRODUCTION

One of the most important parts of preparation is the introduction. What the facilitator says and does in the first ten or fifteen minutes of the meeting will establish confidence that the idea-generation process works. Why are we here? How are we going to play the game? What is everybody's role? You are going to use your introduction to calm down the client, the agent, and the resource group. Even though you have prepared the client, the agent, and the resource group, the introduction refreshes and reestablishes the roles, rules, and process.

By creating an environment where everybody knows how to play, you will make it safe for them to play. A well-prepared introduction will create a safe and inviting environment.

HOW TO WARM UP THE ROOM—USING ICEBREAKERS

To prepare an effective icebreaker, you need to have a clear objective of what you want to accomplish. Your icebreaker should teach people the behavior of making a list, making choices, and suspending judgment, as well as how to take a detour and how to respond to it. The icebreaker gives everybody in the room an opportunity to hear their own voices out loud and introduce themselves to one another. You can choose an icebreaker that has some connection to the product or service that you're getting ready to work on, or one that is related to the target consumer. You can also do an icebreaker that is fun or imaginative and unrelated to the session or the marketing objective.

PREPARING THE TIMELINE FOR THE MEETING

To prepare yourself, lay out the timeline for the meeting. You need to have the discipline to know that even if you're cooking and generating great ideas, you'll have to stop at a predetermined time so choices can be made and a timeline can be created before closing the meeting. Doing the meeting-before-the-meeting means doing the meeting all the way. The facilitator must consider every part of what she plans to facilitate and allow enough time for each step. The facilitator has to remember she is not done until choices have been made, and she's got to make time to do that. Is there going to be a break? If the facilitator tells them to take five minutes, they're going to take fifteen, so she needs to plan for that.

It's equally important to review the timeline of the meeting with your agent and your client. One client asked Sally to facilitate a day-and-a-half-long meeting for her, and she wanted to get a week's worth of work done in that time frame. Sally told her, "I'll get us wherever you want to go, but there are implications in your decision, so let's think it through first. We can do a session for ninety minutes or for three hours, but what you're asking for won't be solved in a single meeting."

The client said, "Sally, we've got to be out of there by four-thirty," to which Sally replied, "Okay, then let's be realistic about what we're going to accomplish on day 1."

Sally then got the client to make choices about the timeline by showing her the path the idea-generation session would need to take: "If you have to be out of the room at four-thirty, then we need to start winding down by four o'clock. I need fifteen minutes to let the resource group make a soft choice, and another fifteen minutes to complete the action planning. If you want to start the meeting at two, we only have two hours of idea generation."

The client said, "Well, that's not satisfying to me."

So Sally suggested, "Okay, then, you will either need to start the meeting earlier or end later. If you extend the idea generation but then don't end the meeting without assigning action, it doesn't matter how great the creativity is; you've wasted the time."

Just like you need to know how to get into a session, you also need to know how you are going to get out of one. When you haven't anticipated how you're going to get out of an idea-generation session, you're in danger of running out of time. You'll be cooking, you'll be coming up with great ideas, and you'll be saying to yourself, "This is going really well." Then you'll look at the clock and see you've got five minutes left, and you haven't closed the session. You haven't made choices. You haven't talked about criteria. You haven't created a timeline and plan of action. So the session just comes to an end.

Unfortunately, this is the typical ending for meetings that aren't completed: "Well, we'll just get on the phone next week and finish it." Next thing you know, it's five weeks later and nobody has called to schedule a meeting.

We never experience a situation where the facilitator has said, "Let's get together and finish it," and the group has followed through. Even if the same group of people manages to get together in a couple of weeks to finish the session, their memories aren't fresh. They won't recall what they were working on and it will take half the session just to regroup and begin to focus on the next step in the process.

Preparing Detours

Before going to the meeting with the radio station's morning team, I bought copies of current women's magazines aimed at the age group of the target listener. For one of the detours, I handed out the magazines and said, "Okay, women's magazines have sections that, in essence, are benchmarks in print. What I want you to do is go through the magazine page by page and when you see a benchmark—for example, a section called, 'What women don't know about men' or 'Do's and don'ts for dating'—call it out, and let's see if we can make a connection to it and come out with a cool benchmark to put on the radio."

The team loved that detour, and it succeeded in adding novel ideas to the list. The detour worked because I had prepared it ahead of time; I decided before the session that I would bring in women's magazines that were relevant to the target and ask the resource group to generate ideas based on the magazines' content. A detour that you come up with on the spot will never be as successful as one that you plan for and have tailored to the needs of the target consumer, the client's brand or product, or the resource group.

As we have said repeatedly, detours are the facilitator's most powerful tool. They will keep the idea-generation session moving forward and the resource group engaged. Your client will see how detours shift the momentum and help the resource group produce a greater variety and quantity of ideas. Prepare more detours than you think you'll need. For an hour-long session, you might want four to six different detours. For a smaller group, you need more detours. You will want to have detours for groups that are reticent to call out ideas or for those that are kinesthetic rather than auditory or verbal. You might want to review what you learned in chapter 8 to be sure you have a variety of detours to generate quantity, novelty, and relevance.

Making Choices

No idea-generation session is over unless a choice has been made. A big misconception about idea generation is that it ends when the ideas stop coming. It doesn't. It ends when the facilitator helps a client make choices from the list.

You have to prepare for how you are going to make choices. Are you going to ask everyone to make a soft choice by voting for their favorite ideas using red dots? You can anticipate this will take fifteen minutes; then you will need another fifteen minutes to agree on a plan of action. This means that the idea-generation portion of the meeting needs to come to an end half an hour before your time is up so you will have time for convergence. If the client wants to make the choices without the group, then the idea-generation session can run longer.

We have to review the meeting in advance so that we can lay out a timeline before the meeting even begins. The facilitator's job is to manage the process and plan time for all that needs to be accomplished.

The client and agent have to be satisfied with what gets done, so communicating the plan to them in advance is important. If you don't, they're not going to understand why we are shutting down idea generation half an hour early.

PREPARING THE ROOM

Sally was once asked to facilitate a meeting for a financial advisory services company in downtown Washington, DC. Two weeks before the meeting the agent told her how beautiful the boardroom was. So she asked them, "Is there any place I'm going to be able to tape paper up on the wall?" The agent said, "Absolutely not!" They moved the meeting. Had she not asked about this, she would have been stuck, because their beautiful meeting room was very small, with expensive woodwork and great big windows.

There's nothing more frustrating than walking into a meeting room at the Bellagio in Las Vegas and seeing million-dollar paintings affixed to every one of the walls. You need to tape up twenty sheets of paper. What do you do now?

I once did a session where we wrote every idea on 8½-by-11-inch sheets of white paper that we "borrowed" from the copier down the hall. Then we stuck the pieces of paper to the wall with tape. It turned out to be a cool technique: If every idea is written on its own sheet of paper in large print, then when the time comes to make choices, you can move and cluster the pieces of paper. This technique will save you when you don't have a flip chart—but not if you can't tape the paper to the walls.

Knowing what the meeting room looks like in advance is an important step toward ensuring a comfortable and smoothly run meeting. You will want to see the room before you get to the meeting so you know whether it will work for what you have planned. If you cannot physically see the room, ask your host to take several pictures and e-mail them to you in advance.

Here are some of the questions you will want to ask yourself about the room:

- Is it large enough for all the participants to fit comfortably?
- Will the icebreaker you've planned work in the space?
- Is there adequate lighting so people can see their work and stay awake?
- If people will be participating via teleconference is the speaker-phone located so they will be able to hear?

You can create an inviting environment by placing colorful toys on tables throughout the room. The toys tell participants as they enter the room that they will be having fun. Toys stimulate thinking and also provide more tactile people an outlet, but stay away from toys that make noise. Here are just a few of the kinds of colorful toys we've used:

- Pipe cleaners
- Play-Doh®
- Neon index cards or sticky notes
- Koosh Ball®

Your requirements for meeting space will depend on what you plan to accomplish—and how. It is often helpful to play the meeting in your mind while you look at the space. Review the *Preparing the Meeting Space and Materials* checklist at the end of this chapter to help identify other meeting room requirements.

LAST-MINUTE CHECK-IN

Sally was preparing to facilitate a session for a nonprofit organization. She had done all her best work. The week before the meeting, the client told her, "Oh, by the way, I've hired a new CFO and he's going to come in a day before he starts the job and join the meeting."

Sally said, "Great! Glad he's joining us." And she went right on with her plans.

Perhaps because it was so last-minute, because her client was so at ease with the situation, or because she had already done her "who's in the room" preparation, she didn't ask her client to think this decision through. She should have. The CFO is the second person in command. That is a big deal. A lot of people in the room were meeting him for the first time.

Before agreeing to such a last-minute change, you need to get the client to think about the dynamics and the implications. Questions you might ask include: What do we need to say to him to get him ready for the room that he's coming into? What's his role going to be in this meeting? Is there any prep we should do with him before he gets there? How should he be involved in the choice making? How do we get a verbal contract with him on what his role will be? Should we get him on the phone?

Sally didn't have that conversation, so it was a very difficult meeting in ways that could have been avoided. For instance, the new CFO was having his first experience with the idea-generation process, which the rest of the resource group already knew. In hindsight, Sally could have pushed for a pre-meeting conference call with the new CFO to review expectations of the meeting with him.

In addition to knowing whether there will be any new people in the room, you will want to be sure nothing else new has cropped up in the company or the market that might have an impact on the dynamics of the meeting.

Here are some sample questions you can ask to flush out the answers:

- What's going on in your business right now?
- Have any changes been made in the marketing plans?
- Has anything changed or is anything new since we scheduled the meeting?
- What concerns do the staff have about the session coming up?
- Tell me what happens after our meeting. How is the decision going to be made?

A last-minute check-in gives both you and the client an opportunity to make sure that you have the same agenda for the meeting.

PREPARATION CHECKLISTS

What follows are lists of the best practices facilitators can use to prepare for idea-generation sessions. Not every session will require preparing each of these items; however, the list can be used to trigger your awareness of the ones that apply to your situation.

Facilitator Preparation

Preparing Yourself

- Meet with the agent and agree on what needs to be done in preparation for the session.
- Confirm the name, title, type of business, and responsibilities of the client.
- Review the results of the marketing analysis.
- Do additional research to learn all about the target consumer.
- Ask the client/agent if primary research is available.
- Search the Internet to find any recent client or category marketing news.
- Cruise the client's Web site.
- Visit the client's business.
- Consume the product.
- Plan an icebreaker that demonstrates making lists and making choices.
- Plan several fact-based and novelty detours.
- Bring samples of the product to the session.
- Bring logos, point-of-purchase materials (like brochures), and current advertising examples to the session.
- Write out your script—customize the introduction.
- Rehearse the handoff with the agent and prepare a timeline for the next steps.
- If you already have key facts, come prepared to post them or distribute them to the resource group.

- If you are from within the company, do your homework to see that you have all the necessary facts available.

Preparing the Client

- Confirm the date, time, and place of the meeting via letter, memo, or e-mail.
- Schedule a "prep call" with the client and the agent to:
    - Review the process.
    - Confirm where you are in the process and set expectations for the meeting.
    - Get the names and titles of people the client is bringing.
    - Explain the role of the resource group.
    - Explain the role of the client and set expectations for how choices will be made.
    - Agree on the length of the meeting.
    - Discuss confidentiality.
    - Explain that the client will need to suspend judgment during the meeting.

Preparing the Resource Group

- Send the resource group a preparation memo with date, time, meeting objective, and a few key facts about the client's marketing situation.
- Ask the resource group to prepare for the session by doing some or all of the following:
    - Visit the client location.
    - Consume the client's product.
    - Check out the client's Web site.
- Distribute a summary of key facts about the target consumer and the brand.
- Distribute primary or secondary research information to help the resource group get to know the target consumer.

- Invite the resource group to the meeting ten minutes before the client arrives to review the process and/or facts about the client.

Preparing the Meeting Space and Materials

- Visit the meeting room in advance of the session to confirm:
  - Good lighting.
  - Good wall space for hanging flip chart paper.
  - Plenty of seating and room for the facilitator to move around.
  - How to find the facility manager if needed.
  - Location of the nearest restrooms.
  - Trash can is in the room.
- Materials you might need include:
  - Easel
  - Flip chart paper
  - Tape
  - Dots
  - Pens/pencils
  - Index cards
  - Note paper
  - Prehung paper
  - Fresh markers
  - Toys
  - Post-it® notes
  - Name tags or place cards
  - Key facts on flip chart paper
  - Seven Rules of Brainstorming on flip chart paper

Now that you have an inside look at the different ways you can prepare so your idea-generation session goes smoothly, let's review how Alesia prepared for the Woodland Nurseries session.

PREPARING TO FACILITATE AN IDEA-GENERATION SESSION
FOR WOODLAND NURSERIES

Alesia, the facilitator, sat down with Eric, the agent, and the two pre-pared for their upcoming idea-generation session for Woodland Nurs-eries. Alesia and Eric had already spoken with Sam, the client, to con-firm what he expected from the session. To start, Alesia said to Eric, "Let's go over what we've learned about the target consumer for Wood-land Nurseries."

Eric replied, "She is an avid gardener who likes to research gardening on the Internet and studies gardening in magazines such as *Atlanta Homes and Life Style* and *Fine Gardening*. She is a homeowner living in Atlanta, between thirty-three and forty-eight years old, and has a family with two children. Early each spring she makes a drawing of her yard to plan her garden, so she is ready by the time of the last frost, which in Atlanta is usually around April 10. Just as if she were decorating a room in her house, she plans what colors she wants in her garden and where. She makes two shopping lists: one for perennials and another for annuals. While annuals can be purchased almost anywhere, perennials are a product that she is willing to pay more for and will take more time to find."

Alesia volunteered to create a briefing package to help the resource group prepare for the idea-generation session. She said, "I have some research on this woman that I want to compile for the resource group to read before our meeting. I'll find some articles from gardening magazines."

Eric said, "Another thing we should do is have the resource group visit Web sites geared toward forty-five-year-old women. There are also gardening Web sites they should visit."

"I'll make sure to include that in the resource group packets as well," Alesia said.

Eric said, "We've got them reading research on the target and visiting Web sites that cater to the target."

Alesia said, "Great. I'll write all this up in a memo and send it to the resource group."

Eric went over the names of the resource group members and briefed

Alesia on who would be attending the session. Eric and Alesia ended their meeting knowing what they needed to do to prepare for the upcoming idea-generation session.

Every minute Alesia and Eric spent on preparation paid off during the session itself. Woodland Nurseries ended up with a cool, custom, and effective program to get Sandy, their forty-five-year-old target consumer, to visit their store right after the last frost.

14

FACILITATOR TIPS

T he following tips have been culled from the rest of the book and collected here as a quick reference and best practices reminder. This chapter is written as instructions for the facilitator and is organized by step of the Creative Resources Process.

PREPARING YOUR LOCATION

Take personal responsibility for preparing the space you will use for generating lists.

Check Out the Room

Visit your meeting room well before you hold a session. Make sure there is room for flip chart easels and posting lists. Many rooms are not suited for idea generation. For example, the walls may be covered with expensive artwork, the room may be all windows, or there may be no room for a flip chart. Leave yourself enough time to book a different room if necessary.

Inventory the Materials You Need

Preparing your environment before the meeting means that you won't have to scramble during the session. Make sure that you have enough 3-by-5-inch Post-it notes or other materials for the resource group to write on, and blue painter's tape (it doesn't harm the paint on the walls), test all your markers to make sure they work, see that you have enough pencils for everybody, check that you have enough flip chart paper on your easel.

Set Up Your Room for Comfort

Make sure the seats are comfortable enough and there is adequate room for the resource group and for you to move around the room as you hang flip chart paper on the walls. Know where the temperature control is and find the restrooms. Have water or other beverages available.

Set Up Your Room to Motivate

Hang balloons and decorations. Have a stash of candy to toss out. Put toys on the table. Create an environment that encourages fun and motivates.

HOLDING THE MEETING-BEFORE-THE-MEETING

Make arrangements to get together with the client and agent before your session. It is important for the client and agent to understand what you will ask of them during the session before they are in front of a group of people. This is also the opportunity for you to hear firsthand what outcomes the client wants from the session.

Set Expectations with the Client and Agent

Set expectations with the client and agent before you bring in the resource group. Prepare them for what will happen during the session.

When the client and the agent know how to play the game and understand the roles of the key players, it will be much easier for them to stay in bounds.

Understand What the Client Wants

Consult with the client directly. The agent is often the person who contacts the facilitator, which leads us to believe that the client's goals are the same as the agent's. Ask the client, "What is it that you expect to happen in this meeting?" Asking the client to clarify expected outcomes will help you tailor your preparation.

Know Your Cast of Characters

Explain the roles each person will play before, during, and after the idea-generation session.

- The *facilitator* is responsible for gently but firmly moving the process along so that the client gets a long, deep list of ideas to choose from that will achieve the marketing objective.
- The *client* is ultimately responsible for making choices from the list.
- The *agent* usually chooses or hires the facilitator, then helps the client implement the chosen marketing idea. When the client is not in the room, the agent will make choices on behalf of the client.
- The *resource group* understands the target audience and the client's company and works under the direction of the facilitator to generate a long, deep list of ideas for the client to choose from.

Identify Where the Buck Stops

Insist there be a single client, even if no one wants to be in the decision maker role. Explain that throughout the process anyone can add to the list, but only one person makes the final choices. That way, when it is time to choose an idea, the facilitator, the resource group, and the client all know exactly where the buck stops.

Identify the Client as Choice Maker

Make sure everyone knows who the client is. Let the client and everyone else know that the client is the ultimate decision maker. When it is time, the agent and stakeholders are welcome to give feedback, but the client will choose the idea.

Establish the Client's Advisers

Find out if the client needs to consult with the agent or specific stakeholders before making a final decision. Make sure these people are prepared to be called upon for advice when needed.

Get the Dirt Before You Begin

Get the political lowdown from the client before you start facilitating to avoid spending valuable session time helping the group sort out their problems. When you know in advance who has issues with whom, you will be able to manage the individuals more effectively.

Confirm Where You Are in the Process

Being able to diagnose the step of the process you have been asked to facilitate is the mark of a truly effective facilitator. The Creative Resources Process is sequential, and all steps of the process usually do not happen in the same meeting. If you are asked to facilitate an idea-generation session, this is the time to confirm that the marketing objective is relevant and is still the one the client wants help with.

Take a Step Back to Move Forward

Successful completion of one step of the process leads to effective facilitation of the next step. Should you discover that the situation calls for a different step of the process, you can ask the client for additional time on the telephone or plan time at the beginning of the session to solidify the marketing objective, for example, before moving forward to generate ideas.

Know What Success Looks Like

Ask yourself: "At the end of this meeting, what will success look like for this client?" If you don't know the answer, it's important that you find out. When you can picture what the client needs for the program to succeed, you will be able to help the group tailor their ideas to the client's marketing goals, increasing the likelihood of success.

Prepare Your Exit Strategy

To create a smooth transition, prepare the agent to take responsibility for the client's idea as soon as the facilitation session is over. Once you have helped the client come up with an excellent solution, it is up to the agent and the client to turn that marketing idea into a reality.

THINGS TO REMEMBER BEFORE YOU BEGIN

No matter what step of the process you are facilitating, there are a few things you should always keep in mind when you are leading a session.

Number and Label Your Lists

Number each idea and number each page. Label the top of the list with its content (wishes, facts, marketing objectives, development, troubleshooting, and timeline). This will make it easy to refer to when the client is making choices and when you go to make sense of the notes after the session.

Keep Yourself Organized

Number each page, and change the marker color for each step to keep your lists organized. After the session, you will be able to unfold your flip charts, or take out your stack of 8½-by-11-inch sheets of paper and know instantly what it all means.

Take a Break if You Need To

As the facilitator you are in charge of managing the meeting, and that includes managing yourself. If you need to take a short break to take stock, organize the room, or take a look at your notes in order to manage the process and the rest of the meeting more effectively, simply excuse the resource group for ten minutes and take a short break.

Make a List and Then Make Choices

Whenever you make a list, a choice must be made. If you get stuck during any step of the process, you have a great tool for creative problem solving—whenever you help make a list, a choice must be made.

Never Leave a List Unchosen

Make sure the client makes a choice at the end of the idea-generation session; otherwise the ideas will remain conceptual and the work will go to waste. While a client might have difficulty making a choice, once made there is a dramatically increased likelihood that the idea will turn into a program used to achieve the marketing objective.

Silence Is Your Friend

Silence allows the group to process information. The more novel the detour, the longer the silence will be. When you use the group's silence to your advantage and tell them you are happy to wait for their ideas, you give them time to think and demonstrate that you are a capable leader.

Rely on Your Process

Keep taking detours and generating ideas, even if you are unsure of how well the session is going. Be confident that by relying on your process, ideas will appear on the list that will move the session forward and generate the quantity needed to give the client a long, deep list of novel, custom ideas to choose from.

Know the Power of the Marker

Recognize that having the marker in your hand puts you in the position of power. It's not your job to give recommendations—just to help the client make choices. When the client turns to you for advice, rely on the process. Ask the client if he would like the resource group to make soft choices or help the client make a list of criteria against which to measure the idea.

Be Aware of Who Should Be in the Room and Who Shouldn't

Know where the client should be, who needs to be there that isn't, and who is there that shouldn't be. Make sure you have the right resource group to work with.

MANAGING THE CLIENT

Keep the client in the forefront of your mind as you facilitate.

Check In with Your Client

A client who is reading the newspaper in the back of the room is not engaged, and you need to know why. A client who is agitated or anxious might have new concerns you need to know about. Avoid getting to the end of the session only to find that nothing is relevant to the client's objective or that the objective itself has changed by periodically asking, "Is there a direction you want us to go that we haven't gone in yet?"

Restate Often That the Client Is in Charge

While the resource group needs to be free to use its imagination, the client is free to dislike any of the ideas generated. In the end, the client needs to choose only one solution from the list that satisfies the marketing objective. Reassure the client of this from time to time.

Don't Let a Judgmental Client Interfere with the Process

A judgmental client participating in idea generation will interfere with the process. When your client can't suspend judgment, it is best to work independently with the resource group to develop a list, narrow it down to the top five ideas, and then bring those ideas to the client to make the final choice.

Avoid a Client's Judgmental Comments

To handle a judgmental client in the idea-generation session, ask the resource group to write their ideas down instead of saying them aloud. Use 3-by-5-inch Post-it notes. This technique allows you to put the group's ideas on the list before the client can throw cold water on them.

Help the Reluctant Client Choose

If a client is reluctant to choose from the list, alleviate anxiety with a reminder: "We are happy to help you with all of these; we just need you to choose the one thing you would like us to work on first."

MANAGING THE RESOURCE GROUP

The resource group should understand or be part of the target audience and should know enough about the client, the client's products, the brand, and so forth to be able to generate relevant ideas.

Create Familiarity

Before they walk into the first session, make sure the members of the resource group have the background information they need to make their ideas relevant. Preparing them might be as simple as reading a fact sheet or as complex as a research briefing package. When the group arrives at the session, they will be ready to come up with ideas.

Make Preparation Fun

Be creative and make the preparation fun. Give the resource group gift certificates to spend in the client's restaurant. Have them ask what customers think about the product or service. Have the resource group visit the client's store, use the product, visit the company Web site, or look at its current advertising. Make a collage clipped from magazines of the target audience's interests, dress, and commonly used products.

Keep the Group on Track

Resource groups with a long history together often spend their time discussing ideas instead of generating new ones. Remind the group to focus on idea generation. If they don't respond, write down ideas from their conversation. This typically breaks them out of their discussion and brings them back to idea generation.

Make the Process New and Interesting

Stimulate the group by making each meeting feel unique and unpredictable. Change your detours, your techniques, and the physical environment. Play music, show the group famous paintings, redecorate the room, and assign different seating for each session.

Be Aware of the Resource Group

Make sure you are not so stuck in running the session that you are blind to what's going on with your resource group. Turn on your radar so you notice who is talking the most, who is disengaged, and who might need help to share creatively.

Don't Give In to the Group's Inertia

Avoid letting the group members control their own inertia. Your job is to rein them in if they're going too fast and to drive them forward if they're dragging their feet. Have enough detours planned to change the momentum when you need to.

INTRODUCING THE GAME

Your job is to empower people to be creative. As the facilitator, you teach the participants how to play the game of generating ideas by creating an environment in which they feel comfortable to bring new ideas to the list. No matter what step of the process you are called upon to facilitate, always begin with an introduction.

Warm Up the Room Before You Begin

Take the group through an icebreaker before you begin each session. This allows you to demonstrate the behavior of making lists and making choices as a reminder of how the meeting will be managed in a fun, low-stakes environment.

Cover the Rules and Reminders

Even if you are working with a group of pros who have participated in idea-generation sessions a hundred times, you still need to remind them how to play the game. This way they will be less tempted to bend the rules—and if they do, you can help them refocus by repeating the points you covered during the introduction.

Review the Seven Rules of Brainstorming

1. During the list-making or idea-generation session, there will be no judgment of ideas, no evaluation, and no criticism.
2. Freewheeling is allowed and encouraged. Wild and outrageous ideas are welcome.
3. We are going to make a long list. Remember that we're striving for quantity rather than quality, because when making lists, quantity leads to quality.
4. We are going to take detours and make connections that create quantity, novelty, and relevance.
5. We need ideas to be specific and clear so that all participants can understand them.
6. All ideas must be written down.
7. Everybody participating in the list-making or idea-generation session is equal in rank. There are no bosses. There is no hierarchy.

Remind People about the Process

Review all of the steps of the process and what the participants can expect to work on during the meeting as well as what will happen next. Remind the group that:

1. The role of facilitator is to be in charge and move the process along.
2. Making a list will generate many ideas to choose from.
3. We will make a list following the seven rules.
4. Detours will give us ideas that are novel and relevant.
5. It is one person's job to choose from the list.

Let the group know how long they will have to complete each phase of the task.

CREATING MARKETING OBJECTIVES

Help your client have something important to accomplish during idea generation by coming up with a worthwhile marketing objective.

The Importance of the Wish

Facilitating a list of wishes helps the client think about all aspects of their business. Asking the client to choose the wish helps the resource group focus their questions and fact-finding on the issue that is most important to the client and the one for which they need ideas.

Ask the resource group to hold their questions until the client has chosen which wish they want to work on.

Fact-Finding—The Marketing Analysis

The effective facilitator knows that the resource group will have to "shop" the list of facts that are generated during the marketing analysis to come up with a list of potential marketing objectives. Scan the list of facts to be sure you have explored target, outcome, product, place, and season and keep asking questions of the resource group until you are satisfied the list contains each element of TOPPS.

Detours as Prompts in the Objective Step

The detours taken throughout the objective step are detour prompts, not side lists. If you are facilitating in the event application, phrase the detour prompts as "Resource group, what do you need to know about the target consumer?" Otherwise the session will become a one-on-one conversation between you and the client with the resource group as spectators.

Transition from Fact-Finding to the Marketing Objective

Be prepared to "teach" the resource group about marketing objectives by explaining that all forms of advertising are striving to get target consumers to do or believe something about a product or service. You may even want to post "Do or Believe" on flip chart paper or look at the list of facts and say what a marketing objective with a TOP for a brand or TOPPS for an activation marketing objective would sound like.

Express a Clear Marketing Objective

Help your client identify a clear marketing objective. An unclear objective, such as, "I wish I had more customers," will generate unclear ideas. A specific objective, such as "To get a forty-five-year-old female homeowner who loves to garden to visit Woodland Nurseries between April 10 and May 15" will generate ideas that are specific and have a greater likelihood of success.

Clarify the Objective with TOPPS

Generate a marketing objective that has TOPPS, which stands for *target, outcome, product or service, place,* and *season.* When the client knows who the target consumer is, has an outcome for the idea generated, identifies a specific product or service, knows the place where the target will interact with the product or service, and knows the season in which all of this will happen, the client or resource group will be able to generate a specific solution to achieve the marketing goal.

Focus on One Objective at a Time

Watch for the word *and* in the marketing objective. The word *and* will alert you that you are dealing with two objectives combined into one statement—for example, "I want the target to believe that we're the best restaurant in town, *and* I want him to buy our hamburgers by Friday." When the client is clear about one objective, the quality and relevance of ideas generated will improve dramatically.

Hover Over the Problem

Resist rushing to completion. Examining the marketing situation thoroughly and coming up with a list of several marketing objectives for the client to choose from is hard work. Most resource groups are more comfortable generating ideas, and a resource group might rush to a slogan before they determine the position of the brand they are trying to label. Avoid letting the group move forward until they have hovered over a problem long enough to define it.

Remember, until the client has chosen a marketing objective he wants help with, the resource group is not ready to move on to the idea step of the process.

GENERATING IDEAS

Know what an idea looks like so you can help the group generate ideas that will aid your client in achieving the marketing objective.

A Well-Written Idea Is a One-Sentence Story

Although it can be tempting to capture ideas as abbreviations, single words, or tools, it is best to write each idea as a one-sentence story. That way the ideas on the list will be clear, and the client will have a long list of custom solutions to pick from when it's time to make choices.

Generate Quantity, Quantity, Quantity

Remember that in making lists and generating ideas, quantity always leads to quality. Don't worry if not all of the ideas are wonderful. As long as you have a long list of novel and relevant ideas, the client is assured of finding a solution that will accomplish the marketing objective.

Give Me Your Idea, No Matter What It Is

Encourage the group to talk and always say their ideas out loud, no matter how silly, off-topic, or impossible they may seem. When the group feels confident that every idea they come up with will be written down, they will be less likely to self-censor and more likely to make new connections that add quantity and variety to the list of ideas.

Make Generic Ideas Specific

Encourage the group to generate specific ideas rather than express their ideas as tools. Respond positively, so as not to embarrass the person who offered it: "Great! It's a gift with purchase. Tell me how that looks in your head." Then invite the rest of the group to help flesh out the idea into a custom concept that can be added to the list.

Balance Novelty with Relevance

If your resource group is cranking out a lot of novel ideas, but there aren't many relevant ideas on the list, add a fact-based detour. Likewise, if you are getting lots of relevance but little novelty, it is time to stretch the group by adding some novelty detours.

Use Ideas to Inspire New Detours

Observe when the resource group responds positively to ideas and comments that come up during a session and use them as detours by asking the group to make new connections to that comment or idea.

Keep Your Ideas to Yourself

Resist the temptation to add your ideas to the list. If you do, the client will be more likely to choose your ideas, not because yours are better, but because you are standing up front with the marker in your hand, and the client thinks you must know more than everybody else.

TAKING DETOURS

Detours allow group members to go away from a problem and come back to it with new ideas. Use detours to create quantity, novelty, and relevance.

Remember Why Detours Are Important

Explain to the group that without detours, idea generation would eventually slow to a standstill. Using detours, the resource group will generate many more options, giving the client a longer list of custom ideas to choose from.

Prepare Detours

Prepare your detours ahead of time—never wing it. A detour that you come up with on the spot will never be as successful as one that you plan for and tailor to the needs of the target consumer, the client's brand or product, and the resource group. Plan your detours to generate quantity, novelty, and relevance.

Take Detours for Quantity

To generate quantity, prepare more detours than you need; that way, your well will never run dry and you will get a long list of ideas.

Take Detours for Novelty and Relevance

Plan an equal number of novelty and fact-based detours. This will help you produce a long list of ideas that are both innovative and relevant to the client's marketing objective.

Take Detours Often Enough

Remember to always take detours, even when idea generation is going smoothly. When the group is on a roll, the ideas they generate will tend to be within the same theme. By introducing detours at regular intervals, you will be assured of getting variety as well as quantity.

Detours as a Side List

Most of the time when you are facilitating the idea step the detours will be taken as side lists. Remember to keep your side list detours separate from your list of ideas and that the side list detours are trash at the end of the session.

Remember Why It's Important to Suspend Judgment

Remind the client and resource group to suspend judgment when you take detours. Creative people are successful because they suspend judgment, allowing them to generate lots of quantity, so they always have excellent solutions to choose from.

Avoid Getting Stuck in Development

Recognize when the resource group has stopped generating new ideas and is instead developing a single solution. Listen for phrases like, "And then we could . . ." Tell the group that you have enough material on that idea, then make it safe for them to take a detour and move on.

Help the Quiet People Participate

When you have a mixture of quiet and verbose people in your group, it's a great time to bring out the Post-it notes. Use a detour as you would normally, but ask the group to write their ideas on individual Post-it notes. Then capture those ideas on the flip chart. This gives the quiet folks a chance to get a word in edgewise and adds their perspective to the list of ideas.

Use Post-it® Notes to Cluster Ideas

Cluster ideas by writing each idea on its own 3-by-5-inch Post-it note or sheets of paper that can be moved around the room and grouped with similar ideas. Clustering is handy whether it organizes the ideas from one large group or combines ideas from several independent groups.

HELPING THE CLIENT CHOOSE IDEAS

Now that you have a long list of cool, custom, and effective ideas, it is time for you to help the client make choices from the list.

Help the Client Narrow the List

Mark all of the ideas the client likes in the first round of making choices, no matter how many. If the client picks more than five, go through the list of choices and help the client eliminate all but the five that best meet the key criteria. Consider making a quick list of criteria the client will measure the success of the idea against and help him choose the idea that will succeed in meeting it.

Help the Client Choose an Idea That Works

Raise the alarm if the client chooses an idea that will clearly not accomplish the marketing objective. Review the key criteria again to help the client choose an idea that will succeed in meeting the criteria.

Label and Group Ideas

Label ideas on the list that are thematically similar using the same number, letter, or color so the client can easily identify ideas that are related. The client can then combine similar ideas to generate a fuller, more involved solution for the chosen idea.

Make Sure the Client Is Satisfied

If the client is not satisfied with any of the ideas on the list, first check in with him to make sure you really are working on the right marketing objective. If you are working on the right objective, then do another round of idea generation to come up with more options. If the client feels the marketing objective is not right, rely on your process and go back to the objective step.

As a reminder, the client must choose ideas he is satisfied with before the group can move on to develop a solution.

CREATING CRITERIA

Criteria are the rules an idea must adhere to—for example, cost, brand compliance, or a safety consideration.

Explain How Identifying Criteria Is Not the Same as Idea Generation

Help the client understand the difference between idea generation and identifying the criteria the ideas need to accomplish.

Use Criteria to Keep You Honest

Use criteria to help the client take a big, unmanageable bundle of information and sift it, cull it, and select only what will achieve the objective. Listing criteria shows how an idea does or does not make sense.

Include Fundamental Criteria

Make sure to include fundamental criteria for the client's marketing program, even if the client doesn't. For example:

- *Brand*: Is this idea consistent with the brand? With the brand promise? With the brand positioning? Is this what the client wants to be famous for?
- *Target consumer*: Will this idea accomplish the marketing objective? Will the target think this is cool? Is it relevant and credible? Is it what our customers expect from us?
- *The client*: Can it be ready by the client's deadline? Will the vendor pay for it?

Using even basic criteria in idea selection creates a much more solid foundation for a marketing program.

DEVELOPING THE IDEA INTO A MARKETING SOLUTION

Development is where the idea is transformed from a concept into a complete marketing solution. The effective facilitator knows that while developing an idea has lots of moving parts, it is really a series of idea-generation sessions rolled into one.

Use Detours That Touch All of the Senses

Use detours that touch all of the senses to help the group generate ideas that the target consumer can experience. For example: "Close your eyes. Imagine what the target consumer sees, hears, touches, and smells. Open your eyes. What did you observe?" The client and the resource group can fully experience an idea before it is brought to life.

Use Tools to Customize an Idea

Use tools as a framework to express your ideas: "When you come to our Web site during the month of June and purchase more than $100 in summer apparel, you will get a free $25 coupon to spend at our store." In this case, the tool of the Web site contains and communicates the custom idea of the coupon-with-purchase, and gives it a context in which to happen.

Know the Difference between a Tool and an Idea

Recognize when the resource group gives you a tool instead of an idea, such as, "Let's do a television commercial to advertise our product." When this happens, write down the tool—"television commercial"—and then invite the whole group to help develop the tool into a one-sentence story. That way, when it's time to pick, the client will have a custom idea.

List the Available Tools

Make a list of tools that are available to communicate with the target consumer. Take a tools detour. Be sure to include all the tools the client has at their disposal as well as other tools that might be used to interact with the target.

A One-Sentence Solution Needs Both an Idea and a Tool

Look out for tools that don't contain an idea, such as "Let's do something on our Web site." Also look out for ideas that aren't contained within the framework of a tool. For example, "When the target spends more than $100, we'll give her a $25 back." In both cases, you need to help the resource group develop a full one-sentence solution that includes both a custom idea and a tool.

CREATING A TIMELINE

Unless a delivery date and responsibilities are attached to every facet of the marketing campaign, nothing will happen.

Make a List of What Needs to Be Done

Begin by taking stock of the program as you see it today and then helping the client and resource group make a list of *what* needs to happen. Your purpose is to get enough on the list to feel confident there will be forward motion on the program. The ideas the client has chosen to include in the program are natural detours to help you make the list of "what needs to happen" longer.

Designate the Responsible Individual(s)

Once you have made the list of what needs to happen, begin to identify the individual(s) responsible for each aspect of the marketing plan, so someone is accountable for completing each task.

A FEW WORDS FOR THE EFFECTIVE FACILITATOR

Facilitate confidently, effectively, and often. The more comfortable you are in your own skin, the more effective you will be at managing the client, the agent, the resource group, and the process.

Know Your Strengths and Weaknesses

Make a note of your strengths and weaknesses when you facilitate, and spend time working on your trouble spots. Figuring out which parts of the process you are uncomfortable with and giving those areas extra practice will help you prepare a well-rounded and balanced session. Also, knowing how you're wired—your learning and behavioral styles—helps you reach those with other learning styles and will greatly improve your ability to run a session successfully.

The most powerful tip for any facilitator is to practice what you have learned. Go forward with confidence that whenever you help clients, agents, friends, or family members engage in the behavior of making a list before they make a choice, you will have helped them improve the odds for success and satisfaction with whatever it is they want to accomplish.

CONCLUSION

NOTHING LEFT
BUT THE DOING

Over the years, we have had the good fortune to teach the Creative Resources Process to thousands of people who have attended our workshops all over the world.

Near the end of our time together, our students are given one last opportunity to make comments or ask any final questions. We have discovered that the tenor of the questions changes from "How do I do this?" to "What if?"

The "What if" questions sound like this: "What if the client wants me to facilitate the process over the telephone?" or "What if I ask every member of the resource group to interview one target consumer before coming to the session?"

Time and time again we find ourselves answering these "What if" questions with a consistent answer: "Try it!"

Now that you've read this book, the most significant difference between you and us is that we have facilitated this process hundreds of times. And whether an idea-generation session was easy or challenging, we always learned something new that made us better facilitators of this powerful process.

For our parting words, we've decided to share with you the same two quotes with which we conclude our workshops. The first is from Erich Fromm: "I shall become a master of this art only after a great deal of practice."[1]

You now know much more than we did when we first started out facilitating this process for a living. So go out there and try it.

The second quote is from that great philosopher Duke Ellington, who wisely observed, "It don't mean a thing if it ain't got that swing!"

We hope this book has given you the confidence to use this powerful process. And we hope that the sessions you facilitate will generate cool, custom, and effective marketing ideas for your clients, your own business, or the company for which you work.

Good luck—and remember to have fun with it!

NOTES

PREFACE: IDEAS ARE THE NEW CURRENCY

1. "David Packard Quotes," ThinkExist.com, http://thinkexist.com/quotes/david_packard/ (accessed February 21, 2009).

CHAPTER 1: MAKING LISTS AND MAKING CHOICES

1. Alex Osborn, *Your Creative Power* (New York: Dell, 1961).

CHAPTER 5: THE MARKETING ANALYSIS

1. William D. Wells and George Guber, "Life-Cycle Concepts in Marketing Research," *Journal of Marketing Research* (November 1966): 362.

2. Ian C. MacMillan and Rita Gunther McGrath, "Discovering New Points of Differentiation," *Harvard Business Review* (July–August 1997): 133–45.

CHAPTER 6: THE MARKETING OBJECTIVE

1. Tom Ritchey, "General Morphological Analysis," Swedish Morphological Society, http://www.swemorph.com/ma.html (accessed February 21, 2009).

CHAPTER 7: IDEA GENERATION

1. Marie-Laure Bernadac, Brigitte Leal, and Christine Piot. *The Ultimate Picasso* (New York: Abrams, 2003).

CHAPTER 8: THE MAGIC OF DETOURS

1. A. B. VanGundy, The Product Improvement CheckList (1985).

CHAPTER 9: MAKING CHOICES

1. Al Ries and Jack Trout, *The 22 Immutable Laws of Marketing: Violate Them at Your Own Risk* (New York: HarperBusiness, 1994), p. 76.

CHAPTER 10: DEVELOPING THE IDEA

1. Chip Heath and Dan Heath. *Made to Stick: Why Some Ideas Survive and Others Die* (New York: Random House, 2007).

CONCLUSION: NOTHING LEFT BUT THE DOING

1. Erich Fromm, *The Art of Loving* (New York: Harper & Row, 1956), p. 5.

INDEX